Cybermarketing

How to use the Superhighway to market your products and services

**Pauline Bickerton, Matthew Bickerton
and Upkar Pardesi**

Published on behalf of The Chartered Institute of Marketing

Butterworth-Heinemann
Linacre House, Jordan Hill, Oxford OX2 8DP
225 Wildwood Avenue, Woburn, MA 01801-2041
A division of Reed Educational and Professional Publishing Ltd

 A member of the Reed Elsevier plc group

OXFORD   BOSTON   JOHANNESBURG
MELBOURNE   NEW DELHI   SINGAPORE

First published 1996
Reprinted 1997 (twice), 1998

British Library Cataloguing in publication Data
A catalogue record for this book is available from the British Library

ISBN 0 7506 2848 0

Composition by Scribe Design, Gillingham, Kent
Printed and bound in Great Britain by MPG Books Ltd, Bodmin, Cornwall

Cybermarketing

The CIM/Butterworth-Heinemann Marketing Series is one of the most comprehensive, widely used and important collections of books in marketing and sales presently available worldwide.

As the CIM's official publisher Butterworth-Heinemann develops, produces and publishes all the titles in the series with and on behalf of the CIM. We aim to publish definitive marketing books for both students and practitioners that help them to achieve the highest possible standards in their marketing education and practice.

The student texts and workbooks are written and developed by leading marketing educators and CIM Senior Examiners for those taking the Certificate, Advanced Certificate and Diploma courses. The titles for practitioners are from leading marketing experts and senior CIM members for use on both vocational programmes and also to deliver the very latest marketing thinking and techniques to the busy executive.

 **The Chartered
Institute of Marketing**

Formed in 1911, The Chartered Institute of Marketing is now the largest professional marketing management body in Europe with over 60,000 members located worldwide. Its primary objectives are focused on the development of awareness and understanding of marketing throughout UK industry and commerce and in the raising of standards of professionalism in the education, training and practice of this key business discipline.

Books in the series

Contents

Read this first!

The first questions a marketer asks about the Superhighway are

1. 'What is the Superhighway?'
2. 'Who uses the Superhighway?'
3. 'How do I contact those people interested in my product in order to increase my sales?'
4. 'Isn't it just a great deal of Hype?'

These critical answers are the starting point of the book.

1. WHAT IS THE SUPERHIGHWAY?

The Superhighway is a global infrastructure of computers connected through an array of communications: satellite; telecomms; cable. Simple as that! However, there are various commercial providers leveraging this network. This book will review each of these in turn: the Internet, Compuserve, MSN (Microsoft) etc. For the sake of simplicity, we will use the term the Superhighway because it encompasses all commercial providers and addresses the concept of the media rather than the benefits each commercial provider gives you.

2. WHO USES THE SUPERHIGHWAY?

This question is just like asking 'Who uses a computer?'
You would answer, 'well, there are business users and home users. Within the business users segment, you can segment by job function. Within the home users, you can segment by interest area.....' You are using exactly the traditional techniques for target marketing. These are

imperative. Nothing is new and every marketing concept still applies. This book is about using traditional marketing models to really utilize this powerful new media to its full.

3. HOW DO I CONTACT THOSE PEOPLE INTERESTED IN MY PRODUCT IN ORDER TO INCREASE MY SALES?

This is where traditional marketing concepts break down. The common misconception of the Superhighway is that it is a mailing list of 40+ million people. This is not the case, the Superhighway is a communications medium where 40 million people can access information that they are interested in. You cannot approach people, you can merely be approached. By the very nature of the Superhighway, 'traditional marketing think' is turned on its head. Marketers talk about penetrating and exploiting niches. None of this language is appropriate to the Superhighway. The Superhighway is a tool for people to pursue selfish desires (hence unfortunately the proliferation of pornography). Unless you can somehow provide value or information, people will ignore you.

> 90 per cent of what you do on the Superhighway must add value, 10 per cent can sell – any other combination fails

You cannot think about being proactive on the Superhighway, sending mail shots out to people. You have to think about attracting people to come to you to find out more about who and what you are. If you are not attractive enough, you have to cope with the rejection and have the courage to try again. It is not about penetrating, it is about romantically, courting and building relationships. The one-night stands (the direct mail shot with the fast conversion rate) are not possible, but you can be rewarded by long and meaningful relationships with your customers which will enhance your product range and enable you obtain competitive advantage.

The paradox of the Superhighway

The ability to understand how traditional thinking can be applied in untraditional ways is how to be successful on the Superhighway. This book is full of success stories of companies doing exactly that. In your world, the same model can bring you professional and organisational success. Read on to put yourself years ahead of your contemporaries.

4. IS THE SUPERHIGHWAY JUST A GREAT DEAL OF HYPE?

The 1980s were about personal productivity and the individual's contribution: e.g. Filofax, personal computing etc., the 1990s are about communication and connectivity - connecting people and information: modems and groupware. Mary Cronin (1995) says 'The defining trend of the 1990's from corporate boardrooms to consumer playgrounds is connecting everyone and everything to everyone and everything else'. The pace of this connectivity is just starting.

Why will it succeed?

Technology succeeds when it adds value to both the individual and the organisation. Personal software (word-processing, spreadsheets etc.) enables an individual to express and present their ideas more directly. It enables an organiation to leverage the personal creativity and knowledge trapped within its people. Whilst the costs of personal computing is expensive (the average cost to an organisation of one PC is £5000 - *Business Technology*, Sept. 1995) which includes software, maintenance and installation) the increased productivity far outweighs the investment. The only reason that personal computing has taken off as well as it has is that it has benefits for the user and the corporation.

The Superhighway offers value to both the user and organisation. It enables the individual to gain and sustain competitive advantage by providing a knowledge base and professional network of contacts. It enables an organisation to gain and sustain competitive advantage by leveraging the creativity and knowledge base outside of the organisation, assess the marketplace and build meaningful relationships with customers. The reasons why it will succeed are:

1. Because it adds value to the individual

Successful people will be working smarter not harder; leveraging a network of contacts rather than re-inventing the wheel; relying on other people's knowledge bases rather than recreating one, communicating will shortly become critical to success and the Superhighway will be critical to communication.

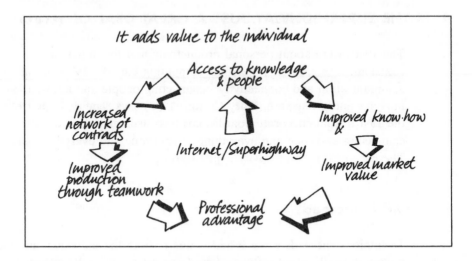

2. It adds value to the organisation.

'Managed strategically, the Superhighway offers more than just a global lifeline to the future. It can become the key ingredient to leadership in the age of interconnectivity', Mary Cronin.

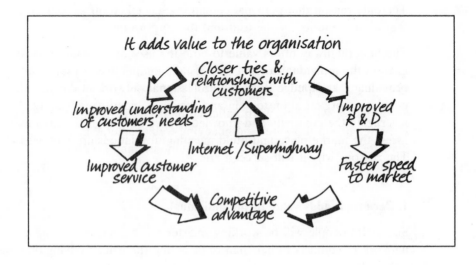

How can. this book help you add value to your organisation and your own professional development?

This book has been written to help you assess the Superhighway for yourself and we have included a disk request form to enable you to have one month's free trial. The book is accompanied by information on the Superhighway at:

http://www.marketingnet.com/cybermarketing

This is what you type into the top line of the software you use to explore the Internet, called a 'browser'. We explain this better in Appendix 2.

We have created an accompanying web-site for three reasons:

- to enable you to experience it quickly and easily without having to invest time and energy in climbing up what is a practically a vertical, learning curve. It provides an easy one-stop shop to searching on the Internet, access to numerous sites which will excite and interest you, giving advice and reinforcing the messages in this book as you go.
- to strip out the Internet gobbledegook which appears in many of the Internet books, and enable you to look behind the hype and the mystic at some of the practical issues surrounding the Superhighway.
- to preserve the shelf life of this book where the web-site can include new and important developments which occur after publication.

How the web site works is that it displays a summary of each chapter and all references (words italicised) made within it are linked to the relevant companies' information on the Superhighway. For example in Chapter 2, there is a reference to *CD-Now* and *MarketNet,* rather than giving the full Internet address, we merely include a link from the accompanying chapter direct to these companies' web sites.

So whenever you see a word italicised in this book, it implies that there is a reference to it on the accompanying web chapter, e.g. *CD-Now* implies a web page which you can visit by jumping from the accompanying web chapter.

CONCLUSION

This book will show you how to apply traditional marketing concepts for successful marketing using the Superhighway. It will also highlight challenges that a marketing person will face when confronted with this new media and illustrate how successful companies have tackled these issues.

REFERENCES

Business & Technology Magazine (Sept. 1995) published by Cromwell Media Ltd, London.

Mary Cronin (1995) *Doing More Business On The Internet*, Van Nostrand Reinhold, New York

1 Marketing with the Superhighway

INTRODUCTION

The purpose of this book is to assist both non-marketing and marketing professionals to integrate the use of the Internet into their everyday activities and in the overall planning and implementation of their organisation's strategic marketing.

For the non-marketing professional

This book gives you a brief overview of the marketing process, concepts and techniques relevant to your successful use of the Superhighway. It is hoped that it will provide you with a marketing framework to help you see marketing as a discipline rather than merely as a set of promotion focused activities.

For the marketing professional

This book gives you a refresher course in some of the core concepts in marketing. These core concepts are critical to using the Superhighway professionally. It is hoped to provide you with a familiar framework in which to understand and best leverage the Superhighway.

The aim of this chapter is to provide a framework of the marketing planning process and to outline how the rest of the book has been structured.

MARKETING

The term marketing has become established in our everyday vocabulary, but unfortunately it is loosely used with many different interpretations.

Many people associate marketing with, or confuse it to mean advertising, selling, packaging or public relations. It is not surprising therefore, to find that many proprietors, managers and employees in organisations invariably quote the words advertising and selling to mean marketing.

This misunderstanding can be explained by the fact that all of us, as employees, businessmen or consumers are constantly exposed to media advertising and selling techniques by large multinational and retailing organisations. We have all been sold something: either in a store; on the doorstep; over the telephone; in the company by a sales representative; through direct mail advertising or even via the Internet. So it is quite natural for employees and the general public to assume that marketing is something to do with advertising, selling or creating a company image.

The explosion in interest in the Internet as a new marketing medium has been accompanied by a plethora of articles, books, guides and on-line publications on 'How to market your business on the Information Superhighway'. Most of these publications have fallen into the classical trap of interpreting marketing to mean advertising, selling, on-line direct marketing and creating home pages to enhance the company's corporate image. Even some seasoned marketing professionals are seeing the Internet only as another means of promoting the company and its products around the globe. One possible reason for this narrow view is that much of the material published on the subject has been written by technocrats. Equally, many of the 'Internet Marketing Services Agencies' that have mushroomed recently are managed by IT and computer specialists who have little understanding or experience of the marketing function.

In order to gain maximum benefit from the new communications medium, it is essential that marketing and non-marketing professionals are reminded of the essence of the marketing function prior to getting into detailed explanation of how to use the Information Superhighway as a marketing tool.

This chapter presents the 'big picture' and has two sections. Section One focuses on the basic question: 'What is marketing?' by examining the purpose of any business organisation and by explaining the Marketing Concept. Section Two outlines the Marketing Management Process and highlights how the Information Superhighway can be used to provide access to valuable information and to the potential target groups of customers around the world.

SECTION ONE

1.1   The purpose of any business

When asked the question: 'What is the purpose of an organisation?', the most common response is to make a profit. Obviously, firms must make profits in order to survive by reinvestment and by providing return to shareholder capital, but it is important to understand that profit comes from sales turnover. There is only one source of sales turnover, and that is from the firms customers. Even in the non-profit making and the public sector, the revenue generated is directly proportionate to the number of 'customers' served. The purpose of any business organisation is much more than simply to make a profit by the manufacture and selling of goods or services.

Peter Drucker (1954) first proposed that the purpose of an organisation is to create a customer or a customer base, and expressed it in the following terms:

'If we want to know what a business is, we have to start with its purpose, and its purpose must be outside the business itself. It fact, it must be in society, since a business enterprise is an organ of society. There is one valid definition of business purpose: *to create a customer*'.

Levitt (1986) reinforced this message by emphasizing that '*the purpose of business is to create and keep a customer.*'

In reality, the ideal organisations are the market-orientated businesses, large and small, that create and meet the needs of the 'customer'. The customer is created by means of identifying needs in the marketplace, finding out which needs the organisation can profitably serve, and developing and offering to convert potential buyers into customers of the firm. It is only through providing customer satisfaction that organisations can achieve their goals, such as survival, maximize profits or the attainment of other social objectives. Drucker's definition of the purpose of the business in society can be extended to provide an overall explanation of what is meant by the term marketing.

1.2 What is marketing?

There are numerous formal definitions of marketing. In the UK, the following definition, developed by the Chartered Institute of Marketing, is accepted as one that encapsulates the essence of the marketing function.

> 'Marketing is the management process responsible for identifying, anticipating and satisfying customer requirements profitably.'

In addition to being an important business function, marketing is an organisational philosophy - a concept, an approach or an attitude to the way in which the organisation is directed and managed. The marketing concept is a business philosophy that Kotler (1984) has expressed in the following terms.

> 'The marketing concept is a *management orientation* that holds that the key task of an organisation is to determine the *needs, wants and values of target markets* and to *adapt* the organisation to delivering the desired satisfaction more effectively and efficiently than its competitors, and to *make a profit.*'

This somewhat long definition can be broken down into four key components (those highlighted above) and explained more fully.

(a) Management orientation

The starting point of understanding the marketing concept is that it is a management orientation. This means that in order to successfully apply the marketing philosophy, an organisation must be headed and managed by individuals who are themselves orientated towards meeting the needs of the customer. This attitude, or approach, to running the business must then permeate throughout the organisation to ensure that it can survive and grow in a competitive environment.

Most organisations operate on the basis of one of the following three orientations.

Production orientation: Making what the firm can or is best at and selling to whoever will buy it.

Selling orientation: Placing major emphasis on advertising and selling to ensure sales.

Marketing orientation: Place major emphasis on prior analysis of the needs of target markets and adapting products and services to meet those needs, if necessary.

Davidson (1987) has argued that in the UK, marketing orientation is an exception rather than the rule. This applies both in large and smaller firms. In smaller firms, the owners and or partners represent the top layer of management and are agents for giving the organisation its orientation and direction. But because most small firms are established by individuals with skills, crafts or ideas, the most common orientation and direction for the business operations is towards production and selling. Such production and sales-orientated businesses fail to create the necessary customer base to survive for very long in highly competitive markets.

The very successful businesses are those headed by entrepreneurial and marketing orientated chief executives. Alan Sugar (Amstrad), Richard Branson (Virgin) and Anita Roddick (Body Shop) are amongst the well known entrepreneurs who have built successful businesses by focusing their efforts on meeting the needs of their customers. Now, as larger organisations, these individuals still provide the management orientation and direction for the business operations, but have marketing directors and other marketing personnel to implement their corporate plans.

Management orientation is a starting-up point of implementing the marketing concept and can be summarized as an attitude of mind, and approach or a philosophy of running a business organisation that regards the customer or the consumer as a focal point around which all other decisions revolve.

Depending upon the size and nature of a business concern, a typically marketing oriented organisation has a marketing director, and middle and junior marketing management personnel. The appointment of marketing personnel is no longer confined to fast moving consumer goods manufacturers such as chocolates, cigarettes and beer. Local councils, hospitals, charities, bus companies and even political parties now employ marketing directors and managers to market their products, services or ideas.

(b) Needs, wants and values of target markets

The marketing concept is based on the principle that all the activities of an organisation should be geared to meeting the needs and wants of its customers. This implies that the organisation must allocate sufficient resources, attention and effort to constantly researching, monitoring and evaluating the needs, wants and changing values of those customers. Organisational survival depends on the firm's ability to secure repeat business amongst its customers. Repeat business or purchase only occurs if, and when customer satisfaction has been achieved. An unsatisfied customer will, on the next occasion, buy a competitor's product or service and may also spread unfavourable work-of-mouth messages about a company or its products. Customer satisfaction only results when the product, service or the organisation meets the exact needs, wants and values of its customers.

Needs

A need can be defined as a state of real or perceived deprivation. It can also be thought of as a state of imbalance or inequilibrium. For example, when an individual has gone without food for some time, there is a feeling of deprivation, or imbalance between feeling hungry and not feeling hungry. All human needs stem from our basic physiological, social and individual needs for food, shelter, warmth, safety, belonging, affection, knowledge and self-expression. A need can also be thought of as a problem. The recognition of the problem prompts an individual towards problem-solving behaviour. A hungry person therefore, will take action towards correcting the imbalance or the problem, and buy or prepare something to eat. A need, or the recognition of a problem is the starting point of all buying behaviour, including the buying behaviour in organisations for purchasing industrial products or services.

Wants

We translate our needs into wants that are heavily influenced by social and cultural norms or individual personality. For example, a need for clothing is not merely to serve the purpose of covering the body, but is translated into want of a fashionable pair of jeans that conforms to an individual's peer group behaviour and acceptance. The consumer in this case has not purchased a physical product but a number of benefits that may accrue from the label, manufacturer or design of the pair of jeans. Likewise, a manufacturer of chemical products may think that farmers need fertilisers and therefore place considerable effort in promoting and selling the features of his chemicals. What the farmers really need is greater yield of crops from their soil. Here, as customers for industrial products, the farmers would be buying benefits of a particular manufacturer's fertilisers and solving a common problem.

Whilst human needs remain constant, for example, we will always need clothing, our wants change in line with our age, fashion, economic conditions, technology culture and society.

Values

All customers have values made up of attitudes and beliefs that affect their perceptions and buying behaviour. Beliefs can also be thought of as knowledge, opinion or faith depending on whether they can be verified by personal experience or by research. An opinion is a belief which has not yet been verified, and faith is a belief that is unverifiable, but nevertheless adhered to.

For example, if customers believe that manufacturers of aerosol based products contribute to damaging the ozone layer, they may decide to stop using such products and look for alternatives. Manufacturers of deodorants and air fresheners have recently changed their products and emphasise their concern for the environment. In marketing terms therefore, we can see this as an example of how a customer's need for social acceptance and belonging has now been translated into a want of an 'ozone friendly' deodorant that would nevertheless ensure effective control of body odour.

An attitude can be defined as an individual's continuous favourable or unfavourable mental evaluation, emotional feelings, or tendency to act towards some object or idea. Attitudes influence beliefs and beliefs influence attitudes. Because attitudes involve thinking as well as emotional feeling and vary in intensity, they can be measured for use in marketing products and services. Although attitude measurement is difficult, there are many methods that can help marketers to change consumer attitudes or change their products to meet those attitudes.

The definition of marketing concept also specifies that organisations must determine the needs, wants and values of 'target markets'. This means that rather than making and promoting products and services to everybody in the hope that they might be bought (a shotgun approach), it is much more effective to target products to groups of customers with different needs or characteristics (targeting).

(c) Adapt

Adapt the organisation to delivering the desired satisfaction more effectively and efficiently than competitors. An organisation attempting to implement the marketing concept may fail to achieve sustained return from its marketing effort due to the lack of the required degree of change necessary to compete effectively in the marketplace. Adapting or changing the way in which an organisation operates is probably the most difficult aspect of implementing marketing orientation in businesses that have a long history of being driven by production or sales considerations.

A pre-requisite of successful marketing orientation is the willingness and ability of an organisation to use the market research data to design the required products and to change its methods of production, sales and customer relations.

(d) Make a profit

If we accept the fact that the purpose of an organisation is to create customers, it follows that marketing is the sole revenue generating activity. In any manufacturing organisation there are four business functions essential to its operation and growth. These are finance, production, personnel and marketing.

- *Revenue* generated by sales turnover have to be managed and controlled or finance for investment raised from shareholders or institutions and the function absorbs cash resources.

- *Production*, financed by revenues and share capital also costs the organisation in terms of factors of production, raw material and warehousing for stock control.
- People need to be found, managed and administered, therefore personnel skills are essential where people are employed, for example, to manufacture the products and administer the operations, and represent an on-going cost to the organisation.

Through these three functions, an organisation can raise the finances, produce the products by employing premises, machinery and people but so far has not generated any revenue. Cash only comes into a company when it has a customer who is willing to make a transaction.

Marketing, although requires an investment (in terms of market research, new product development and promotion), is the sole revenue generating function in any organisation. The marketing function creates the customers that provide a business with the necessary sales turnover from which to release a profit. This fact is often taken for granted by production managers who use the company revenues and financial people who manage and control the money in the business.

The realization of the importance of the marketing function in creating customers and generating revenue has led many organisations to review and change their definition of what businesses they are in. Rather than thinking that they manufacture or sell, they now think in terms of what they market. For example, British Telecom Plc is no longer operating as a telephone company but are in the business of marketing telecommunication systems. W.H. Smiths do not just sell books but are in marketing and retailing of leisure products business. In these and other organisations such as McDonalds (fast-food retailers), Amstrad (electronics) and Marks & Spencer Plc, which fully implement the marketing concept, the whole of the company becomes a marketing organisation and looks to develop, manufacture and sell products and services from the marketing point of view.

Having an understanding of the purpose of an organisation and the marketing concept, it is relatively easy to develop a precise meaning of the term marketing. A simple definition and illustration (Figure 3) of marketing is as follows.

Marketing is a human activity aimed at satisfying customer needs and wants through an exchange process, providing customers with benefits that satisfy their wants for payment and profit.

9

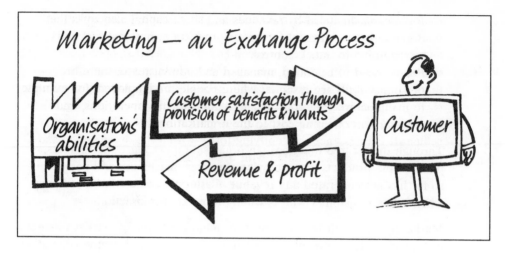

Figure 1.1

Marketing: An exchange process

In simple societies or when demand exceeded supply, business was a straight line transaction between a product or a supplier and consumers. Manufacturing companies made profits by concentrating on producing efficiently. Consideration of customer needs came at the end of a long chain of events. The customer was thought of as a problem solely for the sales force, whose task was to sell what had been produced.

A modern business, operating in an economy of abundant supply, is much more complex. Because consumers are under no compulsion to consume all that is available and there are numerous alternatives to choose from, organisations have to operate by focusing on meeting customer needs. A product idea or service is therefore rarely offered directly to the customers. It first has to go through research and development to meet the precise needs of a target market. Then it has to be produced in commercial quantities and qualities. It has to be carefully priced, promoted and finally distributed and sold in the marketplace. All these activities have to be co-ordinated by a policy making function. That function is marketing in its broadest sense.

Marketing, or the marketing concept, essentially focuses on all the activities of the organisation on satisfying customer needs by co-ordinating and integrating with the other business functions to accomplish the organisation's long-term objectives. The marketing concept as an operational philosophy does not imply that other business functions such as production and finance are secondary. Nor does it suggest that customer needs can only be met through large sales volume. The marketing concept requires integrating, co-ordinating and communicating such diverse marketing activities as product development, pricing, sales forecasting, marketing research, direct marketing, PR, advertising and selling. It is in essence the 'unifying force' within the organisation and therefore closely co-ordinated with other business functions.

Figure 1.2 below illustrates the co-ordinating role of marketing in an organisation.

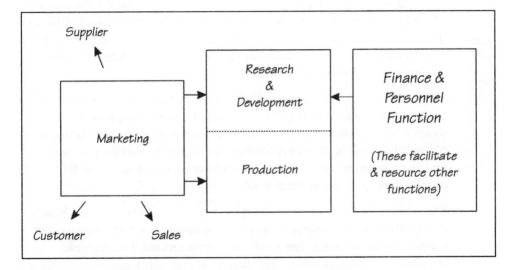

Figure 1.2
The role of marketing in an organisation

COMPETITION AND THE NEED FOR DIFFERENTIAL ADVANTAGE

In a free market economy where competition is encouraged, there tends to be many suppliers of identical products and services. In most markets, when a new product is developed by one company, the competition will follow very quickly with 'Me Too' or homogeneous products. This leads to the availability of several alternatives from which the customer may choose. In some cases, such as cigarettes, chocolate and lagers, it is very difficult for customers to tell the difference between different brands in their physical form or in blind tests. A perfect example is petrol. We do not even see it when we fill the tank with this product, but we are constantly told that one brand is better than another. A service, such as a bus ride or an air journey between two locations, offered by more than one company, is identical in meeting the needs of the travelling consumer. In order to create customer preferences towards their products and services, organisations have to differentiate their offerings from those of the competition. These differences or Unique Selling Propositions (USPs) may not be inherent in the product or service, and may be created through product planning, packaging. pricing, advertising and targeting to specific groups of customers. A good example is the way in which Heineken has been marketed as 'the only beer that reaches parts that other beers cannot reach'. There is no magic ingredient in the beer, but the difference or differential advantage has been created through creative and repetitive advertising.

The strategy of differentiation enables a company to survive amidst 'me too' products and avoid price competition. It helps a company to compete on the basis that its products are different from, and better than, competitive models. It is only through the use of marketing techniques that an organisation can create and communicate differences in its products and gain a competitive advantage.

The conversion of features inherent in products and services into benefits that customers can understand is probably the most effective method of creating differences that can easily be communicated. For example, customers can readily understand that a car has new technology components that makes it much safer in wet conditions than technical details of anti-lock braking systems. In many other cases the differential advantage in selling products and services comes from the reputation or image of the organisation established over a period of time. For example, consumers rarely question the quality of products marketed by Rolls-Royce, IBM or ICI. An appreciation of the need for all organisations to somehow differentiate their products or services is an essential pre-requisite to understanding the role and importance of marketing in creating and keeping customers.

SECTION TWO

The marketing process

The marketing process, or the implementation, has three main components that are closely linked and which together with the company's stated objectives go towards the preparation of a marketing plan. A simplified version of the marketing process is illustrated in Figure 1.3.

Figure 1.3
The marketing process

The marketing process consists of:

1. Environmental analysis

If you recognise that the only constant in business is change, environment in which you operate becomes clearly important as monitoring a basis for formulating strategy for effectively managing change.

Environment analysis basically involves scanning, understanding and monitoring the business environment in which the company operates.

This serves the purpose of analysing market opportunities and monitoring threats arising from factors beyond the company's control. All organisations operate in an environment made up of six uncontrollable variables such as market demand, competition, legal and political regulations, social and ethical pressures, technological and physical environmental change.

- Demand for consumer products is heavily influenced by the condition of the national economy and interest rates.
- Legal requirements have to be taken into consideration in the design, packaging and advertising of the product.
- Social and ethical pressures increase as pressure groups have a more socially aware and interested population, highlighted by the recent calf export issue.
- The dynamics of competition constantly threaten the company's share of the market.
- New technology for components parts and or, for production influence both the way in which a company can differentiate its product or minimize its production costs.
- Physical environment changes also affect numerous industries directly and indirectly.

Demand for industrial products such as steel is derived demand and depends upon consumer demand for products such as cars, washing machines and refrigerators. A major part of the environment is the changing patterns of customer's buying behaviour and emergence of new needs and wants. Demand for new products or services may be created by competitors but which a company can profitably exploit by analysing further market opportunities or gaps in the marketplace. Marketing research can be used to provide the company with useful information on the environment in which it operates. This does not necessarily have to be expensive, the use of desk research can be cost-effective and lead to a breakthrough strategic advantage.

An organisation must also gather information from the marketplace which will help it to forecast future sales of its existing products. Marketing research can provide information on the performance of the company's existing products and the effectiveness of the various marketing strategies, such as pricing, advertising and sales promotion. Marketing research also provides information on competition and the changing nature of buyer responses and behaviour. This feedback from the is essential for the organisation constantly to modify its marketing strategies. Market and marketing research therefore contributes to the company's Management Information Systems which aids management in its decision making process. The uncontrollable variables or factors that make up the business environment and how the Internet can be used for marketing research, forecasting and Management Information Systems (MIS) are used in formulating marketing strategies are dealt with in greater detail in Chapter 2. In addition to scanning the environment an organisation must also identify the strengths and weaknesses of the business. Strengths and weaknesses are always within an organisation, whereas opportunities and threats are in the environment. Together, Strength, Weakness, Opportunities and Threats (or SWOT analysis) are the essentials of an organisation's appraisal of its current situation. These are the core foundations of a marketing strategy.

2. Marketing strategies

A thorough SWOT, or situation analysis influences, often dictates an organisation's corporate and marketing objectives. Marketing objectives are established from an understanding of what the organisation as a whole is trying to achieve within the environmental constraints in which it operates. For example, an organisation may have a long-term corporate objective of increasing the return on shareholders' capital by 2 per cent. The corresponding marketing objective set for the organisation may be to increase its market share by 10 per cent. In order for the organisation to realise its corporate objective, it may be necessary for management to develop various marketing strategies and programmes that would, over the stated time period, attain an increase of 10 per cent share of the market. Objectives therefore signal the level of performance the organisation must achieve at some future date given the realities of its environment, opportunities, strengths and weaknesses.

As discussed earlier, because an organisation cannot control the environment in which it operates, it is forced to change and adapt its methods of operation. For example, a firm has no control over the level and nature of competition or rate of technological change affecting the market. But it does have control over its own operations in terms of product design, branding, pricing, distribution, promotion and market positioning.

Increases in competition and the introduction of new technology (i.e. the environment) will influence a firm's decisions on its choice of marketing strategies, or its controllable variables. It can decide to take its product into another market, or modify the product and launch new models that may appeal to a new class of customers. It may decide to increase or reduce the price of the product, or it may decide to increase its advertising and sales promotion effort and opt for creating greater brand differentiation. All these are examples of how a firm can respond to changes in the environment by developing specific marketing strategies that help to achieve the stated objectives. The three main groups of marketing strategies are: market segmentation, marketing mix and growth strategies.

3. Marketing organisation and control

An analysis of the firm's current situation, forecasting, objectives and selection of appropriate marketing strategies are the main components of a marketing plan. The other element of the plan is the consideration of how the strategies will be implemented in the organisation. This includes decisions on the organisation of the marketing activities, resource allocation (budgets), and control systems. It is important for decision makers to remember that the preparation of a well written marketing plan with creative strategies is only a part of the marketing process. Any marketing strategy must have potential for successful implementation by people within the organisation. If the environment dictates the development of a certain marketing strategy then the firm must ensure that it has or will have the human resource available for its implementation. Marketing organisation structures and budgets are the main means for co-ordinating action.

The purpose of financial control and targets is to monitor the extent to which progress towards an objective is being made and to identify the causes of any failure to achieve it so that remedial actions can be taken. This is why there is a reverse arrow in Figure 1, indicating that marketing organisation and control also influences the formulation and revision of a firm's marketing strategies. Marketing planning must never be regarded as an annual exercise with a plan gathering dust on a bookshelf.

Marketing planning is a process which requires managers to modify objectives, strategies and organisation structures in order to effectively deal with the dynamic and turbulent nature of the business environment in which they operate.

The structure of the book

This book has been structured on the marketing management process framework outlined in the above sections. The essence of the book is to demonstrate how organisations can use the Internet to aid the overall marketing function rather than merely as promotional medium.

This book is organised into nine chapters and a number of appendices.

Chapter 2, 'Finding out about your world and your market' takes a detailed look at the six key environmental variables and demonstrates how the Internet can be used to collect valuable information from numerous sources around the world. The chapter shows, with the aid of practical examples, how information can be scanned and gathered on issues such as the economy, national and international legislation, money markets, company information, consumerism and technological innovation.

Chapter 3 outlines the scope of the Internet as a market and marketing research tool. It demonstrates the ease with which remote databases of marketing information can be accessed to collect secondary data and how the medium is developing into a communication network that will allow organisations to conduct primary marketing research from the comfort of the office. The chapter explores the potential of turning the personal computer into a virtual worldwide library.

Chapter 4 'Building your marketing information system' demonstrates how an organisation can extend its management information system by integrating its internal information with new information captured from a multitude of electronic sources. It outlines how the Internet can be used as the communication vehicle within your organisation.

Chapters 5 to 7 provide you with a detailed explanation and reference to the practical and realistic use of the Internet in the planning and implementation of the marketing strategies.

Chapter 5 'Establishing your global niche - segmentation critical to success' gives you a segmentation methodology which enables you to segment your own market, segment the Superhighway and find whether there is a match. It outlines market segmentation as the foundation of the marketing principle and demonstrates the potential of reaching many different individuals and groups of potential customers.

Chapter 6 'Exploiting your global niche - the best marketing mix' outlines how the Superhighway impacts your existing product, pricing and distribution channels. It outlines ideas of how to tailor these in tune with the use of the Superhighway. It deals with the application of the new technology in product planning, gaining information for pricing decisions and the Internet as a new distribution system.

Chapter 7 'Promoting yourself on-line' deals with the fourth element of the promotion mix - promotion. It covers all the major areas in which the Superhighway can act as a promotion vehicle alongside your existing promotion channels. It is devoted to the Internet as a major new promotional medium and covers many of the latest ideas and development in the art and technology of getting organisations on to the system.

Chapter 8 'Producing your promotional materials in Cyberspace' outlines the considerations and differences in using this new medium. It gives practical advice on the 'do's' and 'don'ts' of producing promotional literature in cyberspace.

Chapter 9 'Integrating the superhighway into everyday marketing' aims to provide technical and practical assistance to enable the Superhighway to become integral within your organisation. It enables both marketing and non-marketing professionals quickly to familiarize and use the Internet as a marketing tool on an ongoing basis. It provides a practical guide to the use of the Internet as a medium to source suppliers, recruit personnel and develop yourself and your team.

Chapter 10 'Where is this all taking us?' provides a final look at the potential development of this exciting medium. It outlines possibilities and implications for the marketer.

The Appendices offer you background support to your use of the Superhighway. They enable you to get on-line, search and understand netiquette and newsgroups.

The marketing management process, techniques, outcomes and the framework of this book is outlined in Figure 1.4 below.

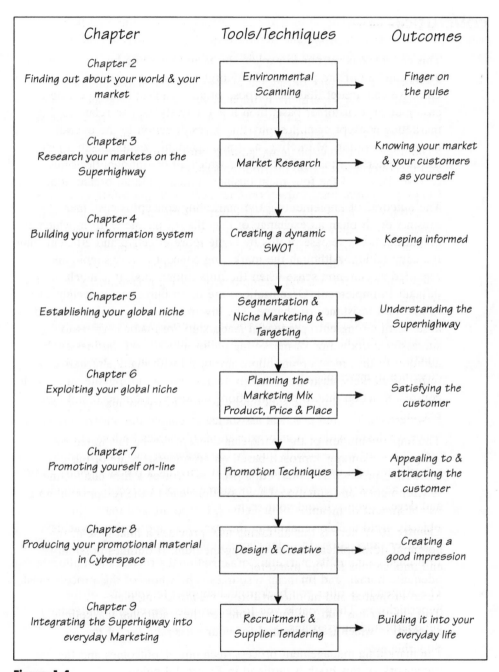

Chapter	Tools/Techniques	Outcomes
Chapter 2 Finding out about your world & your market	Environmental Scanning	Finger on the pulse
Chapter 3 Research your markets on the Superhighway	Market Research	Knowing your market & your customers as yourself
Chapter 4 Building your information system	Creating a dynamic SWOT	Keeping informed
Chapter 5 Establishing your global niche	Segmentation & Niche Marketing & Targeting	Understanding the Superhighway
Chapter 6 Exploiting your global niche	Planning the Marketing Mix Product, Price & Place	Satisfying the customer
Chapter 7 Promoting yourself on-line	Promotion Techniques	Appealing to & attracting the customer
Chapter 8 Producing your promotional material in Cyberspace	Design & Creative	Creating a good impression
Chapter 9 Integrating the Superhigway into everyday Marketing	Recruitment & Supplier Tendering	Building it into your everyday life

Figure 1.4

The framework of the book

CONCLUSION

This chapter has set out to explain the term marketing by developing an understanding of the purpose of any organisation as a starting point. Once we can accept that the purpose of an organisation is to create a customer or a customer base, then it is relatively easy to relate to the marketing concept or philosophy that gives direction to the overall business operation. Marketing, as a management orientation that places the customer as a focal point around which all operational decisions revolve, is one of the four main business functions in an organisation.

The outcome of implementing the marketing concept is customer satisfaction through an exchange of benefits for payments from which an organisation can release profits by being more effective and efficient than the competition. Although the marketing concept is very simple and regarded as common sense when the fully understood, it is much more difficult to implement. Organisations are often burdened by weight of history and resistance to change. The inward looking management and absence of strong entrepreneurial leadership are major barriers to successful introduction of marketing philosophy in such businesses. In addition to this, most organisations are faced with many alternatives in terms of markets, customers and strategies and cannot pursue all possible courses of action due to the limitations imposed by financial and human resources.

The implementation of the marketing concept can be facilitated by adopting a planning approach based on an understanding of the marketing process. The marketing process involves a firm conducting environmental and situational analysis that lead to the re-appraisal and establishment of meaningful objectives. Corporate and marketing objectives aid decision makers in the strategies appropriate to achieve customer satisfaction. In order successfully to implement the strategies, a firm must examine its marketing organisational structures and allocate adequate human and financial resources. The whole of this process must be co-ordinated and monitored through a marketing plan.
This chapter has laid the foundations for the traditional marketing orientation which is so essential for your successful use of the Superhighway.

CHECKLIST

You now know:

The purpose of an organisation.	☐ Yes	☐ No
The difference between production, sales and marketing orientation.	☐ Yes	☐ No
The management orientation of your organisation.	☐ Yes	☐ No
The importance of the needs, wants and values of your target audience.	☐ Yes	☐ No
Marketing is the sole revenue generating function in any business.	☐ Yes	☐ No
The formal definition of marketing and the marketing concept.	☐ Yes	☐ No
The importance of differential advantage in a competitive business advantage.	☐ Yes	☐ No
The marketing process consists of environmental analysis, marketing strategies and marketing organisation and control.	☐ Yes	☐ No
How marketing can be integrated into your business processes.	☐ Yes	☐ No
The difference between promotion and marketing.	☐ Yes	☐ No
How the book is structured.	☐ Yes	☐ No

WHAT NEXT?

The next chapter will enable you to stand back from your everyday business to assess the environment and the influences that impact your marketplace - enabling you to keep your finger on the pulse.

REFERENCES

Drucker, P. (1954) *The Practice of Management*, Harper & Row, New York.

Levitt, T. (1986) *The Marketing Imagination*, The Free Press, New York

Kotler, P. C. (1984) *Marketing Management: Analysis, Planning and Control*, 5th edition. Prentice Hall, London.

Davidson, H. (1987) *Offensive Marketing: How to Make Your Competitors Followers*, 2nd edition, Gower, London.

2 Finding out about your world and your market

'The Internet feels like the 60's, you know there is a party going on, you just don't know where.'

Most marketing people claim that their greatest fear is that they are in abject ignorance of their place in the market. Most marketing people suspect that they may not have fully grasped their full worth in the marketplace. Very few marketers would claim with confidence that they have got their finger on the pulse at all times.

If you can relate to any of the above, this chapter is for you. It is about 'where to look' on the Superhighway and how to go about alleviating those fears. It will help you to design and implement the basis for an effective Management Information System (MIS). This can then improve strategic management decisions and lead to vastly improved marketing.

KNOW YOUR MARKET AS YOURSELF

Knowledge about the marketplace is key to the success of a marketer. The more in-tune with the market, the more successful an organisation becomes. However, the environment changes the marketplace in a dynamic process over time. Forecasting, understanding and assessing the environment remains the marketer's greatest challenge and opportunity. The Superhighway provides a new tool to monitor and test the environment.

The environment consists of six main uncontrollable factors or variables. These are:

1. Market demand
2. Political and legal forces
3. Social and ethical influences
4. Competition
5. Technology
6. Variations in the physical environment of the marketplace.

These pose both opportunities and threats. They need to be measured, monitored and analysed by using marketing research and forecasting techniques. The information collected by using these techniques can then be incorporated with other sources of information to form a Management Information System. Consequently, this becomes a crucial part of informed decision making. The Superhighway plays a vital role for providing this information from a worldwide source. Indeed the Superhighway is such a large and diverse source of data to marketers, the challenge is efficiently to select and filter data so as to provide appropriate and up-to-date information. This is the key to using the Superhighway successfully to monitor the environment.

MARKET DEMAND

Demand for products and services relies on the economic and behavioural aspects of the consumer. The key determinant of consumer demand is the amount of disposable income available to purchase products and services.

People predicted the recession two years before it happened in the late 1980s; those companies which used and planned using that information were the ones that are survived and even prospered in this decade.

Predicting market demand by looking at the economy and government policy may seem a little far fetched. However, the alternative is to react only when it hits the bottom line and often this is too late to take action constructively.

Market demand is strongly affected by political policies. The Government can control the amount of disposable income consumers have by changing the interest rate. A reduction in the interest rate releases money from consumers' mortgages and encourages them to borrow more from banks and save less. The increase in the public's buying power fuels the economy and creates demand for all types of goods and services. Under the pressure of higher inflation rates, the Government can increase the interest rate to slow down or control the growth of the economy. An example of this arose during 1979/80, when the Government slowed economic growth through the increase of the interest rate together with other anti-inflationary measures. This caused higher unemployment through rapid decline for goods and services.

Demand for industrial products, such as machines, chemicals and metals is also dependent upon the demand for consumer goods and services. Demand for industrial products is *derived* demand because industrial products and processes go into consumer products or help in the manufacture of consumer products. For example, demand for steel depends upon the demand by consumers for new cars, washing machines and new houses.

Implications of this for the marketer

It is essential that the individual takes steps to comprehend fully the external influences on the overall marketplace. This year, Bryant and May stopped producing matches. They were badly hit by the production of matches within the Eastern block. This could have been foreseen with the changes taking place in the Eastern block and some desk research into international competition. This would have flagged up the threat of the former Yugoslavia which had a strong and low-cost match production capability.

A professional marketer will understand the wider context of the market environment. To do this, the following factors need to be continuously monitored and assessed:

- General condition of the national (international) economy - interest rates
- Regulations on hire purchase and personal loans
- Inflationary pressures
- Unemployment
- National taxation policy
- International trade policy

> For an updated index to a collection of general economic indicators
> see http://www.marketingnet.com/cybermarketing/economic

The effect of 'lifestyle'

The behavioural aspects of a market such as demographic and lifestyle trends also influence the extent and nature of demand for goods and services. Changes in the demographic composition of the market and in lifestyles can give rise to new market demands and signal opportunities for new product development, thus influencing the direction of an organisation's marketing strategies. Irrespective of income, many consumers will demand products and services that help them to maintain their life-style or the norms of behaviour and consumption defined by their personal social status. Fashion is the other behavioural determinant that influences consumers to buy products regardless of consideration of their economic situation.

Some of the important demographic and lifestyle changes affecting demand and therefore marketing strategies in the 1990s are:

- The increase in the number of working women and their changing role in purchasing and decision making within the family.
- Changes in the nature and size of the family unit. There are an increasing number of divorces, a greater proportion of single parents and unmarried households and more significantly the decreasing birthrate.
- Changes in the age composition of the UK population. The post-war baby boom has resulted in the largest section of the population being in their mid-thirties and early forties. This group represents a market with most significant disposable income and is an important segment for retailers and manufacturers. Superhighway retail outlets such *CD-*

Now and *MarketNet* (see the first section of the book 'Read this first' for an explanation of why these words are underlined) are examples of how marketers are catering for the needs of this age group. The other group of people that represent many opportunities for products and services and problems for the caring authorities is the 65+ group. In this decade, this will become one of the largest sections of the population.

- The increase in the part-time and self-employed sector of society means that 35 per cent of the population are not full-time employed within organisations, according to the classic model of capitalist society. This, combined with the previous point supports the findings of the OECD, related the fact that in 1993 only 33 per cent of the over 55s were in full time employment. For France it was 27 per cent and for Italy this figure is 11%. (Handy, 1995).
- The increase in remote and home working which is becoming more and more prevalent, especially in the service sector. Directory enquiries in Scotland is essentially a network of remote workers where an enquiry to routed out to someone working from home.
- Changes in social class and mobility. This has been facilitated by widespread home ownership, shares ownership and better education, job opportunities and lifting of European barriers will mean new opportunities for organisations to cater for the changing lifestyles and purchasing behaviour of many consumers with increased buying power.

> To access this type of information from a dynamic source contact
> http://www.marketingnet.com/cybermarketing/lifestyle

POLITICAL AND LEGAL FORCES

The political and legal processes in society greatly affect the way in which an organisation operates. Changes in legal regulations and requirements give rise to many new opportunities and threats and influence the way in which products and services are marketed. The deregulation of industries such as gas, oil, telecommunication and other utilities through legal processes has given rise to many new opportunities for competition and marketing to increase customer satisfaction. Other recent examples of opportunities arising from legal changes include rear seat passenger restraints in all new cars, and lifting the ban on advertising by such professions as dentists, opticians, architects and lawyers.

But the most significant and dynamic legal requirements that affect the marketing of goods and services are those concerned with the provision of information to the consumers. The following are just some of the legal mechanisms that regulate the marketing and advertising of products and services:

- Pricing legislation
- Trade Descriptions Act
- Sale Of Goods Act
- Government standards
- Packaging and labelling acts
- Health and Safety regulations
- Consumer rights

A fully developed and regularly updated legal reference site can be found at http://www.marketingnet.com/cybermarketing/legal

ASSESSING SOCIAL AND ETHICAL INFLUENCES

The roles of the consumer in the marketing environment can never be under-estimated. Active involvement by consumer and pressure groups have forced the need for social responsibility and protection of corporate reputation to the fore of marketing and operational decisions. Social responsibility has to be demonstrated by concerted action and communication to the marketplace. Organisations polluting the environment may not only face legal penalties but may lose hard-earned customer goodwill.

In order to maintain good image and reputation amongst the public, companies must avoid the following:

- Misleading advertising
- Poor product performance
- Hidden financial charges
- Inadequate product information
- Unnecessary exploitation of the environment.

For environmental references, we recommend you see:
http://www.marketingnet.com/cybermarketing/environment

SIZING UP THE COMPETITION

Although the size and nature of the market is the starting point for market considerations, an organisation must monitor the level of competition prior to formulating strategies for continuing or entering it. Competition is probably the most dynamic of all the environmental factors. In a free economy, as new organisations enter, others exit, therefore causing unpredictability in the market. Careful monitoring and evaluation of the competition enables marketing management to make informed decisions.

Competition comes from two sources. An organisation normally faces competition from others in the same field as well as from organisations in other industries. For example, a butter manufacturer competes against other butter manufacturers but also competes against soap manufacturers who produce and market margarine from edible vegetable oils that go into the making of toilet soap. Those companies who enter your market with a by-product or subsidiary product can often be more of a threat because they may be able to cross-subsidise investment from their core products in the downturns of your market.

An organisation needs to be pro-active in identifying and exploiting opportunities by anticipating competitive strategies. A pro-active approach requires an organisation to place considerable effort and emphasis on conducting a competitive audit. The Superhighway has over 100,000 companies connected, many using it to present themselves to their customers. Marketers can use the Superhighway to conduct a competitive audit of many companies without even needing to leave their offices!

An effective competitive audit should provide answers to the following questions:

- What marketing strategies are currently being pursued by the organisation's main competitors?
- How are they likely to change their strategies in the future?
- What is the likely size of the market? What is the competitors' share of the market? How are they performing in terms of sales turnover, return on investment and profitability?
- What are the competitors' strengths and weaknesses in relation to the organisation and the future developments in the market?

A competitive audit involves the collection of the following categories of information on the organisation's main competitors:

- Competitors' plans and organisation
- Product strategies including new product development and product-line extension plans
- Pricing strategy
- Advertising and promotional strategy
- Production and investment plans
- Distribution facilities and strategies for developing and using different outlets and distributors
- Other major events

There are many legitimate methods of gathering this information, including scanning annual company reports, promotional literature, price lists, product catalogues and auditing the selling of the product, all of which can be readily obtained off the Superhighway (if published). Sales and market share data can be obtained from syndicated research services. Business and inside knowledge of competition is sometimes brought into the organisation by head hunting and recruiting from within the industry. There are also many published sources of information on the structure, future and current trends of a particular market.

THE IMPACT OF TECHNOLOGY

The rate and nature of technological innovation is a deciding factor on the marketing and operational decisions of an organisation. New technologies create opportunities by providing the means of new product development and improvement in the methods of production.

An example of how new industries emerge from investment in technological innovation is the invention of optical fibre. It was invented to meet the needs of telephone companies and has created new industries in the overall field of telecommunications, including cable TV, electronic banking and other consumer and business information systems.

Over-investment in technology can impose a threat to an organisation. Becoming too technologically driven risks ignoring consumer needs by falling in the trap of first producing the products and then finding a market for them. Research and development should work closely with the marketing function and develop new products around a thorough

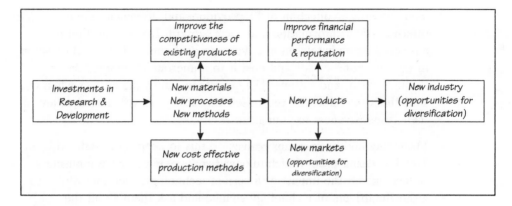

Figure 2.1
The role of technological innovation in the marketplace

understanding of customer problems and availability of alternative products. The launch of the Sinclair C5 best illustrates the pitfalls of technological orientation. Although research indicated that there was significant demand for a personal transporter that would run on a 12v battery and not require a road licence, the company failed to let the potential customer see and try out the product prior to its launch.

Organisations do not necessarily have to be the first in the field of technological innovation. In fact in many industries it is high risk to be the 'first in', e.g. the video industry where Betamax was first in and technically superior but failed to establish itself as the standard. Many organisations survive by monitoring the technological developments in the market and quickly adapting their products to incorporate the latest ideas. Others improve on the research and development of their competitors and launch products with additional benefits to the consumer. It is estimated that 80 per cent of new companies are 'me too' organisations but attempt to differentiate themselves either by product or marketing differentiation.

The Superhighway can facilitate the marketer in three ways:

1. **To provide access to a dynamically updated reference source to technological changes**
   One of the main reasons IT professionals tap into the Internet is that it lets them find out about a subject area in a fast and efficient way.

31

You can visit a collection of IT providers and investigate their offerings, their information and their support. If your question isn't answered immediately on line, you can pose the problem and question in your word-processor and post it to numerous IT support desks through e:mail and forums. They can then return the answer when it suits them to collect the responses; this also gives you an indication of their responsiveness to your needs.

Marketing and business executives do this to keep up to date with the ever increasing pace of technological change. If you have a business concern about the impact of a certain technology, then one way is to go to the drivers of technology change and ask them about the expected growth rate, speed of adoption etc. Ensure that you post these questions to proponents of both the existing and also the new technology. Next use forums to ask how the end users feel about the prospect of this new technology. In this way you are likely to be able to build up a picture of how this technology might affect your business.

Is the innovation demand-led or technologically driver. Often IT companies invest heavily in attaching business needs to their technological developments. Often these business needs are contrived and not a genuine concern of end business users and ultimately the technology fails to make an impact. Neural networks and expert systems were two examples of technological push rather than user demand and have not entered the general business application market because of this. Yet much of the press cited these as 'changing the world as we know it'; marketing people spent time trying to assess the impact on their business but many forums revealed how disappointed business people were with the time taken to utilise and leverage the technology.

If you are an office furniture producer, remote working and portable technology pose a threat to your organisation and here the secret is to assess where the drivers are coming from. Toshiba, Compaq and IBM are heavily investing in promoting remote working as the 'Need' of the 1990s, i.e. they are reacting to the needs of organisations. In fact, remote working was a term derived by the IT world and remote working was not on the business agenda before the portable computer revolution. In fact there is little evidence existing to prove the business benefits of remote working or the supposedly huge demand from organisations, but this technology plays into the human 'want' for ownership and status. Here, you, as a marketing or business executive must subjectively decide for yourself who are the stakeholders and how much are they likely to invest to support the technological change process. In this case, the driving force is the technology companies with access to substantial investment and therefore this technology is likely to prove successful. Whether this results in the majority of executives working from home is a completely different debate.

2. **To provide access to your competitors' use of advanced technology** Companies often promote themselves with reference to their advanced R & D and often give indications of which technology they are experimenting with. This, of course can be a bluff. The fact that some companies have invested heavily in the Superhighway and others haven't is itself an indicator of how easily and quickly your competitors adapt to new technology.

3. **To provide a medium to investigate and gauge customers' reaction and need for new technology** (see product planning in Chapter 6). Many companies use the Superhighway to test market products and services. This is not only cost-effective but low risk. Warning: as obvious as it may seem, a good product development idea posted on an open forum can travel the world as fast as it has taken to type and this is the best way to reveal confidential information to your competitor - so please be warned.

ASSESSING THE PHYSICAL ENVIRONMENT

The environmental factors mentioned above have a human origin in that they result from human activity. Although cumulatively this activity, such as economics, behaviour, law, competition and technological advances are beyond the control of an individual organisation, they can nevertheless be monitored and predicted with some degree of accuracy. The prediction and forecasting of the changes in these variables can help an organisation in formulating appropriate responses and strategies for future operations. But markets are also at the mercy of the physical environment which is more difficult or impossible to predict. The physical environment is made up of geography, location, climate, seasonality and accessibility of the market.

The Superhighway can provide you with:

- Meteorology references
- Climatical forecasts
- Geographical references

For geographical references, we recommend you see:
http://www.marketingnet.com/cybermarketing/geographical

HOW THE SUPERHIGHWAY CAN MAKE MONITORING THE ENVIRONMENT EASIER?

We have provided you with a private chef's tour of reference sites on the accompanying web-site to aid you in the task of environmental analysis. Most Superhighway software (browsers) enable you to bookmark sites of interest to make returning to these areas of interest easier. By book-marking, you can regularly look up environmental indicators and this can become a vital part of your Management Information System. Maintaining a dynamic on-going monitoring system of the marketplace and the environment is one of the most important aspects of the marketing.

If you really want to make the process even slicker, you can set up an automatic search for updates on sites of interest. Simply download a piece of software called 'Webwatch.' from http:/www.specter.com/users/janos/specter/index.html (referenced on the accompanying web site). Leaving this software to run overnight (on-line) gives you a report of any changes found on your list of bookmarked sites. Small changes can be monitored quickly and easily

CONCLUSION

World class marketers know their market and the environment. This chapter has outlined how the Superhighway can help you in this task. It has provided you with references of where to find vital information to assess your environment. It has not been intended to be exhaustive but a starting point for your own exploration.

This chapter has helped you strengthen your knowledge of your environment, appreciate whether your organisation is in touch with external factors and enable you to feel confident that you have got your finger on the pulse. We have taken you back to the necessary theory but provided you with a fast and easy solution to move forward and answer the questions posed for your organisation. So are you in touch with your environment? Is your finger on the pulse? How in touch is your organisation?

CHECKLIST

You now know:

The six variables you need to monitor in the environment	☐ Yes	☐ No
Where to look on the Internet to have access to these six environmental indicators.	☐ Yes	☐ No
Factors which impact market demand.	☐ Yes	☐ No
How to assess the political and legal influences on your organisation.	☐ Yes	☐ No
The importance of assessing social and ethical influences.	☐ Yes	☐ No
How to size up the competition.	☐ Yes	☐ No
How to assess the physical environment.	☐ Yes	☐ No
How to keep your fingers on the pulse with bookmarking.	☐ Yes	☐ No

REFERENCES

Charles Handy (1995) *The Empty Raincoat - Making Sense of the Future*, Arrow Books published by Cox and Wyman Ltd, Reading.

WHAT NEXT?

The next chapter takes you from the general to the specific – helping you explore and research your marketplace and your place within it.

3 Researching your markets on the Superhighway

The Superhighway will become the market research medium of the future. As marketing research is gathering information from many different sources, the Superhighway will become a very powerful medium for companies to scan published data from around the world and also to gain feedback directly and instantaneously from the target groups of customers. This enables people like you to understand your customer easier and more effectively than ever before.

Now, it is all too easy to see the Superhighway as an extension of your own marketplace. Your existing customers may be on-line and it is tempting to use this purely as a new medium to communicate with them. This is the first trap companies fall into. They jump straight in to 'Promotion' rather that take a disciplined marketing approach. This is counter-productive in two respects: firstly existing customers act differently using this medium; and secondly, it fails to take advantage of potential new markets.

Market research will give you the ability to understand how your target segment uses this new medium, what they are looking to achieve and how you can add value to their activity. It will also enable you to identify new target sectors and understand their needs. Again, remembering the 10/90 rule,

> 90 per cent of what you do on the Superhighway must add value, 10 per cent can sell – any other combination fails

unless you fail to add value to your target audiences you will fail to achieve results. You can only add value if you know what is of value to them.

This chapter has two broad aims. Firstly it has been designed to provide an overview of the market research processes and methods as used in conventional marketing. These can be used to understand your customer and their use of the Superhighway. Secondly, it details the sources of marketing information that can be accessed on the Superhighway, i.e. using it to actually conduct the research.

Marketing research is a significant discipline in its own right within the very broad marketing function. The scope of the book only allows for an introductory coverage of this important aspect of marketing.

To date, only a small proportion of sources and methods described in this chapter can be accessed on the Superhighway. The volume changes daily and we are confident that all major suppliers of marketing data will be on-line, selling their services directly through the Superhighway using on-line credit taking facilities. The advantage for the marketer is that this data can then be fed straight into the Marketing Information System and kept dynamically updated through the Superhighway.

MARKETING RESEARCH

Prior to examining the Superhighway as an emerging research medium, it is useful to have an understanding of what marketing research entails in conventional marketing.

There are many definitions of marketing research, and clarification is not helped by the introduction of the term market research. To simplify matters, the term market research should be used to mean the collection of information on a potential market that the organisation may be interested in entering. Because the organisation is not already marketing in that market, the research is concerned with finding out the state, nature, size and buying behaviour of the market. It may include investigations concentrating on researching the needs, wants and values of the potential customers in that market to guide the organisation's efforts to develop a new product. It also includes the development and testing of the prototype of the concept to the test marketing stages of an eventual product launch.

Marketing research refers to the research undertaken when an organisation is already marketing its products and services. Marketing research is used to provide the constant feed-back from the market so that management can formulate the most effective marketing strategies and change their short-term tactics, if needed to counter the effects of competitive actions. Similar techniques and sources are used to collect both market and marketing research data, but which may be modified depending on the objectives of the investigation. Marketing research is much wider in its range of functions than merely to investigate and analyse data on markets. The scope of marketing research can be seen from following two definitions.

(i) 'Marketing research is the systematic problem analysis, model building, and fact finding for the purpose of improved decision making and control in the marketing of goods and services'. (Philip Kotler)

(ii) 'Marketing research is the systematic and objective search for and analysis of information relevant to the identification and solution of any problem in the field of Marketing'. (Green and Tull)

In summary, therefore, marketing research is concerned with the scientific investigation of ALL factors affecting the marketing of goods and services. Its scope is virtually limitless, answering such questions as:

Who? What? When? How? and Why?

Marketing research is employed in the provision of information to aid the decision making process in the following main fields of marketing.

1. Research on markets

- Analysis of market size and level of competition including value, volume and share distribution for products and services.
- Competitive audit of strengths and weaknesses.
- Market demand including buying behaviour, frequency, repeat buying, motivations and demand factors such as seasonal and other fluctuations.
- Market structure, who buys, by age, sex and social class groupings, and industrial buying patterns.
- Market trends and business forecasting, including industry changes and impact of technology.
- Studies of export markets and other opportunities.

2. Research on products and services

- Determining present uses of existing products' characteristics that are most important, and research alternative uses of the products.

- Comparing consumer or customer acceptance of existing products with similar competitor products' strengths and weaknesses.
- Studies aimed at product line simplification.
- Packaging research, design or physical characteristics.
- Test marketing of new or improved products.
- Determination of advantages and limitations of proposed new products.

3. Research on marketing policy and strategy

- Studies of prices – their influence on sales, and in relation to competitors' pricing.
- Evaluation of price policies – discount structures/distribution.
- Appraisal of current sales methods and practices.
- Studies of distribution methods – costs, alternative channels, effectiveness.
- Territorial and individual salesman effectiveness/variations.
- Evaluation of sales incentive schemes – prizes, bonuses.
- Effectiveness and importance of sales/after sales service.
- Analysis of the effectiveness of sales promotion activity – exhibitions, PR, merchandising and point-of-sale material, special offers.

4. Research on advertising

- Analysis of competitor practices in relation to current policy.
- Research prior and during the development of advertising campaigns.
- Pre-testing and post-testing of advertisements.
- Evaluation and selection of media.
- Studies in advertising effectiveness.

5. Other possible areas

- Economic forecasting – both financial/budgets, and model building.
- Transport and logistical studies – distribution planning optimal allocations.
- Plant location studies.
- Marketing intelligence, analysis and evaluation with a view to acquisitions and licensing agreements/joint ventures.

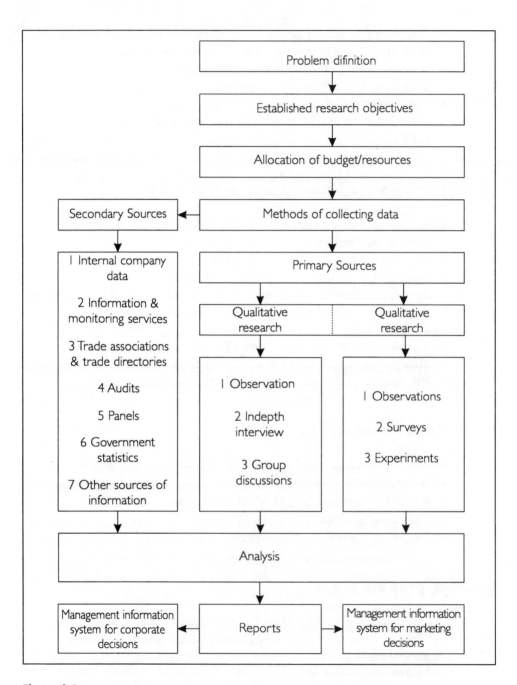

Figure 3.1

Marketing research: an overview of process, sources and methods of collecting data

- Legal aspects of patents, legislation affecting products, labelling, restriction and sale – importance in export evaluation.

WHERE DO I START?

Before deciding on what methods should be used to collect information, it is necessary to be clear about the marketing problem, the aims of the research, the budget available and sources and methods of collecting data. An overview of the marketing research process, sources and methods of collecting data is given in Figure 3.1.

There are two main sources of marketing research data.

1. Secondary sources (or desk research)
2. Primary sources (own research)

Secondary sources

Secondary data is information that has been collected by research carried out by the company, other organisations or official bodies and that is readily available in a published form.

Although secondary data is collected for purposes other than meeting the organisation's objectives, it is nevertheless a very useful first source that should be consulted to gain an overall impression of the marketplace. Secondary sources of information cost little or nothing, but require effort and knowledge of the various publications and reports available.

Finding good research on your marketplace is often the most frustrating but most fruitful place to start. The availability of this information will vary considerably according to the specific market concerned. Consumer and retail market information are a lot more readily available than that for business to business markets.

1. Internal company data

A good starting point is to look internally to your organisation and find out what has worked and what hasn't. What product ranges sell best off the page and which ones demand a different approach. If you are looking to promote your organisation on-line this is essential.

It is very hard to decide how company data should be used and what data is needed as it will depend on the job in hand and the information available. Sales records are usually a good place to start when analysing the market. The sources of internal company data that can be used to gain a useful impression of the company performance in the marketplace are highlighted here.

Marketing data
- Price lists
- Customer lists categorised by business sector; by amount spent with the organisation; by location; by product type
- PR releases, articles and editorials
- Adverts placed
- Direct mail produced

Sales data obtained through analysis of invoices
- By product
- By product line
- By customer class
- By cost centre
- By region
- By salesperson
- By competitors

Annual reports
- Financial Report for the organisation: P& L, Balance Sheet etc.
- ”   ”   for customers
- ”   ”   for competitors
- ”   ”   for suppliers
- Trade association data
- Payroll
- Departmental budgets
- Manufacturing cost reports
- Accounts receivable
- Inventory reports
- Trade journals
- Sales call reports
- Manning tables
- Personnel department reports
- Census data
- Marketing cost reports

Market research data that already exists in the company
- Audit and panel data
- Special projects
- Customer demand schedules
- Questionnaire replies

Marketing personnel
- Turnover ratio
- Hiring ratio
- Transfers
- Promotion
- Absenteeism

Financial information
- Credit
- Discount analysis
- Promotional allowances
- Budgets
- Customer list
- New accounts

This data is an essential ingredient for the Marketing Information System described in Chapter 4 for which the use of the Superhighway as the publishing medium can be very powerful. A good overview of information is essential also when it comes to promoting the organisation on the Superhighway (Chapter 8) because it enables the implementer to have easy access to factual information which can be used to build the credibility of the organisation in Cyberspace.

2. Information and monitoring services

A quick comment about on-line marketing reports

Marketers ask us how much of this information is on-line and unfortunately we have to reply: 'Not very much because it can be sold and why should companies give away what they can sell?'. There is certainly more marketing information available for America than Europe but the same concept applies, only high level information is available with on-line billing for further details. CompuServe offers the best on-line marketing reports for America, but next to nothing for Europe. On a more positive note, as the

---

payment systems of the Internet become more widely accepted, information providers will use this medium for distributing marketing reports.

So our advice to you is, don't waste valuable time and money looking for marketing reports on-line, buy them direct from existing data suppliers or contact some of the suppliers listed further in this section.

However, conducting a general on-line search will give you some idea of the extent of published information about your marketplace. We recommend that you start by conducting some very general searches on key words about your industry, market and your company name. We recommend using a variety of different searches on the Internet and trying 'Find' on CompuServe. If this is not familiar to you, please consult Appendix 5 – How do I search for things? Don't be disappointed or get frustrated – any really valuable market information is not going to be given away for free.

Alternatively visit a public reference library (one that has a business services section) which is normally the best starting point. Try ABI/Inform – it is free and scans all publications and abstracts on key words. Your librarian will give you access to this database and you just need to type in a key word to obtain a list of abstracts of relevant articles places in journals, newspapers and periodicals.

Market survey and monitoring reports
Published surveys and reports are a low cost/no cost starting point as these are the established way of collecting information on markets, products, media, customers and competitors. The main survey and monitoring reports are:
- MEAL
- MINTEL
- Retail Business
- Key Note Publications
- BRAD and ABC
- Financial Times Research Index, amongst many others

MEAL
The Media Expenditure Analysis Limited (MEAL) was originally set up in 1957 by the Daily Telegraph, Daily Express and Daily Mail groups to

monitor all the advertisements in the press and on TV. Like the National Readership Survey, it cannot offer a blanket coverage; but all commercial TV stations and 500 different publications are monitored. The products are sub-divided into 330 different product groups: radio, cinema and poster advertising are not monitored.

MEAL offers a variety of different services, the most usual is the MEAL digest, which is a list of advertisers and their expenditure broken down by months and the moving annual total. In addition to the digest, there are more detailed breakdowns by publications but these are only available to media owners. There are four analyses available to the advertiser: advertisement analysis; brand advertising by media group; brand advertising by TV company and brand advertising by area.

The main criticism of MEAL is that the expenditure is calculated on a rate card basis and is therefore unrealistic. MEAL is useful for an organisation keen to determine how much competitors are spending on media advertising and what media is being used. One of the problems with the data on media expenditure is that it only covers what is being spent on main media and does not show the other promotional expenditure by competitors.

It is an expensive publication and often not held in public libraries for this reason. Most advertising agencies will have invested in this directory and this may prove the most effective access point.

MINTEL (Market Intelligence Ltd), Retail Business (EIU Publication) and Key Note Publications
These three publications are the main reference material on gaining comprehensive information on markets, products and future trends. The publishers produce monthly reports that are freely available in business sections of public libraries or at a reasonable price. These publications specialise in surveying large numbers of fast moving (such as foods and drinks) and consumer durable products (such as washing machines and TV sets). Retail business has a good reputation because of its affiliation with the Economist Intelligence Unit of the *Economist*, and specialises in products sold through retail outlets. There is also *Retail Business Europe* and the publications also forecast the trends in the market and carry out occasional studies on the development of retail outlets in the UK and Europe.

These three organisations exist by charging for their reports so they are not likely to ever offer these on-line for free. But what is useful is

looking up the index which quotes the contents of the reports and the costs. They also offer on-line subscription to their services. Mintel is on the Internet at: http:/www.mintel.co.uk.
Also write to them at:
Mintel International Group Ltd
18-19 Long Lane
London
EC1A 9HE
Tel: +44 (0) 171 606 4533 e:mail Mintel@cityscape.co.uk

Retail Business
On-line retail and consumer market information at present is still primarily focused at the American markets. Nevertheless, a good starting point for this information is 'Business Demographics' (BUSDEM) hosted by CompuServe. The Business Demographics Reports are designed to help businesses analyse their markets. Two types are reports are available by various American geographical units (including county, Arbitron TV markets and Nielson TV markets). This is a premium service and therefore charged on a per time used basis.

BRAD and ABC
British Rate and Data (BRAD) is a monthly publication that provides information on current advertising rates of all the mass media in the UK. It covers all newspapers (including free sheets), magazines (general, specialist and industrial), television (including satellite), radio, posters and cinema. For all newspapers and magazines, BRAD gives their ABC circulation figures which can help a company or an advertising agency to calculate and select the most cost effective media to use. The ABC (Audit Bureau of Circulation) is the authority which audits the circulation of all major newspapers and press media. Circulation (number of copies distributed) figures and readership (number of people reading one copy of a newspaper or magazine) figures from national readership surveys are normally used together to select the most appropriate media in which to advertise.

PR planner
A widely used and popular information databank is provided by Remeike and Curtis called the PR Planner. This is a media database of editors and forthcoming editorials either provided as a book or as a dial-up service. The dial-up service (Media Disk) offers access to 18,000 titles and 34,000

contact names in the publishing business.
Remeike & Curtis Ltd.
Tel: 0171 251 9000.

The Research Index
This is published by Business Survey Ltd and references all published
research papers, articles. This helps you then to find the information you
need within newspapers, periodicals, journals etc.

ANBAR
This is an abstract of research indexes that cover the areas of personnel,
top management, transport and distribution, IT, accounting and auditing.

Financial Times Index
This is a useful first source of information and provides cross references
to special reports, survey, articles and newspaper coverage on a large
number of subjects. These include products, markets, technologies, trends,
economic factors, reports and export markets and other very useful
information. It is also now available on CD from your local reference
library which has a business section.

Other information available on CD
The following research indexes are also on CD:

- INSPEC: this covers the electrical, electronic and mechanical
  engineering industries.
- URBA DISC: this covers environmental issues.
- EC Info: this covers European laws and directories
- Current Technology Index: this covers all the latest technology
  developments.

We predict that in the foreseeable future when on-line ordering is
commonplace, that much of the information provided here will be
available on the Superhighway.

What next?
If you are not in the retail or consumer sector, there is unlikely to be a
one-stop shop on-line, so you need to be more calculating in your search
for data. The next place to search is trade associations who may or may
not be on-line as yet. *MediaNet* looks a promising site to be able to index
trade associations. This might prove to be a good starting point. We have

also highlighted a number of other sources in the accompanying web-site to this chapter.

3. Trade associations and trade directories

Most industries have trade associations with the aim of providing members with information and assistance that is useful for their operation and expansion. Trade associations therefore publish data on new products, markets and technologies that has been gained from surveys of the industry. Studies can, however, be very limited in scope and statistics may be difficult to interpret if important companies or groups of companies are omitted. Because of the restricted number of secondary data for industrial marketing research, trade associations studies can sometimes be very useful in providing a starting point of researching industrial markets.

Trade directories can also provide useful information on companies within a certain industry. Information on suppliers of products is often a useful starting point of studying the level and nature of competition in the marketplace. The main trade directories for marketing research purposes are as follows:

- Bradstreet Register
- Dun and Bradstreets' Guide to Key British Enterprises
- Kompass (Volumes 1 and 2)
- Stock Exchange Year Book
- Kelly's Directory
- Consumer Marketing Manual of the UK
- Industrial Marketing Manual
- Key Note Reports

On-line sources include:

- Dun and Bradstreet
- Medianet
- UK Business Directory

4. Audits

Again, if you are in the consumer or retail industry, desk research on competitive products is likely to be fruitful, especially audits.

Audits for individual companies can be very expensive, and host companies wishing to use retail or wholesale audits tend to use a syndicated service such as A. C. Nielsen.

The method of data collection is retail sampling. Every two months actual stock levels on display are recorded in a series of sample shops. These are classified into different retail organisations, multiples, co-operatives and ordinary retailers and the total sales per month are recorded. Clients may specify particular brands or package sizes to investigate and whether in special areas or the whole of the UK market. In addition clients may commission special analyses or tables on particular products, for example, the effect of special offers. Nielsen also covers advertising expenditure on newspapers, magazines and TV on each brand that is investigated and collates this information with stock movements. It also supplies data for every brand in the market during the period of the report. This is itself secondary data supplied by the Media Expenditure Analysis Ltd. The main use of the Nielsen Index is to provide information on the distribution of the product in the various retail organisations and the level of stocks and rate of turnover particularly for new products.

Additional information such as where the stocks are placed, source of supply, are also included in the auditors record. The data is scrutinised and then itemised and finally grossed up to universe levels. The standard type of information that is computed from these audits is:

- Consumer sales – actual sales in volume and sterling
- Retail deliveries
- Retail stock
- Stock cover
- Average stocks and average sales per shop handling
- Average price paid
- Distribution
- Showings, i.e. point of sales materials.

All this information is broken down by region and shop type. Additional information is available from the data, the most important of which is probably breakdowns of forward and reserve stocks.

The major disadvantage of audit reports to the market researcher is that the Nielsen Index is confidential and may only be used by those who have permission from the client.

The main advantage of audit information is the trend patterns which emerge from national data. Audits are becoming increasingly dependent on the large multiples and if a company such as Boots refuses to participate, the results of the audit can be somewhat suspect. However, the audit does have another disadvantage in that it has a long reporting period of two months, which is not always quick enough.

A good on-line starting point is Consumer Reports (Consumer) by CompuServe. This is not a premium service (i.e. premium priced service) but is still only focused at the American market.

5. Panels

A panel consists of a representative sample of individuals, households, shops, stores, wholesalers or organisations from which data is obtained at regular intervals. It is similar to a focus group in which a group of people are brought together to focus on a key issue or discussion. The main difference between a panel and a focus group is the latter is usually a one-off activity whereas the former is used to describe a set of people who may be used again and again by your organisation. They provide a continuous process and set of data which can be compared over time to provide trend information. The use of panels to obtain information about particular groups, organisations and their behaviour has the following advantages.

Trends can be studied – including sales, brand share, source of purchase, consumer attitudes, behaviour and usage. Although trends can be studied by using a series of separate samples, the use of the panel has some important additional benefits. Use of the same sample provides more accurate information and greater precision in results as sample variations are avoided.

As the sample remains the same the behavioural patterns can be followed through time for individual members – useful for brand switching/loyalty, repeat purchase behaviour.

Costs of sample selection and recruitment are spread over many surveys, and reduce the need for subsequent planning and supervising of fieldwork. Panel members learn instructional procedures, and are usually co-operative in supplying complete data. If interviewing is involved, time is saved, but mainly the benefit is in the quality of the data obtained.

Panels are valuable for conducting experiments under controlled conditions where the reactions of different groups or reactions to different marketing activity can be measured and compared. This is useful for new product development and for assessing the effect of changes to advertising or the effects of sales promotion campaigns. Most importantly, it is one of the best ways to investigate customers' response to the Internet as a marketing medium. One example of this is the collection of TV audience viewing figures run by BARB (Broadcaster's Audience Research Board) where a panel of households around the country have a monitor which records which channel is viewed. The household is also required to complete a diary to record the number of people who were actually watching a given programme.

There are several panel services available in the UK. Examples include Attwood Consumer Panel (household and personal consumer goods) AGB for household products and AGB Index for spending habits, savings and insurance.

6. Government statistics
The Government Statistical Service is made up of statistics divisions of all the major departments plus the Business Statistics Office and the Office of Population Censuses and Surveys and the Central Statistical Office which co-ordinates the system. It is considered to be the largest single provider of statistics in the country.

The Government Statistical Service exists primarily to serve the needs of Government but it is readily used by business managers. It is not expensive, but does not claim to give tailor-made answers to individual organisations' problems.

On-line government statistics include a number of census of populations to local regions. The whole of the UK is not on-line but there are pockets of census data for a number of towns. See *Census of Bristol* and the accompanying web-site for a full list.

7. Other sources of information
7.1 British and statistics
Other sources include published surveys such as the TGI (Target Group Index) which identifies and describes specific consumer target groups and their newspaper readership and TV viewing habits. Omnibus surveys (where a number of organisations share the cost of a survey) and Lifestyles Surveys are the other sources used by companies marketing consumer products. University research departments and other independent organisations also provide valuable information that can be readily available to marketing researchers.

For an overview of a lifestyle analysis of Internet users see the GVU (Georgia Tech's Graphic, Visualisation and Usability Centre) Surveys which are referenced on the accompanying web-site plus being outlined briefly in the next chapter.

7.2 Creating your own marketing information
The two most commonly adopted approaches are:

(a) Identification and monitoring of key players
This is where you would identify and monitor the 5 to 10 key players in your given market. This assumes that they are Limited companies and therefore publish accounts. CompuServe makes this particularly easy by enabling you to set up a regular search which is run overnight on their servers, which then reports back results to you. This means that the costs are kept to a minimum. Likewise you can set up bookmarks on the Internet (see Appendix 2) to reference the activity of key players. You can then use 'Webwatch' (see previous chapter) to monitor any changes but again this assumes that they publish their company's activities on-line.

This approach is particularly relevant to IT-based products and services where all key players are Limited or Plc type organisations and all are on-line.

(b) Independent sales pooling
This is where an independent organisation (most commonly banks) will act as a sales pooling agents working alongside a market research consultant. Here the key players in a given market agree to pool their sales figures through this intermediary. Confidentiality is critical and each member's sales figures are ONLY seen by the sales pooling agent who then publishes the total accumulated figure to identify the size of the market. Each member is also given their share of the market and this is usually monitored on a quarterly basis or monthly basis. Each member agrees to pay the sales pooling agent a fee for providing this service but this is usually a relatively small investment. The most common approach to setting up a sales pooling syndicate is to contact a market research company who will then liaise with an intermediary (e.g. bank) on your behalf.

The most innovative sales pooling organisations use the Superhighway to collect information from the syndicate on-line which help them to:

- collect information from each member quickly and cost effectively
- assimilate and cumulate the data automatically
- disseminate the results at the touch of a button.

Many Internet marketing companies offer to do this service for a fraction of the cost of using conventional methods. Some organisations may perceive using a marketing company through the Internet as less secure than going through a bank and the postal system, but in reality there is no security threat and the contractual arrangements on both sides are identical.

Secondary sources of information for industrial products

Marketing research
There are far fewer sources of on-line information on industrial products and markets than on consumer goods. This is due to the very diverse nature of industrial markets and lack of investment by marketing intelligence companies to research and publish data both on-line and off-line. There is also a lack of syndicated research that can be published. The main sources of information are:

1. Business monitors
   These give data on output by industry and cover almost all the industrial activity in the economy.
2. Government publications
   Many of the Government publications cover industrial production, employment, competition, regulation etc.
3. Trade journals
   There are many trade journals for each of the industrial sectors and these provide useful information on the state and future trends in that industry. Details of trade journals available can be found by referring to BRAD (as discussed above).
4. British Technology Index
   British Technology Index publish a monthly index of articles and research on industrial markets and products.
5. Business Surveys Limited
   Business Surveys Limited publish research index and articles in newspapers, financial and trade journals and can be a useful starting point of further research into industrial markets and products.
6. Sources of UK Marketing Information
   This is published by Neilsen and includes information on industrial products and markets.

Secondary data, due to its very nature, may be of limited initial use to an organisation. In order to answer specific questions regarding an organisation's own products or potential for entering new markets,

53

researchers have to use primary research. However, secondary sources of data can provide a valuable base upon which to design and implement primary research that would solve problems particular to the company.

Primary sources

Primary sources of information is that which has originated directly as a result of the particular problem under investigation. Primary research is normally carried out by an organisation's marketing research department or commissioned through a marketing research agency or company.

Methods of collecting primary data
Methods of collecting primary data can be categorized into two groups:

- Qualitative research
- Quantitative research

Qualitative research
The main characteristics of qualitative research are:

- It is usually exploratory or diagnostic and is normally used to 'get a feel' of the situation. As such it is the starting point on which other research methods can be developed.
- It involves small numbers of people who are not sampled on any statistical basis, that is the sample selected may not be representative of the population.
- Participants may be selected to represent different categories of people or organisations. No hard and fast rules can be made from the data collected by these methods. It is, however, possible to subject it to statistical analysis.
- The findings are impressionistic rather than definitive.
- The researchers are interested in quality of information rather than in quantifiable data.

Qualitative research gives the marketer the best insight into the use of the Superhighway by their desired target audience. We cannot stress enough how vital this is in order to appreciate the relevance of the Superhighway, the target audience's current use of the Net and what potential there is for using it as a promotion and merchandising tool.

There are three main methods of collecting qualitative data, namely by:

1. Observation
Observation research is used in many areas of investigation where people would not answer interview questions correctly because:

1. They do not know the correct reply
2. They are unwilling to tell because of embarrassment or from reasons of pride or prestige.

In this research method the information is collected by observing some action of the respondent rather than by asking questions. It is a cost-effective method of collecting primary marketing information and can be used as a scientific technique when it

(a) serves a formulated research purpose
(b) is planned systematically
(c) is recorded systematically and related to the general proposition
(d) is subject to checks and controls on validity and reliability.

Information can be gathered by personal or mechanical observation.

Personal method involves a researcher to observe respondents taking some action, such as buying behaviour in a store and recording the observations. The personal observations can be followed by interviews with a sample of respondents to obtain additional information. Mechanical observation normally involves the use of electronic or mechanical devices to record or count the action by people or vehicles. Hidden cameras are also useful in gathering data by observation. The methods of collecting data by observation has been successfully employed in the following types of fields of study.

- New product development (for example, cars, kitchen fittings and other appliances)
- Merchandising (store layout and stocking of products)
- Behavioural research
- Advertising copy.

The problems associated with this method of collecting data include: high costs involved in training people, writing up the results, not being able to give underlying reasons for behaviour and the method being unrepresentative of the target market concerned.

The secret to success on the Superhighway

The best way successfully to promote your organisation on the Internet is to:

- Get into the hearts and minds of your potential customers who are using the Internet. The best way of doing this is to watch how people use the Superhighway. Finding out the first place people go when they start using the Internet, what they choose to bookmark and why, and what they like to see on a web page or newsgroup.
- Find out what your competitors are doing both nationally and internationally by observing their presence on the Internet or in some cases their distinct lack of activity.
- Observing the Superhighway activity of industries with a similar make-up to your own.

---

2. In-depth interviews

In-depth interviews are carried out amongst small samples of people to explore a particular issue and to gain a better understanding of a given problem or situation. It requires the researchers to identify respondents who would represent the target market and conduct an in-depth interview using a schedule of topics or an unstructured questionnaire. Depth interviews are normally recorded on a small tape recorder or notes are taken verbatim. Interviewers use visual aids or other material to help illustrate the topics of research. Tape recordings are then transcribed and quotations are used for analysis and reporting of the interviews. Quotations and overall analysis of depth interviews are then used in planning group discussions and or questionnaire design for quantitative research.

One innovative and popular way to elicit general on-line feedback (a little quick and dirty but practically free) is to raise a general subject area and post it into a newsgroup or forum in CompuServe. You would write a message saying 'We are looking for your reaction to: . . . Please reply giving your response, your background, your interest etc.'. Typically you need to offer an incentive which could be a summary of the total responses received.

Example

In order to investigate the potential popularity of this book, Butterworth-Heinemann posted a brief summary and positioning statement into an Internet Marketing Newsgroup on the Internet. They received over 30 responses, fortunately virtually all positive and primarily based on this, they decided to go ahead with commissioning the book.

3. Group discussions

Group discussions provide valuable information by encouraging the interaction amongst a group of people to discuss a topic under investigation. The group consists of eight to twelve participants who take a part in open-ended discussions moderated by a trained researcher. The group discussion provides the researcher with an opportunity to observe the group process directly and helps to chart their reactions to specific questions or to the physical product under investigation. The group also provides the researcher with information on the dynamics of attitudes and opinions that can be provoked with great spontaneity. As with in-depth interviews, the discussions are tape recorded and transcriptions are then used in analysis and reporting.

On-line, this can be done through CHAT on the Internet or a forum on CompuServe. The advantage is that it is practically free but the disadvantage is that you cannot select your respondents and this can give you biased results. However, many innovative marketers using this form of interview as a starting point for designing off-line interview questions.

The other methods of collecting qualitative data are case studies and longitudinal studies. Case studies examine people or organisations in great detail over a short period in time and provide useful information on customer or organisational buying behaviour. A longitudinal study is a detailed examination by observation of a person, setting or an organisation over a long period of time.

Qualitative research frequently provide a framework for more definitive and quantitative research.

Quantitative research
There are three widely used methods of collecting primary quantitative data: Observation, surveys and experimentation. Very rarely do researchers use all three methods on any one project. The choice of method is dependent upon the nature of the research problem, the amount of money, time and personnel available.

1. Observation
This is very similar to the observation technique described under qualitative research but here a much larger sample is involved.

2. Surveys
A survey consists of collecting a large volume of information from a significant number of people selected from a large group. A survey provides an original source of information as is regarded as the only way of finding out the motives, opinions and buying intentions of a large number of people. Survey research is carried out by gathering information by telephone interviews, postal or mail surveys and personal interviews. The method selected for a given project depends on flexibility, amount and accuracy of information required, time and money available.

Telephone interviews
This method has the advantages of speed, low cost, face-to-face communication.

Against the advantages there are a number of disadvantages:-

(i)   Telephones are not universal – industrial versus consumer surveys.
(ii)   Location of respondent, non-contact.
(iii) Difficulty of establishing credentials.
(iv)   Interviews need to be kept short.
(v)   One can't use visual cues, illustrations, motivational techniques.

Postal or mail survey
This method involves mailing a questionnaire to potential respondents and having them return the completed form by mail.

As no interviewers are required, this type of survey is not diluted by interviewer bias and problems associated with the management of interviewers.

The following are some of the advantages and disadvantages of using postal surveys.

Advantages

(i)   Cheaper than any other method despite postal increases – interviewer wages/travelling costs, and telephone charges have all increased dramatically.
(ii)   Immunity from interviewer variations.
(iii)   Respondent can work at own pace.
(iv)   Information may be required from household or group which would be time consuming using personal interview.
 (v)   People more willing to make responses to personal questions e.g. reporting behaviour which is not socially acceptable.
(vi)   Avoids problem of non-contact.
(vii)   Responsiveness to different parts of the questionnaire may indicate different levels of interest.
(viii) It is reliable in the sense that it can be used repeatedly.
(ix)   Useful in locating rare populations for which sampling frames don't exist.

Disadvantages

(i)   Questions must be simple and straightforward; lowest common denominator.
(ii)   Explanation of survey purposes, and covering letter very important.
(iii)   Reduces flexibility in questionnaire design – avoidance of routings/codings/dependent questions.
(iv)   Answers have to be accepted whether, vague or misunderstood.
(v)   All questions can be seen beforehand: can't therefore be used to test knowledge, brand awareness etc.
(vi)   Can't ensure validity of respondent.
(vii)   Can't supplement the questionnaire with observational data.
(viii) You may get a low response. This can mean that it is expensive. One way around this is to use an independent organisation to carry out the questionnaire for you. Another is to use incentives (although you may get a biased sample if you do this). If the information is critical it is best to consult an market research company who can give you advice on which approach is best suited to your objectives.

E:mail questionnaires
This is the most cost effective way to collect data. You can create a
questionnaire form on the Internet and request members of a specific
newsgroup or forum to fill it in. Typically like any questionnaire you
need to offer an incentive but this can be the results of the survey. This
is normally enough.

The disadvantage is that it takes time to collect a large number of
respondents and you cannot select respondents easily.

If you are looking for a large number of respondents and you are not
asking a large number of questions, we would recommend offering an
attractive competition. In the entry form you can ask demographic
questions which you can use to analyse the results and abstract more
targeted data and embed the market research questions within the entry
form. So long as you inform the respondent that you are using the data
for market research – this is not illegal. This process is being very
effectively used by car companies – see www.ford.com who offer a mid-
range car as the competition prize as the incentive to collect market
research data.

Personal interviews
Personal interviews are more flexible than the other two methods because
the interviewer can change the questions and clarify the issues as and
when they arise. The main advantages and disadvantages of this method
are listed below. The main disadvantages are cost, organisation and
fieldworker variations, control and supervision. Costs of using personal
interviews is often prohibitive, may be £40 or more per completed
questionnaire for industrial or commercial surveys where highly trained
interviewers need to be used. Non-response is a major problem and
requires costly recalls to be made when using probability samples.

Advantages
(i)   Advantages are to be had in questionnaire design. This can be
        more complicated, hence shorter, and can be used directly as data
        processing input.
(ii)   Interviewer can explain purposes of survey and can indicate the
        benefits – use of persuasion.
(iii)   Interviewer can explain meaning of questions.
(iv)   Where responses are irrelevant, partial, or inaccurate the
        interviewer can probe further.

(v)   Use of visual matter, checklists, diagrams, rating scales etc.
(vi)   Can be used to test a respondent's knowledge as the possibility of interaction is removed.
(vii)   Can be used where spontaneous replies are required, for example in measuring attitudes.
(viii) Can ensure validity of the respondent.
(ix)   Interviewer can supplement questionnaire with observational data.

3. Experiments
Experimentation is used where the researcher is trying to establish a cause-and-effect relationship. The most important cause-and-effect relationship is between marketing variables such as advertising, sales effort, pricing and sales results. In order to establish cause-and-effect the researcher must attempt to collect data from an experiment that involves the control of all extraneous factors so that any variation in the effect (for example, sales turnover) can be attributed to the change in the marketing variable that is being tested (for example, price or amount and type of advertising).

On the Superhighway, you can actually change the way that a page is displayed according to the country target audience you are appealing to. This would allow you to experiment with which is the best message to use across different cultures, countries and audiences.

CONCLUSION

The marketing research process, sources and methods of collecting data described in this section of the book are summarized in Figure 3.1. The resulting marketing research can be fed into a company's Management Information System of which Marketing Information System forms a sub-system as outlined in the next chapter of the book.

This chapter has helped you strengthen your knowledge of your place in the market, appreciate whether your organisation has fully grasped its potential and enable you to feel confident that you have got your finger on the pulse. It also provides you with a methodology for investigating the appropriateness of the Superhighway to deliver benefits, products and services to your customer in the most appropriate way. Used effectively this approach can enable an organisation to gain a deeper, more profound understanding of the opportunities of the Superhighway (and conventional channels) to leapfrog their competitors for strategic advantage.

CHECKLIST

You now know:

The difference between marketing research and market research.	☐ Yes	☐ No
The importance of research in understanding your customers and their buying behaviour.	☐ Yes	☐ No
The importance of research in scanning your marketing environment	☐ Yes	☐ No
The difference between secondary and primary research.	☐ Yes	☐ No
The range of low-cost, no-cost publications available in libraries and on the Superhighway.	☐ Yes	☐ No
The difference between qualitative and quantitative research.	☐ Yes	☐ No
The use of the Superhighway to cost-effectively conduct initial qualitative research, involving small samples.	☐ Yes	☐ No
The main methods of quantitative research, involving large samples.	☐ Yes	☐ No
That the Superhighway has limited on-line specific market research data but that this will be a growth industry in the years ahead	☐ Yes	☐ No

WHAT NEXT?

The next chapter outlines how you can integrate this information together for an effective decision making tool – the MIS system. This is the key ingredient for intelligence gathering and leverage.

REFERENCES

Kotler, P. (1994) *Marketing Management: Analysis, Planning, Implementation and Control*, 8th Edition, Prentice Hall International, London.

Green, P. and Tull, D. (1977) *Research For Marketing Decisions*, 4th Edition, Prentice Hall International, London.

4 Building your information system

THE NEED FOR INFORMATION

All levels of management need information on which to base decisions, plan, organise and control the various activities of an organisation. Information on its own cannot solve an organisation's problems or capitalise on the many opportunities in the marketing environment. Information has to be used to ensure that key decisions are not made without evidence or in isolation from the marketplace or other parts of an organisation.

Information is gathered by individuals from various sources and by observation and experience of events in and outside the organisation. In medium and larger complex and decentralised organisations, it is not possible for managers to observe and experience all the operations and activities in an organisation. They therefore need formal channels of information for their routine, short- and long-term planning and control purposes.

DISSEMINATING INFORMATION

In most organisations there are many formal systems of disseminating information and which are produced by the various departments or functions. These include reports, operating statements, special analysis, variance returns, balance sheets, and other financial and performance related data. Such methods have the advantage of being comprehensive, accurate and consistent. But they suffer from not meeting the exact requirements of the problem in hand, lacking in flexibility, being out of date. These sources also suffer from telling managers of what is happening internally and do not take the external environment into consideration.

Managers need information that can be interpreted to show the interrelationships between several factors. To be of any use, any such information has to be readily available and in a form that allows access to managers working in all parts of an organisation. The quantity of data available to an organisation therefore needs to be organised into a formalised and integrated Management Information System or MIS.

MANAGEMENT INFORMATION SYSTEM

A marketing information system is an integral part of an organisation's MIS. In order to understand how marketing research and forecasting data is used, it is useful to start with a comprehensive definition of a Management Information System.

MIS is an information system using formalised procedures to provide managers at all levels in all functions with appropriate information from all relevant sources (both internal and external to the firm) to enable them to make timely and effective decisions for planning, directing and controlling the activities for which they are responsible.

The essence of this definition is that MIS is a database of internal and external information that managers can use as an aid to their analysis, decision-making, planning and control purposes. The emphasis is on the use of information and not on how the information is processed.

Influences on the type of MIS
The main factors determining or influencing the type and overall structure of the MIS that is appropriate for a given organisation are listed below.
(a) The primary function of the organisation. The type of business: manufacturing, wholesaling, retailing, services or public authority is the main influence on the type of MIS that will be required.
(b) The scale structure and levels of the organisation:
  • Number of departments, sections and levels
  • Degree of autonomy of departments and sections
  • Number of people employed/sales turnover/capital employed
  • Degree of centralisation or decentralisation.

(c) Interaction with the marketing environment:
- Importance of external information
- In what ways does the organisation need to communicate with customers, suppliers, trade unions, government departments etc

(d) The types of decisions that need to be taken:
- Systematic decision-making
- Corporate long term and strategic timing or urgency of decisions

(e) The management style:
- Autocratic
- Participative

(f) Investment available for using latest technology for storing and dissemination of information.

Irrespective of the size of an organisation and whether the information is in a manual or electronic form, the fundamental structure and the typical sources are common to all designs of MIS. A typical MIS is illustrated in Figure 4.1

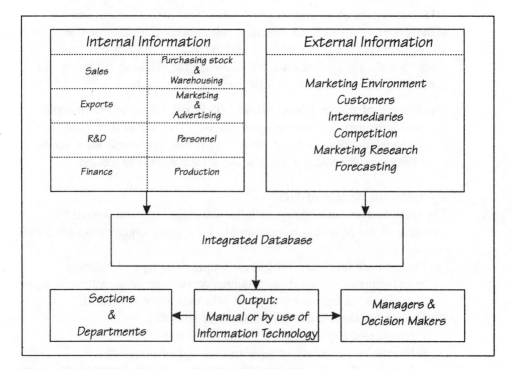

Figure 4.1

Typical inputs and outputs of a MIS

The value of an MIS

As with all types of information, a MIS has no intrinsic value of its own. The value which may be attributed to any MIS can only come from actions of managers that can be measured and evaluated. For example, the use of information must lead to decisions that increase profits, or reduce costs, or utilise resources more effectively or increase the current and future efficiency of the organisation.

The output in form of information reaches managers from a MIS by way of a wide variety of analyses, statistics and statements. These are generally referred to as reports and there are three broad categories of reports.

(i)   Reports providing passive background information

There are normally produced at lengthy intervals and give details of assets, records, depreciation, summaries of annual production statistics and balance sheets.

(ii)   Reports providing control information

These reports are produced more regularly and provide useful information and influence current and short-term tactical and operational decisions. Examples of reports include cost variance reports, credit control information, working capital statements and sales, market trends.

(iii) Reports providing statistical data for planning

These reports include information necessary for forecasting, corporate short-term planning or for longer term strategic planning. Examples of statistical reports include investment appraisals, budget models, market research reports and analysis and selective economic trends and data.

A MARKETING INFORMATION SYSTEM (MKIS)

A Marketing Information System is a sub-system of an organisation's overall MIS. MkIS provides data for marketing management decisions and has been defined by P. Kotler (1994) in the following terms:

'*A Marketing Information System consists of people, equipment and procedures to gather, sort, analyse, evaluate and distribute needed, timely and accurate information to marketing decision makers*'.

The main sources of a marketing information system are the marketing environment, the customers and from within the organisation. The value of a MkIS can be illustrated by examining the inputs and outputs that make an effective information system. Figure 4.2 shows the main components and uses of a MkIS.

The main benefits of using a MkIS are:
- It can contribute to the improvement of managerial performance.
- It integrates and disseminates complex marketing information for decentralised firms that may be dealing in several markets with a large number of products.
- It allows management to exploit and implement the marketing concept more fully.
- It encourages management to use information that the organisation has invested in.
- It contributes to better control of operations, in particular in such decision areas as product withdrawal, modifications, response to competitors' advertising and marketing effort.

A total and integrated MkIS is one which is fully integrated with other functional information systems into the organisation's overall MIS. As outlined in Figure 4.2 a MkIS relies heavily on marketing research information from the organisation's environment and forecasting of the future state of the economy and market demand for goods and services. The previous chapter has attempted to provide an overview of marketing research that can feed into a MkIS to help managers take decisions based on objective data. The aim of this chapter is to give you an appreciation of the role and importance of an information system to hold and communicate this marketing information that you have gathered. The Internet and other technologies based on the same concept enable the marketer to disseminate and leverage this information for competitive advantage.

THE INTERNET AS A MARKETING INFORMATION SYSTEM (MKIS)

The Internet is basically a communication tool. It can be used as effectively to communicate with your internal customers as it can be to

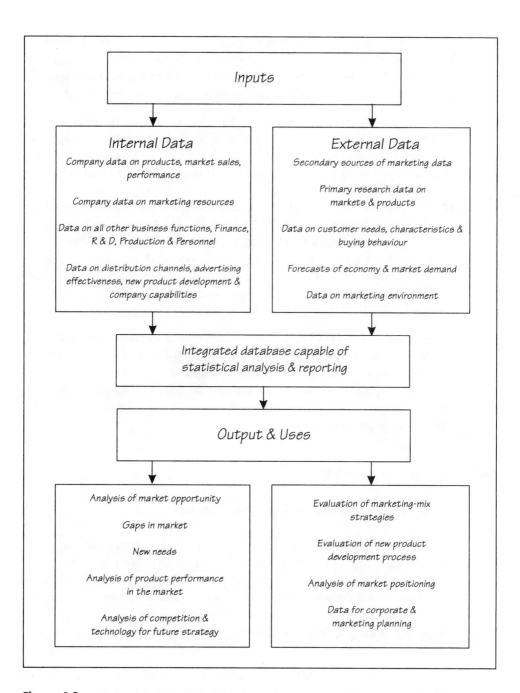

Figure 4.2

Inputs, outputs and uses of a Marketing Information System

communicate with your external customers. Here we are talking about your employees, your suppliers and your shareholders. We are not just describing the e:mail communication functionality although this is still of great value, but describing the publishing aspects of this new media.

The Internet server can be partitioned (and made secure for internal use) to provide an effective tool for creating a Marketing Information System. Here the information taken from internal sources can be collected, stored and displayed in an easy to use manner. It can be used to collect and compare information from external sources. In this way a dynamic SWOT analysis can be created and maintained for the organisation. The Strengths and Weaknesses of the organisation are stored in an internal section; the Opportunities and Threats are maintained in the other. These databases can then be used for analysis, decision-making, planning and control purposes throughout the organisation. The emphasis is on the use of this information as a dynamic source of knowledge and should not focus on how the information is then processed.

Once in place, the MkIS system can then be used to collect dynamic information from salespeople about the environment and competitors: who business was lost to; how competitive the organisation's pricing policy is; customers' responses to new product innovations etc. In this way it becomes self-maintaining and is an exciting tool used effectively by many innovative organisations.

THE DESIGN OF A MkIS

1. External and environmental intelligence

The marketing environment consists of all the factors that affect an organisation's ability to create and satisfy customers profitably. The external environment consists of many factors. The six factors that have a major impact on decision making are market demand, political and legal forces, social and ethical influences, competition, technology and variations in the physical environment of the marketplace as outlined in Chapter 2.

This information is the basis and foundation of an effective Marketing Information System. Successful marketers store this information, disseminate it and make it as widely accessible as possible within their organisation – security issues permitting. They then monitor it by enabling dynamic input from as many sources as possible: shareholders, salespeople, market research organisations, PR agencies etc.

This information becomes the front windscreen for the organisation to widen their vision of the world and focus and prioritise on what is important. It can dramatically change an internally focused organisation into a rapidly evolving and adaptive one.

Just as the web page which accompanies Chapter 2 references sources, where you as a marketer can find information about the external environment, you would provide a window to relevant information for your employees about your organisation's environment. Here you would publish market reports, key note reports, internally conducted research about your market and the environment. Again the same core concepts highlighted in Chapter 8 apply to attracting your target audience, inviting their response etc. which is still very valid. You would design your internal web site with the same care and attention as one you would produce for your customers.

2. Internal control

Some of the organisation's internal information will be published purely as an internal communication tool in order to disseminate information uniformly across the company.

However, within the remit of a Marketing Information System, you would focus on internal information which enabled you to ascertain how effective the match is between the external variables and your internal competencies. This information is likely to include many if not all the factors listed in the previous section within the section entitled 'Internal Company Data' (page 41).

In this way you can build an overview of what your organisation can offer, achieve and deliver – uniformly communicated across the organisation.

3. Policy decisions

The MkIS monitors and evaluates an organisation's opportunities and threats (external and environmental intelligence) against its strengths and weaknesses (internal control). This provides you with a dynamic, self-maintaining SWOT Analysis. This provides marketing management with the information necessary to manipulate the variables that can be controlled and changed in response to the changes in the environment. The Internet ensures that this data is kept maintained and you are not left with a decaying MkIS.

Policy decisions result from this dynamic SWOT analysis which includes changes to products, pricing, promotion, channels of distribution, type(s) of target markets served and line of business. These types of policy decisions can determine the success or failure of an organisation. Therefore, it is imperative that the system provides accurate and timely information which people trust, respect and regularly reference. A key role in this process is to set up a filter mechanism which enables information to be checked before it is published into the Internet. In most cases this filter is the marketing department who validate the external information coming in and ensure that the internal control information is correct at any point in time.

A good MkIS will also document why a policy decision was taken. Highlighting the underlying thinking and assumptions which were paramount at the time enabling a historical review of good and bad decisions. This enables the organisation to learn and improve its decision-making capabilities. It is a brave act on behalf of senior management to reveal this to the whole organisation and most commonly this is kept with restricted access only to those involved in the decision making process. However, this still enables those involved to review previous decisions and understand why and how they worked (or didn't if the case may be!). Documenting this information is also an excellent way to help smooth the process of succession management and alleviate the turning wheel effect where new management unknowingly repeat the same mistakes as those that preceded them.

It is important for an organisation to trap the background reasons why a policy decision was taken. This is typically forgotten in the echelons of time and needed when this policy is revisited and needing to be renewed. Understanding why policy decisions were taken, the environmental and internal variables that impacted the decision is critical for organisation learning. Often companies carefully trap external data but fail to trap the impact this then had on the internal change process. A successful marketer monitors the environment, monitors the impact on the organisation and captures the resulting actions and bottom-line impact on performance. This not only builds a powerful professional record of success but creates a knowledge bank which is a powerful and valuable corporate asset. Novelle would argue that 'the future isn't what it used to be' but the business process does follow patterns and the lessons from yesterday are valid for tomorrow if the variables that impacted the decisions are captured. Examples of this is where price wars repeat and damage all major players in the market. The reason why they repeat is that the knowledge of how badly they affected each player is not harnessed and evaluated at the time the decision was taken.

Results of our survey conducted on the Internet

For the purposes of this book 35 marketing directors from medium sized organisations (100–500 employees) were asked whether they had a Marketing Information System. Thirty-two said 'yes'. Of those 32, 30 were in a paper-based format and 2 were in an electronic format. Of the 32, 28 said they only stored external data on competitors, market indicators and marketing reports. Four said they stored internal data in addition and compared this to what decisions arose.

Most said that they conducted some sort of yearly SWOT review, analysed how external factors should affect internal decisions on pricing, product development and promotion. Most said that they were looking for a system to help move the process from a once off event to a dynamic process. All said that resources were their major obstacle. Interestingly none appreciated that the Internet could be used for this purpose.

The feasibility of this option depends heavily on the size of the organisation and its budget. This is not relevant for an SME (small, medium enterprise of less than 100 people) because it requires a significant investment in having an internal web-server (a computer that is permanently attached to the Internet). If you are not looking to buy your own web-server, please skip this chapter and move on to Chapter 5.

THE INTERNET AS AN INTERNAL COMMUNICATION TOOL – INTRANETS

The whole of communicating even the most simple of initiatives across the whole of a large organisation can not only be costly and time consuming but often ineffective. Pockets of the organisation can become saturated whereas others can be left in ignorant bliss. Often it is the sales people who are not within the organisation's physical location every day, that are most poorly communicated with. Ironically it is exactly these people who need to understand and relate to major changes within the organisation. Senior executives need a tool to enable them to communicate changes and initiatives consistently, efficiently and continuously. Internets make the ideal solution.

The research findings discussed in the previous chapter are examples of information which, once shared with the whole organisation, can impact onto the commitment and acceptance towards your Cybermarketing campaign. What better communication tool to communicate the use of the Internet than the Internet itself.

What we are describing is a relatively new application for the Internet. An organisation will purchase a web-server to host its own Internet site to the outside world. At the same time, it will partition a part of this computer to host its internal web site. The organisation reserves a dedicated part of the machine on which to publish internal information. Customers and Internet users cannot access these pages because they are kept secure within the organisation. Security is a major issue and it is essential to use a 'Firewall' and we discuss this later in Chapter 9.

In this way:

- The corporate business plan can be posted throughout an organisation and kept dynamically updated.
- The marketing plan can be integrated with the marketing activities so that internal team members can see how the overall plan is being implemented.
- The corporate policy documents (appraisals, expenses, holiday entitlement etc.) can be stored in one place and updated regularly without having the paperwork mountain that so many organisations wrestle with.
- The company's newsletter can be read on-line.
- Price lists and product descriptions can be referenced throughout the organisation, even by salespeople who work remotely.
- Interactive forms could be used to configure, price and print quotes for fast delivery to customers.
- Stock levels can be queried remotely.
- Discussion forums can be hosted to improve intra- and inter-departmental communication.
- A quality control feedback system can be implemented and all the documentation and proformas can be stored and updated without incurring the huge paperwork changeover process.
- A suggestion scheme can be initiated with anonymity built in.
- New versions of software can be collected by employees and so enable them to receive the latest version of software.

Centrally publishing internal communication is only one benefit. The real benefits are derived from the ability to interact with employees in respect to this communication. Senior manager can create response forms which enable employees to feed back their response, ask questions, comment or extend the corporate 'think'. Just as the Internet can provide a closer link between the manufacturer and the customer, so too can it create a closer link between senior management and the worker on the shop floor. It is a brave step to implement. Done well it can flatten the structure and innovate the company through a change process which would otherwise take years to implement. Many of the large American organisations use the Internet primarily for this purpose and have found the benefits greatly outweigh the initial investment needed to build the IT infrastructure. Many of the universities throughout the world produce a web-site solely for enabling fellow academics access to their e:mail addresses and research publications.

There are many tools to enable this process to become easier and slicker. All the main software houses produce 'internal web-publishing' tools; making it easy for senior managers to design their own internal web pages. Many companies are already doing what has been described here using other software products. The huge growth rate in the sale of Lotus Notes™ (a corporate e:mail and internal communication tool) has come about primarily based upon organisations' need for faster dissemination and collection of information. Lotus Notes acts in effect like an Internet system (Intranet) and can be much easier for SMEs than implementing an Internet server. The success of Microsoft Exchange™ is predicted for exactly the same reason. Our recommendations are to review these software products alongside the use of the Internet for a MkIS system.

CONCLUSION

There are many sources of information, both internal and external to an organisation. The relevant information has to be collected and made available to management in an accessible and employable form. The most valuable Marketing Information System is one which relates how the external variables were responded to (or not responded to) over time through an internal change process. This then builds a valuable and powerful knowledge base to improve future decision making. It is time-consuming and expensive to setup and maintain but this needs to be compared with the potential benefits and improved decision making ability it could offer an organisation. The Internet offers the ideal tool to publish and maintain this information.

CHECKLIST

You now know:

The difference between an MIS and a MkIS	☐ Yes	☐ No
The key ingredients, inputs and outputs of an MIS and a MkIS	☐ Yes	☐ No
The issues relevant for the design of an MIS to your organisation	☐ Yes	☐ No

The value of an MIS system to your organisation   □ Yes   □ No

The use of a webserver as a MIS and MkIS
publishing and monitoring facility.   □ Yes   □ No

The use of a webserver as an internal communication
tool with remote workers and for cascading information
quickly throughout the organisation.   □ Yes   □ No

The use of the MIS to monitor, record and trace
policy decisions to changes in internal or external
    factors.   □ Yes   □ No

The security issues surrounding the use of the
Internet as an MIS tool.   □ Yes   □ No

WHAT NEXT?

So you've seen how to consolidate your internal and your external
marketing information to provide a marketing intelligence system for
your organisation. Next you will want to find out more about how to
segment your market and match this with a segmentation of the
Superhighway. The next chapter provides you with the theory behind
segmentation and then proceeds to segment and update you on the
Superhighway.

REFERENCES

Kotler, P. C. (1994) *Marketing Management: Analysis, Planning, Implementation
and Control*, 8th edition, Prentice Hall, London.

Lotus Notes™ is a registered trademark of the Lotus Corporation.

Microsoft Exchange™ is a registered trademark of the Microsoft Corporation.

5 Establishing your global niche – segmentation critical to success

Successful marketers break down markets into sub-groupings by reference to the different needs and characteristics of the customers. This process is essential to producing targeted effective promotion rather than a machine-gun approach which is not only costly but ineffective.

In the previous chapters we have identified how you investigate the environment and your marketplace. You now need to use this information to define customer groupings. These are collections of people who are your target markets. If you are at the conception stage where you have no previous sales history information to analyse, you may need to conduct further research to identify your target audiences. In this case, we recommend that you return to Chapter 3 to investigate this further.

The main objective of this chapter is to give the marketer an understanding of the process of segmentation and assess the business opportunity the Superhighway provides as a method of reaching and communicating with identified segments. The chapter is broken into four sections: what is segmentation;how can I segment the Superhighway; how can I use the Superhighway to segment my market; and, lastly, is there a match.

5.1 WHAT IS SEGMENTATION?

Segmentation, or target marketing approach to business operations, centres around the recognition that customers (for consumer and industrial products and services) have different needs and characteristics and that what is on offer can be changed and targeted at specific groups of people. For example, women of different ages and backgrounds require different types of cosmetics and jewellery. Many production-orientated businesses rely on the 'shotgun' approach by trying to sell the same product or service to anybody who will buy it through mass distribution and mass marketing. Some businesses adopt the 'half-way' approach and produce two or more products that have different features, styles, quality, size, etc. and offer variety to a large number of buyers rather than appeal to different groups of customers.

A simple definition of the term segmentation is given below.

'Segmentation is the breaking down of supposedly uniform markets into sub-groupings by reference to the different needs and characteristics of the customers'

We can further simplify this definition by examining its main components.

Supposedly uniform markets

Many organisations that adopt the 'shotgun' or mass marketing approach make the mistake in believing that the market in which they sell is uniform, that is, that all the customers are the same and that they will buy whatever is available. This is also the classic approach adopted by many companies on the Superhighway, seeing it as one homogeneous entity. Markets are only uniform when the product or service is very new and there is little or no competition. For example, when computers were first invented, the market was uniform – anybody who had a need for a computer was a potential customer for the products on offer. All markets slowly attract competition and many 'me too' similar or homogeneous products become available on the market. In order for many businesses to survive in such competitive markets, different organisations start to differentiate their products by addressing the different groups of customers that make up the market. Gradually the market becomes fragmented and offer opportunities for organisations to target their products to distinct groups or segments of the market.

Different needs and characteristics of the customers

The essence of a market orientation is that the customer is the focal point in running the business. The starting point or the foundation therefore of any business is its market or customer base built upon an understanding of customers' needs and characteristics. Customers for consumer products such as clothes, cosmetics, jewellery, cars, electrical appliances, holidays, trains and buses can be grouped as segments by reference to their age, sex, social class and life style. Customers for industrial products can be grouped by analysing their geographical location, types of industry, end use of products and customer size. Analysis of all types of markets can also give rise to the identification of gaps in needs that are not currently met.

Criteria for successful segmentation

Segmentation begins as part of an overall market analysis. To successfully target a market, an organisation must ensure that it meets the following basic requirements before manufacturing products for that segment.

1. Identification of a target market. This requires imagination and an ability to interpret market research information (both statistical and qualitative) and to identify the characteristics that can be employed to segment a market.

2. Measurability of the size of the identified sub-market. Once a target market has been identified, it must be measured to ensure that it is large enough to make it viable for the organisation to enter. The organisation must be able to gain information on the make-up, nature, size and any variations in demand of the sub-market. A cosmetic company highlighted that a key target audience was 30–40-year-old women who had a AB demographic profile and worked in London. Unfortunately, less than 5 per cent of them used the Superhighway and therefore it was not an appropriate or cost effective mechanism to reach these people. Another cosmetic company researched and identified a market for a luxury gift ordering and delivery service for packaged cosmetics. They wished to target 30–40-year-old males with high disposable income. The Superhighway offered this company a huge target audience.

3. Accessibility. If it had been decided that the sub-market is substantial enough to justify investment in manufacture and marketing, the organisation must research whether it can reach that group of people. The organisation must be able to communicate with the sub-market and therefore ensure the availability of media that will reach them. Also the product has to have channels or outlets for distribution to reach the target customers.

4. Appropriateness. The company must be able to match the needs of the target audience with the ability to produce the right product at the right price in the right quantities. These considerations may prevent the organisation from entering a recognised market segment. For example, it would be inappropriate for a plasctic toys manufacturing company to attempt to enter a market segment that requires wooden toys. Essentially the organisation has to decide whether the needs of the target market are within its agreed definition of 'what business are we in?'.

5.2 HOW CAN I SEGMENT THE SUPERHIGHWAY?

To help you appreciate what segmentation is really all about, we thought it appropriate to segment the Superhighway in just the same way that you would segment your marketplace. It also has the hidden advantage of giving you a segmentation of the Superhighway to match with your own to identify if there is any correlation.

There are many ways of segmenting a market. An organisation has to apply different variables such as age, sex and social class, either singly or in combination. The various consumer characteristics and patterns of behaviour can be clarified into the following four main groups.

1. Geographic segmentation

Markets can be segmented into sub-groups by reference to the different geographical location of the customers. The sub-groups can then be defined as towns, cities, counties, regions or countries.

Unfortunately, no-one can give you an accurate breakdown of users by town or even by country. This is because the only monitoring device of the Internet is the number of host machines. Each provider will have one or more of these host machines and will know how many users are connected to these. But this data is not collected or pooled at present to identify users by geographical area. There is no doubt this information will be available in the near future but at present it is the major frustration for all marketing and business executives wishing to target more effectively.

However, we do know the global breakdown of host computers for 1995, courtesy of the Internet Services Group through the Internet Marketing Report:

Country	Number of host computers
North America	3,372,551
Western Europe	1,039192
Pacific Rim	192,390
Asia	151,773
Eastern Europe	46,125
Africa	27,130
Central and Southern America	14,894
Middle East	13,776

Surveys offer some further geographical segmentation

Although much of the recent press asserts that the British are reluctant in coming to terms with the Internet, the actual figures are quite promising. In their third Internet user survey, GVU (Georgia Tech's Graphic, Visualisation and Usability Centre) discovered some promising information. For instance, the UK has the fourth largest population of Internet users in the world (after California, New York and Texas). The GVU survey places the locations of Internet users into three categories, namely USA, Europe and all, (which represents the rest of the world). Over 13,000 people responded to the survey which took place between 10 April and 10 May 1995.

Response to the GVU survey from Europe is significant when observed internationally, after the USA which provided 80.59 per cent of the replies, came Europe with 9.81 per cent, followed by Canada and Mexico with 5.52 per cent. The UK appears to be home to a larger number of Net users than anywhere else in Europe. By studying the pages on the Net you can see that there is very little text in any other European languages other than English and, to a lesser extent, German). The response to the GVU survey in Europe showed the UK to be the most interested country (3.81 per cent), followed by Germany (0.85 per cent). Other interest came (in descending order) from the Netherlands, Sweden, Finland, Switzerland, France, Norway, Italy, Belgium, Denmark, Austria, Ireland, Iceland, and finally Spain (with 0.08 per cent). By looking at the

European results in the survey it is possible to form a picture of the interest shown in the Internet in the UK.

Percentage wise, Europe has a greater share of the 16–20, 21–25, 26–30, 31–35 age groups. There is also a higher percentage ratio of male users in relation to female users and 'single' without dependents in this continent than in the USA or the rest of the world, (N.B. according to a recent survey 72 per cent of CompuServe users are married). In relation to race there is a higher percentage of white users in Europe (93.5 per cent), than in the USA (82.12 per cent), and the rest of the world (82.32 per cent).

2. Demographic segmentation

Demographic segmentation involves analysing the observable and measurable features of the population. Such features or variables include age, sex, family size, stage of the family life cycle, income, occupation, education, religion, race and nationality. Segmentation by reference to demographic variables is used most extensively because consumers' needs, preferences and usage rates are directly related to these variables. As many of the variables are observable, they can be measured and used more readily than other methods of segmentation. The main demographic variables are expanded below.

Age and family lifecycle stage

Most consumer markets can be segmented by reference to age groups. For example, the market for toys start with babies aged between 1 month and 1 year for such products as rattles, teethers and pram toys, and then expand to 1–3 years, 4–9 years, 10–13 years and so on. A organisation has to identify or construct such groups and analysis the customer needs prior to develop products for each target group.

Family life-cycle refers to the progress of life through its various stages, which can be classified and used as a useful method of segmenting markets for such products and services as insurance, cars, domestic appliances and furniture. Life-cycle stages can be grouped as follows:

- Young and single
- Young and married
- Young, married with child under 6
- Young, married with youngest child 6 or over

- Older, married with children
- Older, married with no children under 18
- Older, married with grandchildren.

On the Superhighway, there appears to be a significant difference between users of the Internet and those using on-line services such as those offered by CompuServe (or in America Prodigy). For those using the Internet only, 7.9 per cent have three or more dependents, 16.9 per cent have two, and 14.5 per cent have one dependent. For those using on-line services, 9.8 per cent have three or more dependents, 20.9 per cent with two dependents and about the same for one dependent.

63.1 per cent of females on line had no children, 60 per cent of men had no children.

GVU also researched age groups. It discovered that the average age of the Internet user was 35 years old. This had increased by four years, since the survey six months previous had found the average age to be 31 years old. European users tend to be three years younger than the Americans.

They discovered that people using on-line services (e.g. similar to Compuserve) were three years older than people just using the Internet.

Overall 50.3 per cent of users were married and 40 per cent were single, 5.7 per cent were divorced. 58.8 per cent of Europeans were single, 34.1 per cent were married.

We can conclude that the largest two segments on the Internet are young and single and young and unmarried people. However, the trend and growth of the Superhighway implies that the user profile is shifting to the older, married with dependents category. This trend is extremely fast if six months later the average age has changed by four years.

Sex

Segmentation by sex of consumers is most common in marketing fashion goods, jewellery, hairdressing, magazines, cosmetics and certain food products. Recently there has been a trend to market products such as cosmetics and diet products to men and cars, beer and cigarettes (such as Kim) exclusively to appeal to women.

The April 1995 GVU survey reported 15.5 per cent of users are female and 82 per cent are male (2.5 per cent would rather not say!). This compares to 10 per cent female – 90 per cent male reported in Oct. 1994 and 5 per cent female – 95 per cent male in Jan. 1994. Men outnumber females by a four-to-one ratio but the balance is being addressed very quickly.

Income

Income is used as the basis for segmenting markets for cars, holidays, clothing, houses, furniture and many services. Incomes can be grouped to give rise to target markets for given products. The level of income does not always link directly with people's occupations (or social class) and occasionally there is high demand for the product from people belonging to the lower social class. For example, plumbers and carpenters are skilled manual workers but may earn more money than a teacher or a doctor.

GVU reported a significant difference between on-line service user (such as those offered by CompuServe) and Internet users. The former had an average income of $80,000 compared to $69,000. Whichever value you wish to accept this still highlights that the Superhighway is used by those in the top income bracket and these values are conservative when you reflect that there is still a high proportion of students on-line.

In summary, GVU reveal that the average Superhighway user:

- Is male
- Is 31 years old
- Earns 65,000 a year
- Lives in North America
- Has a college degree
- Has a professional or technical job

We would argue that this is not particularly useful because it fails to help the marketer target and segment and would only be useful as an introduction. Companies that have published globally ignored billboards have used just the basic information and failed to appreciate the subtlety of the needs of the sub-groups. The best way to really understand the Superhighway is to look at the kind of people they are (see the next section) how they use it and
their motivation behind using it in this way (see section 4).

3. Psychographic segmentation

Segmentation by reference to customers' psychographics involves sub-dividing the market on the basis of how they live rather than on how much they earn. The maintenance of quality or standards of living are determined by social class, lifestyle and personality.

Social class

Social class of a person is based on his/her or the head of the household's occupation. The head of the household is that member of the household who assumes the financial responsibility for the welfare of the family and for the maintenance of the household. The numerous occupations are grouped into four categories commonly known as AB, C1, C2 and DE. Social class can be used in conjuntion with age and income to provide a strong base for targeting such products as cars, clothes, home furnishing, leisure activity, entertainment, etc.

When studying the employment of Internet users GVU discovered that Europe's surfers were largely made up of civil servants, college lecturers, college students, engineers, those in the entertainment business, homemakers, those working with Information systems, micro-computer specialists or people who are networking.

Lifestyle

The type of lifestyle people wish to maintain or aspire to achieve influence what they consume and purchase. Lifestyle, therefore, refers to the patterns or modes of living that have been adopted by people as their approach to life. Target segments are formed on the basis of differences in which products and brands are used to facilitate and improve the life style. In order to identify lifestyle segments, organisations have to measure consumers' interests, activities and opinions. For example, there can be five lifestyle segments for men's clothes:

(1) The conservative consumer
(2) The fashionable consumer
(3) The brand conscious consumer
(4) The outgoing consumer
(5) The price orientated consumer.

This will vary according to the product type and is an ideal area of discussion within a forum with your customers. This can be particularly advantageous to investigate prior to moving to promoting on the

Superhighway. Understanding this can enable you to customise the web site according to the brand image your customer will find most attractive. This is explained in the third part of this chapter.

Personality

Segmentation by personality types is used in marketing products and services such as sports cars, luxury items, expensive holidays, credit cards, leisure and sports activities. The analysis of personalities of end users is employed to design features into the products and the ways in which they are advertised. Personality characteristics such as extrovert, introvert, risk taking, sense of adventure and self-confidence help to build the product's personality and helps with the messages that go into the advertising. For example, from a demographic study it can seen that the heavier users of shotgun ammunition tend to be men aged 25–44 in a skilled trade, with lower income range and often from a rural area. The psychographic data show that the shotgun user is an outdoor type, more attracted to violence, less worried about risk and with lower levels of internal control (conscious). This type of information helps with decisions on where the product should be sold and what should go in an advertisement.

The personality types on the Superhighway are heavily dependent on the interest area to which the user is applying the technology. It would be true to say that the typical personality type would tend towards the 'introvert' because the use of the Superhighway is a personal and quite lonely activity, even if you can converse with 40 million others!

The best way of assessing personality types is by 'lurking' inside (listening into) newsgroups (Internet), forums (CompuServe, CIX) or Sigs (Delphi). Each newsgroup has a personality style of its own, each one has its own rules and the major contributors set the style of the discussion. This also gives you a feel for the extent of virtual communities brought together by this technological innovation.

4. Behaviour segmentation

Behaviour segmentation involves dividing people into sub-groups on the basis of their knowledge, attitudes and use of a product or service. These behavioural characteristics can be used to analyse customers and group them according to their:

User status

These can be non-users, ex-users, potential users, first-time users and regular users of a product or service. Products and marketing strategies are designed to encourage the maximum usage of the product.

People reveal their personality in different ways on the Internet. The first is in the way that they use the Superhighway. Every person using the Superhighway uses e:mail to some degree or other. But beyond this users decide to go down one of two tracks either to become a global villager or a global beachcomber (our own terminology). Because both take up time, there are very few people who are extreme examples of both. There are two types of personalities on the Superhighway.

The global villagers
Some people use it only for electronic mail to communicate, others exchange ideas in global Usenet 'newsgroups' or forums dedicated to particular subjects. Typically people like this subscribe to CIX or CompuServe. Their primary motivator in using the Superhighway is person to person networking, communication and information sharing. They may use the Internet for searching for specific information but their primary focus is networking. The extreme version is the self-employed consultant who is looking to sell his/her services on-line. They come home after a hard day and tap into their virtual office and find out who has been talking to whom, about what. They are anxious about how they appear on-line and often state their judgements in black and white to retain the ethos of an expert. Many genuine experts go on-line to talk to the populace and declare that the responses they get take a huge amount of time to answer and of often of low value.

The global beachcombers
Others use it to search, abstract, source and order. They are looking for something for nothing. When they find something of value, they have proved that they can be a loyal advocate of the provider. At the extreme, these people scour magazines for interesting places to visit, desperate not to miss out on hidden treasure. They regularly use the search databases and would boast that they know the Internet as a Londoner knows the Underground.

The global workers

These people use it as part of their everyday process of working. Contacting customers and suppliers. Referencing suppliers as bookmarks on the world wide web and using it as a communication tool with that supplier. Asking and answering business questions on line. Researching issues and technological changes. At the extreme, these people very rarely use the telephone but prefer fax and e:mail. They see the Superhighway as a critical information base to draw knowledge from and will remain loyal to sites which enhance their knowledge, ability to perform better or give them some leading edge information. They are also likely to use it personally to source domestic suppliers: hotels for holidays, presents, CDs etc.

Usage rate

Markets can be segmented into light, medium and heavy usage groups.

The GVU Survey highlighted how many hours people use the Internet. The results showed that the average user used it for less than 5 hours a week (47.1 per cent Europeans, 32.5 per cent US) but a significant number used it for between 6 and 10 hours (33.4 per cent Europe, 19.61 per cent US).

Education seems to be one of the key factors in explaining the usage of the Internet throughout Europe, not only are users on this continent more likely to be based in or receiving higher education, they also tend to be both younger and less affluent than their counterparts in the USA and the rest of the world. Percentage wise, Europeans spend less time using the Internet as a source of fun than anyone else, as the world wide web has grown in popularity it is the Americans that have shown the most interest (see figures for 'Number of months/years on the Internet).

Buying habits

This can be used to segment markets because of the differing types of products purchased and the levels of repeat purchase. The University of Michigan Business School surveyed 3,522 people in Oct./Nov. 1994 predominantly in North America and Europe. Their findings were as follows:

	Bought	Requested further information
Music	11%	35%
Electronic products	7%	36%
Videos	5%	42%
Travel services	5%	31%
Concert tickets	4%	20%
Clothing	3%	5 per cent (significant when there are few clothing retailers on-line)
Legal services	1%	7%
Jewellery	1%	4%
Sun-glasses	1%	1%

People appear to use the Internet as a part of their buying process and the more complex the variables needing to be compared the more likely they are to use the Internet as their starting point. This is why computer dealers, car dealers and music retailers are proving successful on the Internet.

Motivation factors

What people do on the Superhighway reveals their motivational factors. People who use the Superhighway use it for selfish reasons. If you appreciate these selfish reasons you can attract attention and where you attract attention, interest and desire, you will normally be able to elicit action. Many companies promote themselves on-line without the first understanding of who it is they are trying to attract and what motivates them.

This method of segmentation is much less rigorous and heavily subjective. However, it is a useful and practical way of conceptualising this huge user base in such a way as to target and promote it effectively. We have created a tiered triangle showing time progressing downwards as the user base expands.

The top of the triangle is dedicated to the people who use the Superhighway from a purely technical perspective who are seeking to understand, program and professionally and/or commercially leverage the resulting knowledge base. These were some of the first people to use the Internet and as such are an established community with some common behaviour traits. We have called these people the '**techno-lusters**'.

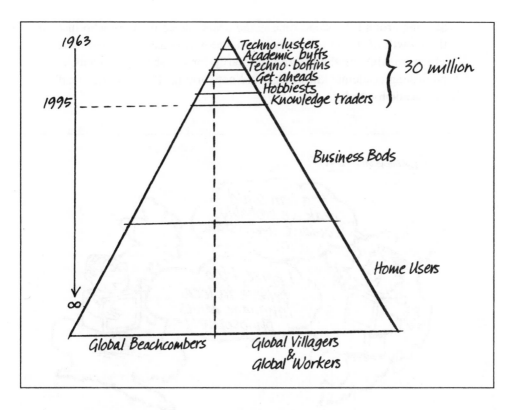

Starting around the same time is the academic community who instigated the growth of the Internet, they remain an established and cohesive subgroup who use the Internet primarily for the sharing of ideas, publishing academic knowledge and networking. These we have called the '**academic buffs**'.

The next community on line were a derivative of the techno-lusters but who were not just interested in the technology but also of reaching out to other techno-lusters. They use the Superhighway to network with other like-minded people to exchange information. Often these are IT professionals needing support for technical problems where experience is the key and re-inventing the wheel is costing them either commercially or professionally. We have called these people '**techno-boffins**'. The vast majority of forums on CompuServe and the newsgroups on the Internet have a strong IT focus for specifically this target audience.

The next tier down are the '**get aheads**' who are trying to tap knowledge banks to improve their marketability and increase their knowledge banks. They may or may not be technically minded. They are either imparting

or seeking knowledge or creaming off information for their presentations. They have a clear perception of their goals and are using the Superhighway as one mechanism to achieve them. E:mail is the main driving force behind their use of the Superhighway and speed of communication is of paramount importance to these people.

Alongside these people are the **'hobbiests'** who are similar to the 'get aheads' in that they are using the Superhighway as means of achieving a desired outcome. This time the desired outcome is less of a professional focus and more of a personal focus. Almost every hobby and leisure pursuit is covered and these people will use the Superhighway to meet people of common mind, share ideas, source information and purchase products from referrals.

One significant sector within the hobbiest community are the **'music buffs'** who want to create a interaction with their favourite group, keep abreast of the music scene, buy CDs on line and sample demo releases of music. One other significant group are of course the **'surfers'** who surf for surfing's sake and enjoy the design, graphics and culture of the Internet.

As remote working grows and portable computing grows in popularity, the growth of the **'knowledge trader'** continues. These people are similar in profile to the **'get aheads'** but are not drawn to the Internet for reasons of competitive advantage or marketability but more for communicating their knowledge back to their organisation or linking up with other knowledge workers. Often these people are lonely and use the Internet as a means of creating a virtual team environment. They are often more giving than the '**get aheads**' and spend more time searching on the world wide web for things of interest to challenge their knowledge bank.

The last two sectors '**business bods**' and '**home users**' are the growth potential of the Internet. They are not easily segmented because they are vastly under-populated or represented on the Internet at present but these are the target audiences of CompuServe and all the major providers. The light at the end of the tunnel and the gold at the end of the rainbow! As the *Guardian* point outs out (21 September 1995) 'the Internet is growing in every direction at more than 10 per cent per month. It is also becoming easier to use and navigate thanks to significant improvements in the friendliness of the technology required. When the Superhighway really develops it will be as easy as watching TV'.

Of course we are simplifying things and in the real world people may be in one or more camps.

(The words we have used to describe these target groups are not intended to cause offence and our apologies go out to people who find them in any way insulting – this was not our intention.)

5.3 HOW CAN I USE THE SUPERHIGHWAY TO SEGMENT MY MARKET?

The Superhighway is a meeting place for people with common interests, needs and worries. Forums (in CompuServe) and Newsgroups (on the Internet) offer a virtual meeting room for people to discuss relevant issues. If you can identify the people who are most likely to be interested in your product, you can then eavesdrop into their meeting and see what they are interested in, what concerns they have. You will have an ear to the ground, constantly listening to your customers.

The best way to be near your customer base is to talk to them every day. This is, for the most part, impractical for marketing and senior business executives but not if their customer base is on-line. For the large IT companies, the Internet has offered a dream come true. They set up a forum in CompuServe and invite their customers to talk to them and to talk to their other customers. They have created an instant dialogue with their target audience and by listening to what they say to other customers they can see where they are failing and where they are succeeding. This dynamic interchange has enabled IT companies to be closer to their customers. This has enabled them to react faster to customer service offerings, product development and new product planning.

The first question you need to ask yourself is 'Are my customers on-line using Forums or Newsgroups yet?' If they are, then the Superhighway has got something to offer you as a mechanism for effective segmentation. If not then you have two options: either return to traditional marketing research techniques such as questionnaires as highlighted in Chapter 3 or get your users on line by creating a forum for yourself. Many companies create user clubs and host forums just for the purpose of market research and segmentation whilst providing their customers with added value services such as a direct link with the organisation, support and other customer contact.

Assuming your customers are on-line using forums there are different approaches according to whether you are in consumer marketing or business to business marketing.

Consumer marketing

If you are a consumer marketer and need a clearer segmentation of your market, the Superhighway may offer a great observational starting point.

If you sell photographic equipment, you can discuss in a photographers' forum what people look for when they are about to buy a new piece of equipment. You may be able to elicit a response about how they liked your product. But what you are really interested in here is what defines your customers as distinct from your competitors. Observing the discussions between people can be a key ingredient to this.

A word of warning: the culture of the Superhighway is open, honest and caring to the most part. There are of course exceptions. Generally speaking though, people offer advice, opinions and reactions freely. Often the motivation is egotistical (people like being asked for their advice) but more often than not it is to be friendly as one would help somebody who is lost in the street. This friendliness and openness is one of the main attractions for people joining this culture. It is very important to appreciate this as a critical ingredient to the culture of the Internet and avoid exploiting it at all costs. Therefore, if you are looking in forums and newsgroups to identify target sectors, you may be tempted to ask person questions and in doing so offend. Please take note here to observe all the rules of netiquette outlined in Appendix 4, before contributing to any forum or newsgroup.

Business to business marketing

This is slightly more difficult because the forums on-line are by interest area or by company and what you are looking for is typically by job function. In an ideal world there would be a forum for every job function: HR professionals, finance directors etc. Because this list is changing daily, we cannot answer your question, 'are X-type people hosted in a forum?' We recommend you contact CompuServe, CIX and a few of the Internet providers for advice as to whether your function area is covered.

Our best advice is to use observational research to investigate where your customers go when they use the Superhighway, which forums they subscribe to and what magazines they subscribe to on-line. All you need to do is follow their route around and listen to them, elicit feedback in every way possible and use that feedback to increase your understanding of your target market. This book is all about finding your customers on the Superhighway and attracting them to your products and services. This sounds obvious but out of all the books on the market about the Internet very few advise you to investigate your customers' use of the Internet.

By getting really close to your customers by way of a forum, you have the opportunity of identifying what products and services they are failing to be supplied with – in other words niche marketing.

Gap analysis or niche marketing

The methods of segmenting described above can be employed to market existing products and services to distinct target groups. The other approach to differentiating the company's products, increasing sales turnover and market share is finding and filling a gap(s) in the market. This involves the thorough analysis of all existing products offered in the marketplace and to ascertain what needs are not currently being met. The identification of a possible gap or niche in the Superhighway is easy and potentially very lucrative, but is then subject to the criteria for successful segmentation and by deliberate design, manufacture and marketing of a product that would meet the needs of the customers.

5.4 IS THERE A MATCH BETWEEN THE SUPERHIGHWAY SEGMENTATION AND MY OWN?

Whether you are carving out a niche market or tailoring a product to suit the Superhighway, it is important to stand back at this point and ask the question 'Is there a match between the demographics of the Superhighway and the demographics of customers buying my product?' If the answer is 'No', we would suggest that you do not dismiss the Superhighway as a promotion medium because the demographics are changing daily. With a growth rate of over 10 per cent per month it will not be long before the demographics include your existing target audience. However, do ask yourself the question 'How important will technology be to our target audience in the medium term (approximately 2 years)?' If significant, we would suggest you start to experiment with the Superhighway. It is relatively inexpensive and the learning curve that you will develop as a result may put you years ahead of your competitors.

However, if you have reviewed the demographics and conducted some research with your target audience, not seen a correlation or a desire in your target audience in the medium term, it is wise decision to do nothing. It is a brave organisation that makes the decision to take no action. It is very easy to be swayed by the hype and press excitement about the Superhighway but it takes up valuable marketing resources where the opportunity cost of not directing them to a more worthwhile area could have a severe impact on your business. In this case, the Superhighway may act as a great diversion for your competitors where you can gain competitive edge through the use of another medium.

CONCLUSION

The key to making best use of the Superhighway is segmentation. It is the only way to be successful in the long term as well as the short term. Segmentation, very simply, is the breaking down of supposedly uniform markets into sub-grouping by reference to customer needs and characteristics.

In this chapter we have segmented the Superhighway and shown how you can use it to segment your target audience. This will give you the background to your decision making of how important it is for your organisation to leverage this new medium. But to really get to grips with segmentation, we would recommend some structured targeted research outlined in Chapter 3 to encapsulate who your target/s should be, how they use the Superhighway and how you can approach and attract these people to your company's products and services. This will set the foundations for where you should progress when it comes to your marketing strategy outlined in the next chapter and how much resources you need to allocate to it when it comes to reviewing the decisions outlined in the Chapter 7 (on promoting).

CHECKLIST

You now know:

What segmentation means and why it is critical to
your organisation.   ☐ Yes   ☐ No

What factors you need to consider when you attempt
to segment your marketplace.   ☐ Yes   ☐ No

How the Superhighway can be geographically
segmented. □ Yes □ No

How the Superhighway can be demographically
segmented. □ Yes □ No

How the Superhighway can be psychographically
segmented □ Yes □ No

How behaviour patterns can be used to segment
Superhighway users. □ Yes □ No

How you can use the Superhighway to segment
your market. □ Yes □ No

The importance and meaning of niche marketing. □ Yes □ No

How the segmentation of the Superhighway matches
the segmentation of your marketplace. □ Yes □ No

How relevant the Superhighway is to your
organisation at this present moment in time. □ Yes □ No

WHAT NEXT?

Now that you have assessed the Superhighway as fitting or not fitting
with your target audience, you now need to assess how it affects your
marketing mix. Even if there is no correlation with your target market,
the Superhighway still has a huge amount to offer you in the process of
product planning, price testing and channels of distribution decisions.
Read on to discover the help it can offer you when you put together
your marketing strategy.

6 Exploiting your global niche – the best marketing mix

Every business organisation, whether manufacturing products, retailing or providing a service, has a marketing mix. Many production-orientated organisations do not realise that they have a marketing mix and therefore do not plan or devise strategies to gain maximum return for the business. Marketing mix is one of the essential concepts in modern marketing and is very simple to understand.

Marketing mix can be defined as a set of controllable marketing variables that a firm can plan and use to influence the buyers' responses towards the company's products or services. In a free market economy, we cannot force people to buy our products. All we can do is to understand their needs and wants and plan our offerings in such a way that it will attract buyer towards purchasing our products or services rather than choosing what competitors have to offer.

The marketing mix consists of all the things the management can do, and the decisions that are in their control. The many decisions can be grouped into four sets of variables, namely:

- Product   (the goods or services that the firm offers its target markets)
- Price   (the amount of money that is charged by the firm to its customers, including decisions on discounts and allowances)
- Place   (the distribution of the product/service to make it available to the customer)
- Promotion   (the communications that are needed to make customers aware and persuade them to buy goods and services)

The marketing mix is known as the 'Four Ps'. The marketing mix decisions should be made on the basis of having decided the target markets or segments the company is going to cater for as outlined in the previous chapter.

The Superhighway affects all four in a unique and distinct way. It is also a major new promotional tool and as such deserves a chapter dedicated to the options and considerations within this area. This chapter will help you review your current marketing mix in respect to decisions about product, price and place.

The over-riding message of this chapter is that your organisation's efforts in Cyberspace needs to totally integrate and reinforce all aspects of your existing marketing strategy. The Superhighway should not be seen as a separate variable but as additional dimension which supports and is supported by all the traditional marketing activities.

PRODUCT RE-PLANNING

By this stage, you will have identified whether there is a marketing opportunity using the Superhighway i.e. your target audience is approachable through Cyberspace. But:

Is your target audience currently buying your type of product on the Superhighway?

If they are then you have a basis to research what they look for, how they make their buying decisions and identify opportunities to position and sell your product on-line in a way that differentiates it from other on-line retailers. Here we recommend conducting primary and secondary research into the buying behaviour of on-line shoppers to answer the following questions:

How do purchasers search for suppliers on-line?

What do they look for in a supplier?

How do they evaluate alternatives?

- By the physical look of the product?
- By product features and options?
- By the brand name?
- By the packaging?

- By the guarantee or warrantee?
- By the quality of the product?
- By the fit inside an established product line?
- By the service level provided?

How do they then take action: credit card on-line, telephone to obtain unique reference, go to retail shop, mail order etc.?

Our belief is that this research is unlikely to have been comprehensively conducted by your competitors and will be the mechanism by which you can leapfrog the existing on-line retailers.

Relatively speaking, there is little on-line shopping at present on the Internet, which is why the statistics in the last chapter about 'buying habit' are even more surprising. It implies that people would, given the right products, promoted well, with easy on-line payment system, shop regularly on-line. Mat Tor in a recent article in Direct Response (leading direct marketing magazine in the UK) indicates that at present the on-line shopping industry is worth £10 million, with expectations of £21 billion in 5 years.

Because on-line shopping is so new and as such not established, it is more likely that you are faced with the answer 'No' to the above question. This is a bit like the story of two sales people going to a desert island and the first responding back to headquarters 'Returning home: can't sell any shoes: no-one wears shoes here', the second wires back to base 'Am setting up a new franchise: 20,000 people need shoes'.

The opportunities are vast here and done well can produce a revenue earning business with relatively low set-up costs. But to do this you need to replan your product for its suitability for on-line shopping.

How do I adapt my product for on-line shopping?

The term product can be used to describe a physical item such as a computer, a can of beans, a bar of chocolate or a machine tool. It is also a service such as public transport, dental treatment, healthcare or consultancy. Marketing of both applies the same principles.

People buy the benefits of a product, not the product. You buy the perceived **quality** of a product, together with the **features and options**, because it has a certain **style or brand name**, because of its **packaging**. It may be that it fits within a **product line** which is attractive. It may offer a **guarantee or warranty** which makes the risk taking of buying easier. A integral part of the product is **service**. If this is good either pre or post sale, it may even compensate for lack of benefits in other areas of the product.

All the above will have no doubt been considered in great depth when the product was planned in respect to conventional marketing. All of these attributes need to be reviewed in respect to this new medium and the following section outlines some of the issues involved in adapting the product to meet the needs of on-line shoppers:

1. Quality

The quality of the product has to be communicated to the customer. Quality is perceived by the customer and is a subjective measure of a product's worth. Quality can be communicated by strong branding, labelling and packaging. Using an endorsement of a product is another approach especially if a new concept. Quality can also be communicated by putting seals of quality or stickers claiming quality control procedures in the manufacture of the product.

In conventional marketing, the quality of the product can be displayed by the look and feel of it in physical terms. This may be difficult to convey on-line and therefore it is an important starting point. It your existing product relies heavily on physical differential in the area of quality, you need to find a way to emulate this on a computer screen. Graphics can go some way to achieving this but other methods may need to be added to convey the same quality image. A shaving oil company called *King of Shaves*® used Will Carling (then captain of the English rugby team) to endorse their new product. This conveyed the quality because it was used and endorsed by a 'quality' person. This worked well on the Superhighway because they positioned their product alongside a picture of Will Carling. Another example, is that of *J. Sainsbury Plc* who published Jancis Robinson reviewing their wine on their web site.

2. Features and options

Every product should incorporate certain features and options to attract customers away from competitors' products. These features and options must be translated into benefits for the end customer. People often use the Superhighway for specification comparisons and it is important to ensure that these enable the customer to compare like with like. *Dealernet* offer an on-line car directory showing all the car manufacturers' specifications. It enables a customer to compare one car easily and effectively with another. Little of these features and options are translated into benefits but this is not necessary the purpose for giving specifications and options. To actually translate the benefits of their features and options over the competitions, many car companies have created their own shop front (*see Chrysler*).

3. Style

For physical products, the finishing or the container is the style. AS400s (a mid-range computer sold by IBM) are now only produced in black. The style of the box is deliberate to indicate the new integration of the PowerPC chip as a major change. For services, style can be incorporated in the way that the service is presented or communicated. Style can be used as a powerful means of achieving differentiation for the company's products. The opportunity of re-styling the product on-line are huge and the costs of doing so are negligible compared to the costs of re-styling in conventional terms. The greatest advantage the Superhighway offers in this respect is that of experimentation. You can assess how attractive a product is to the target audience by the number of hit rates (number of visitors clicking on pages that reference that product). You can then re-style it to find the most suitable fit with your target audience.

4. Brand name

Every product and service has the potential for branding. A brandname helps to establish and differentiate a product from the competition. As the Superhighway puts a downward pressure on pricing, branding becomes a critical issue. The fact that small players can seamlessly position themselves alongside major players means that customers become more brand sensitive and loyal on-line than in the real world. This alone may enable you to premium price. Hotel companies with an existing brand name have found significant advantages of the Superhighway against lesser known hotel suppliers and this has been due to the fact that people like to reduce the risks of purchase by going with a name they know and trust. If you have an established brand name with international respect, you have a significant competitive advantage over your competitors when it comes to Superhighway marketing.

If you haven't already got an established brand name, one of the major benefits of being an early adopter on the Superhighway is that you can build up a brand name as people searching for a given product will see your brand name first and foremost and perceive you as a major player.

5. Packaging

The product's promise and quality can be enhanced by the way that it is packaged and presented. Packaging is an integral part of the product and is the first point of contact with the customer. The Superhighway offers a marketer the dream solution to packaging if the product is to be sold on-line because they can test the effectiveness of different packaging at the touch of a button. The presentation of the product on-line can be finely tuned to suit the target audience interactively by careful monitoring of viewing figures (hit rates). There are negligible costs in re-packaging your products on-line.

If the customer actually receives the product on-line, the packaging on receipt also needs careful planning. Buying books on-line is less aesthetically pleasing than seeing the cover and presentation of a physical book. Downloading CDs in the near future will not give the customer the all important box and sleeve cover. Some creative ways around this must be the prime product replanning initiative.

People are prepared to pay a substantial amount for good packaging and the ability to convey and deliver this remains a major challenge to most on-line marketers.

6. Product line

A product line is a group of products that are closely related in terms of their similar function and are aimed at the same group of customers through the same type of outlets and that fall within a similar price range. for example, Kelloggs Bran Flakes have a product line with Branflakes with sultanas, Branflakes with fruit and All-Bran. In this example, the product line has been extended and this helps the company to use its manufacturing and marketing capacity to its fullest and ensure that they provide the customers with a choice. The basic product is the same but variety has been introduced at a similar price range. Product line extension is a useful strategy with which to fight off competition. In conventional marketing, the cost of extending the product range involves re-branding and re-packaging and this can be costly. On the Superhighway, product line extension can be purely cosmetic: offering 'virtual' extensions to products that do not have to be produced until the order levels have warranted their production. This is particularly useful for service based companies where they can offer a plethora of services, all derivatives of their core product which gives the variety of choice to the end customer without the costs involved in production. It is also a fantastic mechanism to test how far consumers are prepared to have the product line extended.

7. Guarantees and warranties

Customers can be influenced to buy a particular brand by giving them peace of mind. Guarantees and warranties are very much a part of the product because like the benefits and features, customers look for how the inconvenience of paying for a product failure or breakdown can be avoided or minimised. Every product should carry a guarantee or a warranty which has been designed with customer satisfaction in mind. The customer's post-purchase doubt about the product can be reduced by the completion and postage of a guarantee registration card.

The Superhighway offers the ability for any individual or organisation to set up shop. With good creative design this can make it very difficult for the end customer to differentiate between established reputable organisations and cowboys. Because of this consumers are correctly dubious of company names or product names that they are not familiar with. Guarantees offered in a published format on-line are legally enforceable and therefore this can be very important for the peace of mind of the customer.

N.B One word of warning, the costs involved in suing an international company outside of your own legal domain is expensive, and consumers are usually aware of this, so guarantees and warranties usually only offer benefits to those within your own country.

8. Service level

Customer service either pre, during or post sale of a product is another important factor in planning and making the product (or service) complete. A customer buying a washing machine or a car must be assured that the company can provide an adequate service backup in case of repairs or spare parts. In respect to service products such as consultancy and training, the level of service should be demonstrated in terms of customer care and attention.

Added value
The usual indication of the future level of service that a company is likely to provide is relayed to the customer at the first point of contact. On the Superhighway this will be the amount and quality of on-line information of value to the customer. Ensuring that you obey the 10/90 ratio of salespitch to value, your customers will perceive you as giving good service. A company merely promoting its products is providing no service and therefore unlikely to build up customer loyalty. The more added value you provide the better perceived level of service you are providing.

Your responsiveness
Another indication of service is the organisation's responsiveness to on-line requests. We asked for further information from twenty six organisations on-line, five came back the same day, five came back the following day, ten came back the same day, two came back within a month and four never responded. Again your organisation's responsiveness on-line should reflect your organisation's responsiveness through conventional communication mediums.

Customer friendliness
Every organisation tries to make it as easy as possible for their customers to buy from them with a positive feeling in the process. This desire is translated into the user friendliness of the screens when people visit you in Cyberspace. So many companies make it difficult for their customers to order by not giving their customers easy access to them by a variety of different ordering mechanisms: phone, fax, post and on-line. This would be one way of demonstrating service on-line.

The ability to extend the product line, style, quality and service on line means that product testing has never been easier. Neither has it been easier for your competitors to see what you are trying to achieve. The next section describes how the Superhighway can be used to develop your products

Product development

New product development is an important activity because a product has a restricted life and there is a need for a balanced portfolio. It is also necessary to introduce new products if the company is to grow and become profitable. Defining segments as in the previous section and creating a dynamic interaction with them will not only eventually prompt them to buy from you but can be used as an invaluable source of concept and product testing. The first reaction we have from marketers is that the Superhighway is not secure enough and that they fear that a competitor will steal the idea. This is absolutely valid if we were to suggest publishing the plans as web-sites for people to visit. We are not suggesting this. We are suggesting that you follow the traditional approach to product development as outlined below and you include the use of the Superhighway when and if appropriate.

The product development process

1. Product development objectives
2. Idea generation and product screening
3. Concept testing
4. Technical feasibility analysis
5. Product testing

6. Profitability analysis
7. Test marketing and market introduction

(1) Product development objectives

It is imperative that the objectives of product development are clear. Which target audience the product is designed for; what revenue stream is it expected to produce; over what period; to what cost etc.

(2) Idea generation and product screening

Both these tasks are components of formal product planning and their efficient organisation and control can reduce the high risk of waste and product failure. It is estimated that the overall success rate for new products (both consumer and industrial) is only 65 per cent . The main reasons why new products fail include:

- Investment in managerial ego – that is, management or a high-ranking executive pursue a favourite idea and the product is developed without much market research.
- Over-estimation of the size of the market.
- Bad or inappropriate product design to meet customer needs.
- Lack of resources allocation for advertising and marketing.

The new product ideas have to be screened in order to eliminate the greatest number from further considerations. Successful screening requires the use of a systematic method of appraising and shifting the alternatives. One such system is the use of a score-card that requires the company to score points (say out of 10) to a series of considerations for each idea. The ideas with low total scores are rejected. The key areas for scoring including such questions as:

- Is it a unique product or with a number of unique features?
- Is it patentable?
- Is it within the 'business we are in' category?
- Can it be manufactured with existing plant and skills?
- Will it sell to existing customers or is there a ready-made market for it?

The Superhighway can act as a good link with academic research institutions for their knowledge and understanding of this field especially if the product lies within a high technology or engineering field. It can also be used as a supplier search directory to find interested parties who may wish to manufacture your product and be able to give you an indication of manufacturing process issues and costs. In summary the Superhighway can offer a one-stop shop to feasibility and can save you a huge amount of time and effort searching for information by conventional means. (Please read Appendix 5 on searching.)

(3) Concept testing

Once a large number of ideas have been screened and rejected, those remaining can be taken to the next stage. Concept testing involves explaining and demonstrating the product idea to a sample of the potential market to gather their views on them. This requires the production of prototypes (and/or graphic illustrations) and use of qualitative and some quantitative research. It is also useful, at this stage, to research the views of retailers, wholesalers and experts in the field.

The Superhighway enables you to talk to customers about the concept through the use of either forums in CompuServe and/or newsgroups on the Internet. Yes, these are open to your competitors but you can discuss a huge number of different concepts which will at worse confuse your competitors and at best mislead them down an avenue which you have already identified as unfeasible. You can also put a general request out on a forum, collect interested parties' e:mail addresses and talk to them privately away from the forum or even using traditional forms of communication.

Alternatively, you can use a secure server and set up a security system which permits only careful vetted people to access the information through a password front screen. The advantage here is the reduced costs of an evolving prototype and the distribution costs of sending it out to the concept testers.

(4) Technical feasibility analysis

Concept testing usually results in the rejection of more ideas and the remaining ideas are then subjected to technical feasibility studies to:

- Determine if the firm can design a product which implements the new product idea.
- Estimate the investment required for development and manufacture.
- Estimate unit cost of production.

The Superhighway can be used for tendering where you invite manufacturers to request a fully documented specification for them to reply to giving implementation plans, prices and service agreements. The invitation to tender can be posted on a forum or a web-site and the full documentation sent by post after various vetting processes have taken place. This is widely used by large organisations and the Government.

(5) Product testing

Product testing provides information on the following and is used on only one or two of the ideas remaining from the elimination process.

- Product shelf life.
- Product wear-out rates.
- Problems that may result from its improper usage or consumption.
- Potential defects that will require replacement.
- Appropriate maintenance schedules.

The Superhighway is unlikely to offer much assistance here because this stage relies on the prototype being tested in physical reality.

(6) Profitability analysis

Many new products fail to survive in the market, not because they are not wanted by customers, but because the company fails to achieve acceptable levels of profit contribution. Profitability analysis is therefore an important stage of new product development process that provides information on break-even points, operational costs, cash flow projections, profit contributions and return on investment.

However, testing the market's elasticity of demand can be done in a painless and cost-effective manner by asking customers on-line how much they are prepared to spend on a given product. This is very rough but a result of a price which is close to the cost margins will give an early indication of the potential unprofitability of the product before further costs are invested. The reverse is also true where consumers may be prepared to pay premium prices for a product. Many companies constrain their product development based on perceived low margins without first testing the propensity of their customers to buy.

(7) Test marketing and market introduction

All new products should be subjected to test marketing amongst a sample of the potential market. Although test marketing is an expensive and time consuming exercise (that can give competition time to launch a similar product first), it is justified because it can provide a valuable trial run prior to national launch. Test marketing provides information on product acceptability, reactions to pricing policy, effectiveness of advertising and other sales and distribution policies.

As outlined before, the Superhighway can be used as an effective way to invite customers to test market the product. You may get a biased sample this way and it would be important to also test market non-on-line customers. However, this can be one of the most cost-effective recruitment methods if used well. If it is software that you wish to test, the Superhighway can be used to distribute the product for testing where security can be built into the web-server to restrict assess to only those people you wish to access the software. Many IT companies use the Internet to test early releases of their software, e.g. Netscape.

Product re-planning in summary

The term product means the physical item, service, event, idea or organisation that is offered to the market as a means of meeting customer needs, solving problems or providing benefits. As such, the product is the most essential ingredient of the organisation. But in order to be successful the product must be planned and completed (in terms of quality, features and options, style, branding, packaging, product line and service) before it is offered in the market. If this product is to offered on the Superhighway then all eight factors need to be re-planned in accordance with the target audience and the target audience's use of the Superhighway in respect of the product.

PRICING

Very few Internet books currently on the market address the issue of pricing. Yet the effect of the Superhighway has the potential to radically alter pricing systems. There are various new forces driving down pricing:

1. The potential closer link between the manufacturer and the customer.
2. The ability for the customer to shop around internationally.
3. The reduced costs of distribution can be passed onto the customer.
4. The reduced sales costs can be passed onto the customer.
5. Global competition can be fierce.

6. The costs of entry into some markets are reduced, so smaller players with smaller cost bases can compete at reduced prices.

Any industry which has maintained prices at premium rates compared to international counterparts is threatened by the Internet. The effect of globalised trading means that the least-cost producers can go on-line early to increase market share. This is certainly true of CD suppliers in America, see *CDNOW*. The threat to the music industry in Europe is only tempered by the cost of postage and VAT charged on the import of CDs. Even this barrier will go down when people can download music onto their PCs when read/write CD players become cost-effective. However, the current explosion of bands and pop groups marketing themselves and samples of their music on-line is causing much concern amongst the traditional music distribution channel providers.

Ultimately the customer has everything to gain from the Internet. In the true classical economic model, consumer sovereignty reigns through improved product and pricing information. The customer can make more informed buying decisions which drives price down. The seller can no longer drive price up through restricting supply if supply is available from the global marketplace. The seller can no longer restrict information to drive up price if it is freely available on the Superhighway. The seller can no longer join up (informally or formally) with other sellers to agree pricing if the products are available from global suppliers. All this is power to the elbow of the customer – marketers and senior managers should prepared to fight globally as well as locally.

The way forward for marketers to combat this potential global price war is to plan their marketing mix in such a way as it clearly differentiates their products in areas other than price. This brings into play many of the issues described in the product section of the book. The eight factors (quality, features and options, style, branding, packaging, product line, guarantees and warranties and service) can be carefully planned and presented so that the consumer clearly sees the reason for premium prices. Branding still remains the most effective way to differentiate your product on-line – people will always be attracted to a name that they know on-line.

On a more positive note, although there are downward forces acting on prices, the Superhighway offers many opportunities to premium price.

The Superhighway can enable organisations to create a meaningful dialogue with customers and carve out niche positions. This means that companies can increase their speed to market and premium price as a result. It will only be established recognised products that will be so price competitive. The Internet offers speed to market and therefore increased time to benefit from the benefits of premium pricing. There are also few products on-line at present so early entrants can typically choose their price (subject to competitive pressures in the real world).

It is now easier to charge for information. On-line charging for information is becoming commonplace and what better place to deliver it than through the Internet. On-line services can be sold by almost any organisation and this can be the route to take to compensate for the margin reductions in the core product. Software prices have reduced vastly but software companies have recouped their margins by charging for support and training. In this way, they move from being software vendors to information providers. Many industries are following along the same lines, where they sell the product at near cost but make their profits by selling the associated information which accompanies the product.

In summary, the Superhighway has the potential to revolutionize the pricing structure of an industry. We have outlined the music industry here because it has gained much coverage in the recent press, but many industries are threatened by the same model. The answer is to replan pricing objectives with the Superhighway in mind.

Price objectives

As with other components of the marketing mix, the first step in setting prices should be to establish objectives. Pricing objectives are particularly important because they are closely related to the company's corporate goals. A company that has set itself a corporate goal to achieve 10 per cent return on shareholders' investment provides marketing managers with a framework on which they can decide prices and hence contribute to the corporate goal. Likewise, a firm that establishes a corporate aim to dominate the market requires marketing managers to engineer prices in a flexible way so as to ensure high market share.

Any pricing strategy adopted by a company therefore, must take into consideration the five following types of overall company objectives that the overall marketing strategies must achieve:

(i)   To achieve a given target of profitability
(ii) To support a planned market position
(iii) To pre-empt, meet or follow competition
(iv) To differentiate product or company image
(v)   To achieve stabilisation of price.

Methods of determining price

There are several formalised methods of determining price levels, but a very large proportion of British industry apply the cost-plus system. The five main pricing methods are outlined here.

1. Cost-plus pricing

Cost-plus pricing is the simplest and most commonly used technique of building a price by allocating costs to the product and adding on a percentage profit margin. This method has a major weakness in that there are far too many arbitrary allocations which do not relate to the product. Also this method does not take into consideration the market and is not related to volume. If applied to selling products on the Superhighway, reduced sales and market access costs would imply a downward pressure on prices which may or may not be required to generate demand.

This method provides a benchmark for the company and should be used to compare the price determined by this method and other methods.

2. Breakeven analysis and target profit pricing

Target profit pricing – uses the concept of a breakeven chart. An analysis of the breakeven chart shows the total cost and total revenue that can be expected at different sales volume levels.

This method is an improvement on cost-plus pricing because the firm can examine the inter-relationship between fixed and variable costs and also the effect price has on sales volume. Once the firm decides on the price to charge, fixed costs cease to be a relevant factor – the simple objective of pricing then becomes to maximise contribution to fixed costs. However the same criticism applies in respect of the Superhighway. Reduced sales and market access costs would imply a downward pressure on prices which may or may not be required to generate demand.

3. Competition-based pricing

In this method, the firm bases its price largely on competitors' prices, without paying too much attention to its own costs or demand. The firm can decide to price above competition, below competition or the same as competition. This may be a situation that the company is forced into by an established industry presence on the Superhighway where products are sold which are identical. The software industry is the prime example here where UK software companies are forced to compete with their American competitors on price. It poses a difficult problem which can only be addressed by product differentiation or differential pricing described later in this section.

4. Contract or tender pricing

This method also relies on estimating what competition would charge to win certain contracts or tenders. The firm bases its price on expectations of how competitors will price rather than on a rigid relation to the firm's costs or demand structure. The firm is keen to win the contract and is willing to set the price lower than other competing firms. But because the price set cannot be lower than operating cost, the contract is priced around expected profit level.

The Government uses the Internet for tendering and many organisations are following suit. The use of the Superhighway becomes a fast and effective route to getting the best price for a given standard of quality and is another downward pressure on prices. Many supplying companies have had bad experiences of this approach and have committed to loss-making projects which have proved mutually disadvantageous. Some supplying companies have stopped putting in tenders as a result.

5. Market-orientated pricing

In market-orientated pricing methods, costs and profitability are considered but the primary basis for setting price is the 'elasticity of demand'; how reactive customers are to changes in prices. There are three specific forms of market-orientated pricing.

Premium pricing (also known as 'skimming the market')
This involves setting a price higher than competition to reflect the high level of product quality. This approach also provides a means of differentiating the product and is a sound strategy for products

manufactured to cater for very clearly defined target markets. In the case of a new product, where there is little or no competition, the firm can skim the market by setting a high price in the knowledge that it will attract customers from a distinct segment of the market. Premium (or skimming) allows the company to maintain higher contribution margins.

The Superhighway offers many companies the opportunity of being 'first in' with the luxury of premium pricing. This is particularly true of the retail sector where there is a proven desire from Superhighway users to buy but a notable lack of products for them to purchase. Here, a strong price is often seen as a reflection on quality and with a supportive style, brand or packaging quality or guarantee can afford a lucrative short-term business. A good example of this is *Joe Boxers*.

Going rate pricing
This is a popular way to price, especially on entry into an existing market. This is where the company adopts the market price on the basis that it represents the collective wisdom of the industry and will yield a fare return. This type of conformity will preserve industry harmony and is advantageous for all concerned. The classic examples of this are petrol, steel, opticians, Internet access provision.

In these oligopoly type industries, the products and services on offer are very similar in appearance, function and quality. The main concern of the firm is price stability and target return on capital employed, with steady long-term growth.

Penetration pricing
This involves setting a price below competition in order to stimulate an increase in demand and to achieve high market share in a short term. A product should be of equal or better quality than the competition to attract buyers. Companies operating this policy will only sustain growth if:

(a) market is price sensitive, for example video recorders, personal computers and compact disc players;

(b) the company's price advantage over competition is at least 10 per cent . A much higher price difference will make the customer suspicious of the product quality;

(c) the company has a technical or material advantage which earns at least equal gross margins to the rest of the industry, despite the lower price. The Japanese, for example, adopt penetration pricing on most of the products exported to the UK and Europe. They ensure high quality products at medium price ranges and gain a foothold in the local markets from which they grow by dominating the markets.

Pricing strategy

Once the company has established the method that is to be used in setting price levels, marketing management can then formulate the pricing strategy that will most effectively achieve the business objectives. The main types of pricing strategies available to management are given here.

1. Product differentiation

One of the critical objectives of pricing policy and indeed of marketing as a function, is to cater for customer preferences for the company's products and services. This is achieved through a closer understanding of purchasing motives and the features of value considered important by each market sector. Objective and subjective values can be reflected as a greater or lesser willingness to pay a specific price and is the basis of price discrimination through product differentiation. Examples of these factors are:

Objective	**Subjective**
Quality	Quality
Design/style	Design/style
Efficiency	Colour
Reliability	Packaging
Running costs	Advertising
Sales service	Promotion
Delivery, advice	Salesmen's personality
and installation	The price itself
After sales service	
Spares, repairs	

In many cases it may be easier to differentiate the subjective product differentiators in traditional marketing as opposed to Cybermarketing. Packaging, design and style need to be approached in a different way and the learning curve created from scratch. The product may need to be 'merchandised' in a completely different way and this will be discussed more fully in the section within this chapter that specifically addresses merchandising.

2. Differential pricing

There is considerable scope for both consumer and industrial product manufacturers to practise price discrimination through the selling terms and conditions which determine the price the customer actually pays.

The Superhighway offers a marketer the opportunity to price differentially and indeed may be forced to in order to activate demand. Many IT companies offer one set of prices mail order and another retail. Many organisations charge less for products on-line than they do selling retail in order to promote this cost-effective route.

Such price differentials come from:

- Cash discount (for example, when buying direct from the Superhighway)
- Quality/volume discounts
- Sales or return policy (for example, book clubs and direct mail purchases)
- Advertising support
- Credit, deferred terms (e.g. storage heaters – buy now, pay nothing for three months)
- Reciprocal trading
- Cumulative discounts (where previous purchases are taken into consideration for calculating discount).

3. Pricing new products

There is no established pattern for pricing new products and companies adopt a variety of strategies. The choice generally is between entering the market at high price (skimming) to recoup the development and promotional costs early in the launch and to make successive price reductions in response to long-term competitive reactions; or entering the market at low prices to discourage competition from following (loss leading). This can help the company to build a significant volume share of the market which competition will find difficult to attack. Because price is often an indication of quality and people are naturally more hesitant buying on-line, premium pricing supported with warranties is more common on the Superhighway than loss-leading.

It is often argued that considerable benefits accrue by several companies introducing a new product idea simultaneously, since promotional costs are shared and volume share is more easily acquired in the short term. This gives directory providers, brokers and agents the marketing opportunity of putting a trade directory or supplier index on the Superhighway. The benefits to all are the reduced costs of climbing up the learning curve independently of one another and the reduced cost of providing only one web site.

Price constraints

There are several constraints to free pricing that limit the scope of pricing opportunities. The main constraints that marketing managers have to take into account when setting price levels are:

1. **Uncertainty of demand** – Price relationship may inhibit speculative pricing exercise and deter marketing decisions, particularly in the case of new products.
2. **Derived demand** – The market may be so removed from the factors determining primary demand and particularly if there are many substitute products, that price changes will have a negative effect in attracting sales volume.
3. **Government legislative controls** – increasing government measures aimed at 'fair trading' and counter inflationary measures can inhibit the company from charging higher prices. Legislation is a primary price consideration in specific industries, for example gas, water, electricity, telephones, oligopolies and other nationalised industries (see the legal references under Chapter 2 of the accompanying web site).
4. **Price changes** – Alterations in price changes can in themselves deter sales. If a company shows a history of frequent large price changes, customers will begin to speculate and switch brands or supplier in anticipation of price movements.

Pricing in summary

Pricing policy is one of the key marketing tools and must be established in the context of a company's overall marketing strategy. It requires a systematic planned approach and should not simply be based on the cost-plus method or posing the questions:

- What do competitors charge?
- What does it cost to make?
- What can we get away with?

The rational process of setting prices should involve:

1. Having a clearly defined target market for the product
2. Establishing clear pricing objectives in relation to the company objectives
3. Analyse price elasticity, competition and the product's profitability, taking pricing constraints into account.

Once a method of setting prices has been fixed, the company can then select the most appropriate pricing strategies to achieve the objectives.

It is exactly this approach which will enable a marketer to create a strong and robust position on the Superhighway just as in their traditional marketplace. Without this thinking and careful planning, the organisation is in danger of entering a global price war, damaging the brand image and potentially ruining the profitability of the company.

You can go out of business easier, quicker and more effectively than ever before.

PLACE

The Superhighway has the potential to revolutionise an industry's established network of distribution channels. The music industry has been cited as the best case in point and there are many relevant learning points we can take from this example. Here is an industry built around the problem of the manufacturer (the musicians and recording studios) not being able to deliver their product to the end customer (the listener). The profits in the industry through the mark-up on CDs are substantially gained by the distribution channels: the retailers. The ability for the Superhighway to create a direct link between the manufacturer and the customer poses a direct threat to this distribution channel. This model is true in many industries and this section outlines how a marketer can review the impact of the Superhighway on their own distribution network.

Channels of distribution

Channels of distribution are the means by which an organisation gets its product to the target group of customers. As such, most channels of distribution consists of inter-dependent businesses that engage in product movement and availability. The manufacturers, wholesalers, retailers, direct mail houses, brokers and sales agents that make up such channels represent a system because they work together to buy, sell, deliver, store, display and demonstrate the products that customers want. In the past, manufacturers managed distribution channels as they had the responsibility of ensuring that the product is efficiently distributed to reach the consumer. But now many large retailers (and wholesale groups such as Sainsbury, Marks & Spencer, Comet (electrical appliances), Dixons and some national department stores operate as the channel leaders because they can exert considerable control over manufacturers.

The decisions regarding the choice of distribution is as important as the product itself. It is of little value if the firm invests heavily in researching the target market and developing the required product if it cannot effectively make it available in outlets or channels that are most convenient to the potential user. The channel decision therefore has to be made on the same systematic and often creative basis as product planning, pricing and promotion – as an integrative approach to marketing planning.

Channel systems

The different types of channel systems that consumer and industrial products (and services) manufacturers can use are summarized in Figure 6.1.

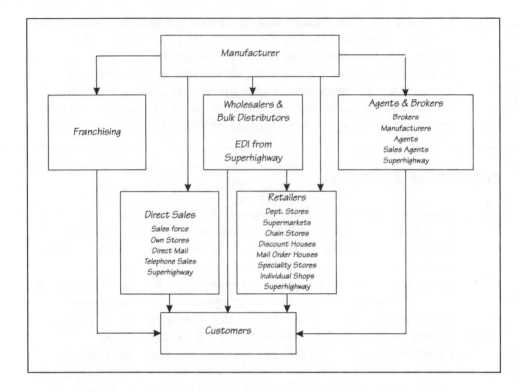

Figure 6.1
Channels of a distribution system

Direct sales

The distribution channel most affected by the Superhighway is of course the direct sales channel. In traditional marketing, direct sales is often the most costly to instigate and the hardest to maintain. The Superhighway makes direct selling a more viable option. As such the Superhighway potentially enables the manufacturer to attract, sell and take orders from the customer direct.

Examples of the benefits of the Superhighway in the area of Direct Sales:

- Artists display their pictures on-line and selling direct to the art-buyer without paying around 30–50 per cent commission to galleries.
- Contractors offering their services on-line without having to use agencies.

- Hotels offering on-line booking without having to use booking reservations agencies.
- Industries creating their own directories on line rather than paying a middle agency to create and distribute paper-based directories.
- Theatre and concert bookings direct rather than going through ticket reservations agencies.

In the examples above, the manufacturer takes all the benefits of cutting out the middleman. Examples of where the benefits of direct sales are shared are:

- Authors by-pass book shops and provide books on-line for people to sample a given chapter and then pay by credit card to download.
- Musicians offering reduced priced CDs if ordered on-line.

What about on-line ordering – is it popular and secure?

At present there is much hesitancy by companies to offer on-line ordering due to the widespread belief that it is not secure enough at present. This hesitancy is a reflection of users' hesitancy to give their credit-card details on-line. Companies like Visa, Access and Netscape are investing heavily to improve security. This is as much to do with changing attitudes than it is to do with the technical security. It is still safer to give your credit card number over the Internet with a secure provider than to give it to a waiter in a restaurant or over the phone.

The most common approach around this issue is to offer an account number or password over the phone in exchange for credit card details. The best approach is to offer your customer a selection of ordering mechanisms, in this way they can decide the most appropriate for them.

In summary, on-line ordering is growing and peoples' attitudes are changing. What is known is that on-line trading was worth £13 million in the year 1994 and is expected to grow exponentially to £20 billion by the year 2000. The technical issues around security on the Internet is covered in Chapter 7.

Agents and brokers

These are the middlemen who do not take the title to goods but facilitate distribution by bringing buyers and sellers together. They are directly threatened by the Superhighway as this conceptually could replace their importance in the supply chain. Agents differ from brokers by serving as an extension of the manufacturer's sales force. They are usually independent of the organisation, work on commission basis and normally specialise in certain lines of business. Examples of agents include Avon Cosmetics, insurance agents, sales agents for industrial products like computers, heavy machinery and agents for exporting. Brokers do not have continuous relationships with one seller. They inform sellers of possible buyers and negotiate deals directly with buyers on commission basis. Brokers are used in such businesses as insurance, certain food produce, financial securities and commercial property sales.

They will continue to prove important in dynamic marketplaces where the number of buying variables are complex or require the consumer to spend significant time upskilling their knowledge base.

The 'virtual' equivalence of these people are commercial on-line information providers offering translation services, insurance quotes etc. These people have taken the opportunity offered to them by the Superhighway and created a parallel to their value in the supply chain in the real world to the value they can offer in Cyberspace. Any directory supplier, brokerage or agency needs to consider how they are going to react. If they are innovative they will provide value to the end customer and the supplier for whom they broke, print or buy from. If they are not, the Superhighway may well replace their need in the supply chain altogether. For examples of successful innovations see *Hotelnet, Dealernet, Thisco, Lawnet.*

Retailers

The Superhighway threatens this distribution channel severely. If home shopping takes off, retailing will be revolutionised. Their present initiatives reveal their anxiety and the first companies to take advantage of the Internet have been retailers. They see it as both a huge threat as well as a great opportunity and the jury is still out as to which one it is. Certainly retailers offering generic products which can be purchased without sampling are at most risk. Argos, Tescos, Sainsburys and Toys 'R Us all offer products of this type and are some of the first retailers to take advantage of the Superhighway.

Wholesalers and bulk distribution

These are organisations that buy in bulk and sell to other businesses. They are threatened by the Superhighway because retailers and customers may well be able to go direct to the manufacturer, assuming that the manufacturer can afford to supply in smaller volumes. They are unlikely to benefit directly from the Superhighway except to find new products and attract businesses to their services.

Where the Superhighway doesn't threaten wholesalers and retailers

There are many examples where wholesalers and retailers add value to the interaction between the manufacturer and the customer:

- Their knowledge of the local markets and contacts with customers are so specific that without it the manufacturer's products would not appeal to the customer.
- They break bulk – i.e. they buy in large quantities that helps the manufacturer with the costs of delivering to large numbers of small quantity buyers.
- They provide storage facilities for the stocks of products that otherwise have to be stocked at the company's expense.
- They absorb the risks, especially of maintaining inventories and product obsolescence.
- They provide credit to customers to facilitate the sale of products.
- They provide a one-stop shop for their customers rather than force the customer to go to multiple retail outlets, e.g. food shops.

So long as they continue to add more value (to the interaction between manufacturer and customer) than their resulting costs, the Superhighway offers no real threat.

Franchising

Franchising is one of the fastest growing forms of distribution. A franchise is a contract – a legal agreement between the franchiser (usually a corporate body) and a franchisee (usually a sole trader or a small business) which allows the franchisee to process, stock and sell the franchiser's products, methods or machinery, and to trade under his name. Another term for franchising is licensing. A manufacturer can grant or sell another business a licence to make and sell its products or services. The Superhighway makes it easier to both attract interest in a franchise opportunity and ease the contractual process.

The Superhighway is not going to revolutionise existing franchising systems but it is going to affect the way that franchised products are promoted. If current use in the US is anything to go by, we would suggest that it is likely that franchisers will use this new medium to add value and market the brand name, attracting enquiries that are then fed out to the respective franchisee. Examples of this approach are Pizzahut, Interflora and many hire companies. In this way the Superhighway reinforces the brand name, adds value to the franchise and provides business for the franchisee in a cost-effective manner.

Selecting channels of distribution and strategy

The process of selecting a channel system requires the following key considerations.

1. Setting distribution objectives
These should clearly specify the target market that the product is aimed at, the extent to which these markets need to be penetrated and the promotional and other activity that is necessary to encourage and support the intermediaries.

2. Customer requirements and purchasing behaviour
An understanding of the needs, wants and values of the target markets will enable the company to select the channel system that most closely matches the customer's requirements, lifestyle and buying patterns. The buyer behaviour should provide information on the customer's motives for buying the product, the personality types, influence of peer groups, culture and family situation. It is only with this understanding can the organisation decide if the Superhighway is relevant to their target audience. For example, the Sinclair C5 personal transporter failed partly because the company used an inappropriate method of distribution when the C5 was launched. The only method of purchase was through direct mail order. This distribution strategy did not take account of customers'

needs and buying behaviour. A product like the C5 needs to be seen, 'test driven', demonstrated and actively sold by trained personnel. Is the direct sales channel through the Superhighway really going to appeal to your customers' needs and buying behaviour?

For industrial products the buying behaviour and the knowledge of the decision making unit, specifiers and influencers is a major consideration in developing channel strategy.

3. The product

The channel system used by a company should match the product and its benefits. The following types of products require direct selling rather than using intermediaries:

- Perishable goods – these require quick delivery.
- Complex goods – large and complex products such as industrial machines, computer installations etc. require technical assistance that can best be provided by the firm.
- Bulky goods – these types of products should avoid multiple transportation and handling operations.
- High priced goods – these usually carry considerable financial risk to the company and requires direct control over its physical distribution.

In the near future, even these will be able to be sold through the Superhighway. For example, there are various test projects in the UK aimed at on-line home shopping for perishable food items.

In general, it is true to say that products that are smaller, standardised, packaged, and lower priced with longer shelf life are much more suited to distribution through intermediaries and for direct selling through the Superhighway.

4. Selecting intermediaries in distribution channel

Once the company has considered the factors influencing the distribution system, it can proceed to select the intermediaries that would make up the most efficient channel. For this the company has to decide on:

- **Length of the channel system – or the levels or intermediaries that are to be used.** Industrial channel systems are short compared with those for consumer products. Shorter channels give manufacturers greater control over intermediaries. Some consumer durable products such as cars, television sets, personal computers, etc. are sold through the use of one level channel of dealers to sell them because the companies want some control over the way in which their products are sold.

Obviously the shorter the channel system, the more likely the customer is of obtaining a good price. Shortening distribution channels can be achieved through the use of the Internet and it only takes one or two major players in the industry to reduce the channel for the whole distribution chain to collapse. We discuss the most topical one, the music industry, later in this section.

- **Differing lengths in the distribution chain.** This is where the manufacturer uses a combination of channels varying as to how far detached they remain. The direct sales approach may be used alongside dealerships. This can be attractive for the manufacturer for many reasons: improved price margins, feedback from the marketplace etc. However, communication is vital because the customer can be the victim of differing service levels and pricing structures depending on whether they bought direct from the manufacturer or dealer. It can also be costly to maintain over time when dealerships can adapt to the market quicker than the manufacturer.

  Dealers are faced with a dilemma when their suppliers use Superhighway direct, because they cannot be seen to disclose prices that conflict and attempting to offer service differential can be politically difficult on a screen media. Car dealerships and software dealerships are the obvious examples but there are many others to explore. The most obvious way around this dilemma is for all parties not to discuss prices and service level, but one could argue that this may possibly defeat the purpose of the game.

- **Intensity of distribution can vary with the nature of the product.** Some products like fast moving consumer goods such as goods, drinks, chocolates etc., need to have intensive distribution via all sorts of outlets and locations. Other products, as part of a company's strategy, need to be sold through selective types of outlets in order to enhance the product's quality and name. Selective distribution is most often used when the product is relatively new and for such products as compact disc players, video cameras, musical instruments (Yamaha for example) and furniture. Some manufacturers grant dealers exclusive territorial rights and make the distribution exclusive to few intermediaries in each geographical area. This gives the company greater control and also helps retain the image and reputation of the product. Examples include cars such as BMW and Rolls-Royce and other products such as jewellery and certain domestic appliances. Companies may wish to choose to have their product only promoted and sold by themselves on the Superhighway, equally they may wish to promote it as an inclusion into many other organisations' on-line product ranges. Ultimately it will depend on the nature of the product and its attractiveness to the broad spectrum of Superhighway users.

5. Evaluating and modifying the channel system

The selection and use of a channel system should not be a static activity. The effectiveness of the chosen system should be constantly monitored and evaluated against such measures as volume turnover by the system members, market penetration, customer reactions and inventory data – i.e. statistics on product movement, sales, and unsold stocks. The channel system should be renewed during the product's life cycle and additional intermediaries or outlet types added to fight competition.

The Superhighway may be an effective launch distribution channel to a new product or brand name. Many companies use the Superhighway to attract dealers to then take the product and include it within their web site. In this way the organisation can move from a direct sales channel to an intermediary approach. Alternatively, it could work in the opposite direction where you currently use intermediaries and find that the direct sales approach is more effective and profitable.

Place in summary

A company must develop a channel system to ensure that its goods are made available to the target markets to buy at the right place and at the right time. A company can choose to distribute through intermediaries such as wholesalers, retailers and agents, or direct to the customer, or by franchising its operations. The Superhighway can potentially affect many of these traditional distribution channels and give the opportunity for the manufacturer to create a closer link with the end customer. However, intermediaries perform several valuable functions for the company, including breaking bulk, providing storage space, facilitating buying by providing credit and by taking on the risk. The whole distribution channel network needs to be reviewed when thinking about the Superhighway and our recommendations are not to see it as a separate distribution channel.

CONCLUSION

We have outlined only three of the four elements of the marketing mix in order to dedicate a whole chapter to the issue of 'Promotion'. However, what we have attempted to do here is to give you a feel of how the Superhighway affects your product, price and place decisions at a macro (industry wide level) as well as at a micro (company specific) level.

CHECKLIST FOR EXPLOITING YOUR NICHE MARKET

You now know:

How integrated your use of the Superhighway is within your existing marketing strategy.	☐ Yes	☐ No
Why and how your target audience currently buy on the Superhighway if they do.	☐ Yes	☐ No
How you are going to either product and/or price differentiate yourself on the Superhighway	☐ Yes	☐ No
How appropriate it would be for you to use the Superhighway to develop new products.	☐ Yes	☐ No
What impact the Superhighway is likely to have on the existing pricing structure of your industry.	☐ Yes	☐ No
What impact the Superhighway is likely to have on the existing pricing structure of your organisation.	☐ Yes	☐ No
What impact the Superhighway is likely to have on the existing distribution channels within your industry.	☐ Yes	☐ No
What impact the Superhighway is likely to have on the existing distribution channels within your organisation?	☐ Yes	☐ No

WHAT NEXT?

We will now cover the last and most exciting element within the marketing mix – promotion. This is what marketing is commonly mistaken for but with the marketing concepts and research behind you, you are now ready to explore the use of the Superhighway as a communication and promotional tool with your target markets.

7 Promoting yourself on-line

**A company's web-site is essentially an empty billboard
waiting to be filled with a corporate message...
But who is going to read it?**

There are also a vast number of global billboards being globally ignored!

'You too can have a globally ignored billboard.'

The main message of the book is that marketing on the cyberspace is not conceptually different from marketing in the real world. You need to have a deep understanding of your market, why people buy, what benefits you offer over and above your competitors and what marketing mix most suits your target audience. This information will prevent you from publishing a globally ignored corporate billboard. Basically, you need to have a clear marketing strategy in place before you consider using the Superhighway as a promotion mechanism. This chapter reviews the role of promotion within your marketing strategy, the decisions involved in selecting the best promotion channel to meet your communication goals. The Internet is a new medium which can be applied in various ways but must be seen in the overall context of promotional planning. To provide you with a framework to conceptualise your use of the Superhighway, we have forworded this chapter with an in-depth look at promotion.

WHAT IS PROMOTION?

Many people associate the term marketing with advertising, selling, corporate image, sales promotion and publicity. This is because we all get exposed to these techniques every day of our lives. All of these means of communications can be grouped together under the term promotion. Even selling, an activity in which many organisations place considerable emphasis and organise as a business function, is only one part of the overall promotional programme. Promotion is one of the four elements of an organisation's marketing mix. Most organisations, large and small, use promotional tools to help them sell goods and services. But many companies do not make effective use of promotion because of the management's lack of understanding of the roles of, and difference between the various tools available. The promotional mix is made up of the following main methods of communicating with the marketplace.

- Advertising
- Sales promotion
- Merchandising
- Publicity and PR
- Direct marketing and personal selling

These tools, or methods of communication have distinct purposes and are interrelated in terms of how and when they should be used. Many organisations invest in advertising and personal selling, but without any sales promotion effort to support the campaign, nor any effort in projecting the company image. In order to achieve some return from such investments, management should understand the capabilities of the different promotional tools and carefully co-ordinate their use to meet specific communication objectives.

This chapter sets out to deal with the five main promotional tools and highlight how, why and when they should be used within the overall context of an organisation's marketing effort and the use of the Superhighway within this context. As a result of reading this chapter you will have a much clearer idea of the use of the Superhighway as a promotion tool as well as how it fits within your overall communication plan. You will be positioned light years ahead of your peers as they perceive this new medium as a separate and disparate promotion mechanism. The next section deals with advertising, sales promotion and merchandising, and the last section briefly covers the main aspects of personal selling.

In most marketing situations, competitive or differential advantage can be established and communicated through the use of promotional techniques. For example, when a new product such as a chocolate bar is launched, it may have the novelty factor or some other distinctive features through its design or use of technology. But this differential advantage will be lost when competitors launch similar products on the market. Likewise, the new product may be priced lower than competing brands to gain an advantage. But economic pressure may mean that this is only a temporary measure used to promote the product at an early stage of its life. Or a company may decide to use different means of distributing the product. Again, this advantage may only last until competition follow the same strategy. A company, however, can use the promotional mix to create and communicate lasting differences and advantages in a competitive market. Advertising, sales promotion and merchandising can help to give products and services brand personalities and create an image or reputation for an organisation. These techniques can help to create and communicate unique selling propositions or differences in products and serves that may or may not exist in them. Examples of brand differentiation through the use of promotional mix include Guinness (the drink for the thinking person), Green Giant (quality canned vegetables), Volvo (safe cars). The promotional mix of any organisation should have the following aims.

- To create an awareness of the availability of products or services and how they can benefit the customer.
- To encourage sampling of the products or services on offer, or of an organisation as a supplier of goods and services.
- To encourage repeat business.
- To establish and maintain a corporate image that will help the overall marketing effort.

Figure 7.1 shows how the promotion mix can help achieve these objectives. These three techniques are concerned with persuading retailers, wholesalers (and other marketing intermediaries) and customers to:

Communication goals	Promotional tool
1. Create an awareness of the availability and benefits of products and services, and existence of suppliers.	Advertising
2. Encourage sampling.	Sales promotion, direct marketing and personal selling, and merchandising
3. Encourage repeat purchase.	Sales promotion, direct marketing and personal selling, and merchandising
4. Establish and maintain good corporate image.	Merchandising and advertising

Figure 7.1

Use of promotional mix to achieve communication goals

The result is that your customer:

- buys more of an existing product or source
- buys more a new product or service
- buys a new or modified packed, size or version of a product or service
- buys at a different frequency level
- buys from a particular outlet or supplier.

The outcome of using these techniques should be to create a favourable image of the company and its products or services by reinforcing existing positive attitudes and changing negative attitudes or misconceptions. The three techniques that can help to achieve this are described in this section of the book.

ADVERTISING, SALES PROMOTION AND MERCHANDISING

Advertising, sales promotion and merchandising are the three main communication techniques that make up the promotional mix, and if properly planned and implemented can help to sell products and services and gain a competitive advantage for an organisation.

Advertising

Advertising can be defined as a one-way, non-personal presentation and promotion of ideas, goods or services. Advertising is an indirect form of communication in that it takes place outside the immediate environment of the product or service. That is, the message is communicated to its target audience through the use of mass media, and the receiver is not in contact with the physical product or service. For example, an advertisement for a new motor-car is placed in a quality national newspaper that can reach half a million people representing the company's target market. The advertisement is read in isolation of the physical product. The message is therefore relayed from the manufacturer to the potential customer by an indirect and non-personal means and received outside the immediate environment of the product.

Organisations have to communicate with very large numbers of potential customers who may be geographically dispersed locally, regionally, nationally or internationally. In order to communicate with these people, organisations cannot use personal and direct contact, but have to rely on advertising. Because advertising is the only technique that uses mass media (such as the Superhighway, radio, television, posters, cinema and press) it assists the sale of the maximum number of units of product (goods or services) at a minimum cost.

How advertising works

In order to make the most effective use of advertising, it is essential to have an understanding of how it works. In most marketing situations (with the exception of the Superhighway where a customer can place an order for goods directly as a result of the advertisement) advertising on its own cannot create customers for the company. Sales result from a combination of factors including the product benefits, pricing, distribution, the sales force effort, advertising and other promotional tools. There is also a lagged effort of advertising. That is, a customer becomes aware of the product benefits and the brand name through advertising, but may not take any buying action for some considerable length of time. As discussed in previous chapters, people only buy when they perceive to have a need or a problem. This lagged effect makes any measurement of the effectiveness of advertising very difficult. An understanding of the advertising process can aid and guide managers in the four main decision areas in advertising management. Figure 7.1 shows how these decision areas are closely interrelated and form part of the overall marketing programme. The target market selected for the company's products should dictate or influence the marketing mix strategies. The product should be planned to meet the needs of the target market, with the right price and channels of distribution.

The promotional mix must be planned most effectively to communicate with the potential customers. The media or medias that should be used depends on how much the company has to spend and what it is trying to achieve. The target market and message or copy decisions also influence the selection of media. Likewise the media that can be used within the allocated budget influences how and what types of messages should be portrayed.

An understanding of how advertising works can help the setting of advertising objectives which then influence the other decisions.

A number of models and theories have been developed to explain the advertising process. Although the number, stages and terminology involved in these models tends to vary, their common theme is concerned with indicating that the influence of advertising is a sequential process.

One simple model is AIDA which stands for:

Attention
Interest
Desire
Action

This model, also known as the Hierarchy of Effects model, suggest that advertising must gain consumers' attention, hold the person's interest, arouse desire for the product and stimulate action towards the purchase of the product. This model is useful in design advertisements and web pages.

Another useful aid to advertising management is the more recent and comprehensive flow-model of advertising known as DAGMAR (Defining Advertising Goals for Measured Advertising Results). It was developed on the basis that all commercial communications that aim at the ultimate objective of achieving a sale must carry a potential customer through four levels of understanding or stages as outlined in Figure 7.2

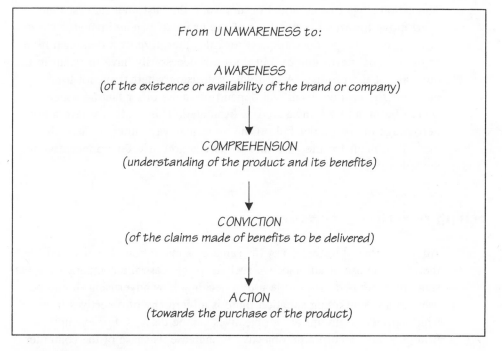

From UNAWARENESS to:

AWARENESS
(of the existence or availability of the brand or company)

COMPREHENSION
(understanding of the product and its benefits)

CONVICTION
(of the claims made of benefits to be delivered)

ACTION
(towards the purchase of the product)

Figure 7.2
The DAGMAR model

In this model, the first objective of advertising is to create an awareness amongst the target audience. The advertising may be of a product, service or ideas (e.g. policies of a political party) or an organisation. This is the primary problem area for companies trying to use the Superhighway as an advertising medium. Creating that awareness involves attracting people to their site and it is often difficult to identify easily how to do this. The next step is to ensure that certain attributes of the advertised item are known and understood, for example, brand name, pack size, technical features and benefits and where it is sold. This is effectively merchandising on the Superhighway which is covered later in this chapter. The third stage involves convincing the customer of the claims made in the advertisement. This may take the form of scientific evidence or testimonials from people with credibility. Credibility proof is extremely important on the Superhighway due to the low cost of producing material and needs careful and thorough design and testing. The action stage of the model occurs when the customer makes some overt move towards the purchase of the product. It may involve a closer inspection of the product, request for sales literature or a demonstration of the product performance, but does not necessarily have to result in the purchase of the product. A customer's decision whether or not to purchase the product itself will depend on many other factors which cannot be monitored, measured or evaluated. This is often where a high percentage of companies fail on the Superhighway either because they make it difficult for the customer to take action or offer no incentive for immediate action.

Setting advertising objectives

An advertising objective is not the same as a marketing objective and therefore the use of an objective such as 'to increase the company's market share by 5 per cent' is of little use in deciding how advertising should be used. In any marketing situation there is a hierarchy of objectives from which specific communication objectives can be derived. For example, a firm may have a corporate objective to increase its share of the computer market by developing computers for the financial services sector (banks and building societies). This corporate objective will help management in setting sub-objectives for the different functions within the business – for R & D, marketing, production, etc. The marketing objective may be to increase sales turnover in a segment of the financial services market by £1m over the next twelve months. The specific advertising objective set to reflect the marketing objective may be to create an awareness and understanding of the firm's range of products, services and reputation.

In using the hierarchical model of advertising, the objective must be:

- Capable of being communicated with management and those involved in its execution, in a written form.
- Measurable.

- Involve a starting point.
- Aimed at a defined target audience.
- Over a fixed time period.

One example of such a specific advertising objective is as follows.

> Setting an advertising objective is the most critical but often missing starting point of looking at the use of the Superhighway. As in the famous words by Lewis Carol, 'The Madhatter said "If you don't know where you are going – you probably won't get there"'.

The most useful information that can guide the setting of objective is that concerning the buying behaviour of the potential market. Effective advertising decisions cannot be made without a thorough understanding of how customers are influenced in their purchasing decisions. In industrial marketing, the Decision Making Unit (DMU) is much more complex than is the case with consumer goods for industrial products. The Decision Making Unit has to decide on what product (the systems choice) will solve the problem and from whom to buy (the brand or supplier choice). The DMU consists of:

- Decision maker – The person who makes the financial commitment.
- Specifiers – Technical people, engineers, designers, architects, buyers etc.
- Influencers – End users of products or services, marketing department, buyers.
- Gatekeepers – People who control the flow of information to decision makers, for example, receptionists and secretaries.

An analysis of the buying behaviour (covered in Chapter 2) gives information regarding the target audience that can be useful in setting advertising objectives and also provides a useful guide for selecting media and designing advertising copy. The setting of advertising objectives helps to integrate the advertising effort with the other ingredients of the marketing mix to form a consistent and a logically developed marketing plan.

Media decisions

The choice of media in which to advertise is largely determined by objectives to be achieved, amount of money available and the target audience to be reached. Because each marketing situation is unique with each product having its own problems and objectives, there can be no specific rules to cover media selection. As a general rule, media selection should be guided by a thorough understanding of the buying behaviour and the DMU operating in a particular market. Buying behaviour and, in particular, the evidence of who act as influencers, specifiers and final decision makers (or financial commitment) aid the process of assessment, evaluation and comparison of the media available to reach various targets for communication. The process of media selection can be further aided by asking four basic questions of each medium available.

- Does it deliver an audience which corresponds to the target audience in the right quantity and at an economical cost?
- Does it offer a particular valuable form for presentation of the message?
- Does it provide an opportunity to motivate the target audience?
- Has it the correct atmosphere, or will the circumstances in which the message is perceived by the audience help to sell or promote the product or service?

Use these questions to review again the decision as to the feasibility of using the Superhighway as a promotion vehicle. It may be a valid decision to use an alternative media as your primary advertising mechanism and see the Superhighway as an exploratory initiative in the short term. The alternative five other mass medias are:

- Press – National dailies, National Sundays, local morning, evening and weekly, general interest magazines, magazines and journals.
- Cinema – Gives flexibility to targeting local or national markets
- Radio – National and local independent radio stations.
- Outdoor advertising – posters or hoardings.
- Television – Local and national network of independent television companies. Now includes satellite television with possibilities of reaching international markets.

We would strongly recommend that you consider using at least one of these other mass medias in addition to your use of the Superhighway. This is because the Superhighway is not strictly a mass media. With all the other mass medias, you can be sure that your advertising will be seen by a given number of people. Yes, people can choose to turn over your advert on the page of a magazine, they can choose to make a cup of tea when your advert is shown on TV but they are exposed to your message.

However, the Superhighway acts in a very different way – people choose where to go and what to look at. There are very few places that all users go to, even the search engines (see Appendix 8) which are the most popular starting point for using the world wide web are not frequented by everyone. Just as people read different magazines, people use different areas of the Superhighway. It is still a mass medium but should be qualified that although there are 45 million users – you do not have the opportunity to place an advertisement where all these people are exposed to your advert. So it is important to return to your research as to where your customers do frequent on the Internet if you are to ensure they read your advertisement. In summary, it acts in a very different way and the next section outlines the opportunities this brings.

THE USE OF SUPERHIGHWAY AS AN ADVERTISING MEDIUM

This section helps you evaluate the benefits of the Superhighway as an advertising medium for your organisation. It outlines where the Internet is today, what it is predicted to become and some case studies of successes. It then outlines your options on how to get your company on-line.

Where is the Superhighway today?

Although there are a huge number of sites in America devoted to marketing on the Internet, the evidence shows that, as yet, the United Kingdom and the rest of Europe have not shown comparatively similar enthusiasm. In 1995-6, estimates ranged from 1-7 per cent of the UK population being on-line, with Europe being less. Only recently have European businesses begun to appreciate the full marketing potential of the Internet in the UK.

There is a Catch 22 working here. The cost of using Internet in Europe is more than in the USA due to the price of local calls. This means that the userbase was initially slower to grow in comparison (only 10 per cent per month rather than 20 per cent in built-up areas of America). Because the userbase has been slower to grow, the incentive for European companies to invest has been less. However, as commercial organisations offer more added value the incentive to the end customer grows and this process is just starting to compensate for the costs and reverse the initial slow uptake.

When marketers ask what the UK Internet userbase is, there are unfortunately few statistics.

Mat Toor reports on the future impact of this new powerful medium: 'Companies that will succeed with this new medium need to learn these lessons for themselves by actually getting their hands dirty by going on-line as soon as they can. Don't expect to make a million overnight but the fact is that within three years every company will be on the Internet in some form or another. Those that get on-line now and learn about working with the medium while it's still in its infancy will be the ones that clean up when it matures into a genuine mass market medium'. (*Direct Response*, Sept. 1995.)

Why is the Internet a different advertising medium?

The belief amongst marketers is that the advertisements on the world wide web have to be different to those that currently exist in traditional media and should instead be interactive. In order to approach the world of the Internet, the prospective web marketer should make themselves fully aware of all the current dilemmas, possible shortfalls and the changing attitudes towards the Internet. They also need to experience it first hand from the customer perspective. To facilitate this, we have provided an easy entry into searching and finding your way around within the accompanying web-site for this book. It will reduce the high frustration levels that you may experience otherwise.

Considerable care is needed by those wishing to market on the new medium. A lot of care is needed when putting together a package to go on-line and people should be aware that a code of ethics exists which defines what is acceptable and what is considered unacceptable. Please see Appendix 4 (Netiquette).

Despite these cautionary measures there is a strong belief that with sufficient knowledge a company can establish a distinctive presence on the Internet. There is a strong belief that the Internet marketing should be of use to the customer.

Despite fears that the frequently referred to '50 million users of the Internet' may be an exaggeration. Marketeers are quick to point out that the Internet's audience is very large and is increasing rapidly. There is also the belief that on-line marketing is really very easy. This is not the case and the best analogy is the launch of desktop publishing where users perceived that design of marketing materials was suddenly made easy. All that happened was that between 1987 and 1990, there was a proliferation of badly designed marketing materials. On the Internet, there is a proliferation of badly designed corporate brochures, obviously arising from the IT department with little effective marketing. Sales messages are not translated to this new target audience. Graphics are included in tune with the corporate logo which add nothing to the end customer for which he/she is forced to pay for, etc.

The need to be innovative and not replicate your conventional advertising material on-line is stressed with great frequency. Offering free gifts to consumers may attract some initial interest but, in the long run, it does not advance the situations of the marketeers themselves.

The Internet is developing its own specific identity with its own language. New marketing techniques need to be adopted but the application of traditional marketing thinking will prevent the mass marketing mess that appears in segments of the Internet at present.

But people wanting to move into marketing must do so now, before it is too late. Marketeers must be realistic and fully aware of the limitations and never over-estimate the medium and proceed with caution. The medium should not be used simply because it is there as it should be surveyed to see how it can enable the interested party to improve their business, most importantly in the form of information and entertainment.

'Successful Internet marketing involves developing a whole new collection of attitudes and words to accompany them' – a widely used remark that shows that the Internet is set to become the medium of the future and that it will revolutionise our everyday lives.

Putting your company on the Superhighway

This is where you publish your company as an entity on the world wide web. The options in this area are vast and complex. This section is not intended to give you every option available as this changes by the day as suppliers in the industry make it more affordable and easier to implement corporate initiatives. It will however provide you with a decision tree to outline the various choices, the benefits of each and some of the cost implications. It will give you a checklist to enable you to talk to providers and make good purchasing decisions.

Question: How serious am I?
The first question you need to ask yourself is 'How Serious Am I?'

In traditional promotion terms, do I want a black and white A3 flyer or a 20-page four-colour embossed, pull-out brochure. Budget will be the major constraining or enabling issue when it comes to deciding your route to successfully publishing your company on-line. Again, the decision of how much to spend in reference to the Superhighway needs to be seen in the overall context of the advertising budget bearing in mind that the Superhighway presence also needs to be advertised in its own right.

The advertising budget
There is general tendency by many companies to decide on the amount of money to be spent on advertising before thinking of what needs to be done. Advertising budget is also, in many cases, the first to be sacrificed when there is a shortage of money in the business. Advertising expenditure should be regarded as an investment rather than a cost, and

the money should be spent to help achieve the marketing and corporate objectives of the organisation.

How much you decide to spend will depend on how important your company image is in your marketplace and also how interactive you wish to make your Internet presence. This is, of course, similar to the issues of producing an advert. Too inexpensive and it may cheapen your corporate image in the eyes of your customers, especially if they are used to high quality advertising and marketing materials. Too expensive and it may be costly to warrant and maintain. However on paper you can produce a high quality, low cost item with some good creative work, good design and some imaginative copy. In Cyberspace, this is also true but you do have an additional concern – your 'address'. Every page of marketing material needs to have a reference under which a customer can locate it. This address reveals how much or how little you are spending. For example: http://www.demon.co.uk/widget is a page produced under an existing company on the Internet called Demon. You are placing your marketing materials inside their company's Internet site. This implies that you have spent less than £1,000. http://www.widget.com on the other hand implies that you have committed to this technology and have created a unique corporate domain name which is registered to your company and are likely to have your own dedicated computer for your customers to access 24 hours a day. This can cost in excess of £5,000.

We have just touched on the concept of domain names here because it does affect your budget. For a more in-depth discussion about domain names, please read the next section.

> The exception to the rule is Guinness. They heralded one of the most successful Internet campaigns in 1995, giving away an amazing screen-saver. They received 45,000 requests in the first two months. They did not use their own domain name but placed their pages under an existing provider and used the address:
> **http://www.itl.net/guinness/**

Low budget promotional options
You have four options:

1. A Directory Entry
There are many companies offering this service. They recognise that not all companies wish to produce their own web-site and therefore they

offer an easy and cheap way to publish your company's information. They also offer the end customer a 'one-stop' shop. Because they offer benefits to both sides of the supplier chain, they will continue to prosper and are the best starting point for your investigations even if you are considering producing your own web pages in addition. They usually offer the complete service from helping you design your entry all the way through to producing your web pages and maintaining them over time. Additional benefits to your company and your customers is that you may be able to make use of a shared security payment system, a shared enquiry response form or a fulfilment system which would normally be out of your budget threshold. In other words a directory provider may offer a secure credit card payment system which would enable your customers to buy products direct from you on-line.

The downside of this option is that you are often contrained by the style and amount of pages you wish to publish. You may also find that your pages are costly to change and incur either high monthly maintenance costs or high credit card commission rates.

The best option is to find a provider who specialises by industry type. A good example of this is *Dealernet* who offer a car dealer directory with specifications of cars and contact addresses. All the big car companies in America are contained within here. Dealernet are commonly cited as a success story, reputed to have sold 57 cars directly off the Internet. Interestingly most of their customers also have their own web-site in addition. Entries into this type of directory service vary between £20–£1000. If you can find an American supplier, this is of course much cheaper because the market is more mature. However, many European customers will not search through an American based directory to find a European company – so it may be better to pay for a more expensive European supplier. Another good example is *THISCO* who provide a one-stop shop for hotel bookings across hotel chains: see *Hotelnet*, *Virtual Tourist*, *accommodata*.

If you are a consumer marketer, the equivalent to this is the shopping malls. *Barclays Square* and the *London Mall* were two of the first in the UK and an entry in one can cost as little as £500. The downside of this type of promotion is that it fails to provide your customers with a one-stop shop and puts you alongside insurance brokers, chocolate suppliers etc. However, this may be to your advantage if you are wishing to promote a product which is not something that a customer would key into a search engine to look for and you are looking to catch the attention of an existing on-line purchaser. CompuServe host Tescos and Toys 'R Us and are building a retail environment, so this provides another good place to start.

Just as the three key issues when buying property is 'location, location and location', the three key issues when looking at placing a directory entry is 'readership, readership and readership'. The only problem is that only the directory provider knows what the readership is and it is in their interest to lie to you to attract you in, in order to increase their readership. We recommend returning to the marketing research chapter and how your customers would typically try and find you in Cyberspace and if directories are a key channel then use them immediately – maybe even all of them! You may even want to create your own directory. This is not significantly more than producing your own web-site and it can produce a revenue stream to offset the cost. A common approach is to loss-lead for the start-up period and offer listings free and only charge when you become established. It is very much a dog-eat-dog type of game at present as many companies are trying to compete in this directory market. A list of directories offering listings at a fee is hosted by *MMG* and referenced on the accompanying web page for this chapter.

2. Publish your company within a provider's web-site
This is the second most cost-effective way of putting your organisation on the Internet. This is the cheapest option if you want complete control of how your pages look and how the customer can access them. Most of the major providers in Europe offer this service.

This is where you create your own pages either yourself or using an external provider and you request that your provider publishes them under their existing Internet site. You do not need to have your company registered as a unique entity (i.e. your own domain name) and the provider names a certain area (or directory) with your company name. Your web address will be:
http://www.yourprovider.com/yourcompany.

Although this reveals that you do not have your own web-site, you have more degrees of freedom to make up for your lack of investment on the creative design of your pages. This is the cheapest way of having carte blanche on your creative design and image. You are also less constrained as to how many pages you can have as compared to a directory entry.

If you want to offer a response form, credit card payments and other advanced Internet services, this is usually provided at an additional cost. We strongly recommend you investigate the cost implications of these options before you commit to publishing with a provider.

First you need to investigate provider prices for including you in their web-site. These prices vary considerably and it certainly pays to shop around. CompuServe has offered this service for free but this is typically aimed at the individual or self-employed market allowing users the ability to experiment with HTML (Hypertext Mark Up Language – the programming language that presents the format of the pages on the Internet). Ultimately you are paying for the provider's brand image and their technical infrastructure. In the marketplace. Pipex has a better brand image than Demon at the present time due to the fact that Demon received some early bad PR on the lack of organisation and structure they had in place. You also pay more with a brand leader for their technical infrastructure. Where for example they have a backup telecommunication link to America so it is unlikely that you will ever lose your service to America. Some of the cheaper providers may not have such a backup and it is more likely that you will lose your service. Therefore you pay more for being hosted by Pipex. The service that your end customer will receive will not vary considerably, speed of access being your only need for concern. However, the service that you as an organisation receive may vary considerably. Some providers will offer you monthly statistics of how many people are accessing your pages, others won't. Others offer the whole process from designing your pages all the way through to helping you maintain your site.

N.B. Typically these providers are IT focused and your pages will be designed by technical people with minimum marketing creative and design skills. Although the prices may be tempting this alternative is the equivalent of having your corporate brochure designed by a printing company.

ALWAYS CHECK OUT YOUR PROVIDER

We recommend you investigate at least five providers before making a decision. Always test any supplier. It is easy to test out their web-server and look at what they have done for other clients. Things to look for include:

Pricing structure?

Some providers look very attractive by hiding costs by a complex or different pricing structure. Examples of these are:

> Per message charges for e:mail
> Per hit charges for your customers' access to your pages
> Hidden costs for transferring your web pages or domain name to another supplier.

Do check out the prices and options for domain names? There will be different prices depending on which URL you desire. Some providers cannot register your company.co.uk domain names because their servers are based in America and can only offer you *.com (which implies an internation company). Some providers will only enable you to have http://www.yourname.com/directory name. Ones that can provide you with http://yourname.co.uk/ will charge premium rates for this because it gives the end customer the impression that you have your own server.

Do they have a sound technical infrastructure?

What is their speed of response today?

You should try their server at different times of the day and if time permits, spot check it over a number of weeks. What you are looking for is how reliable is their equipment: is it ever off-line or ever running really slowly. Although this is easy to test, this only tells you what their speed of response it today. It is worth investigating their investment plans into new equipment. Particularly if they are good value for money, they will attract a large number of customers and without the right levels of investment, their service will drop off. It is strongly recommended that you pay extra to increase your chances of a sustained good service.

Reliability?

How many connections do they have to the Internet. If they only have one connection, and it goes down, your customers cannot access your pages.

References?

Also ensure that you have a look around at other companies they are 'hosting'. Ask the provider to give you the name and telephone number of an existing customer to talk to. Alternatively e:mail a number of companies that are being hosted by the provider and ask them whether they are satisfied and any response they have received from their customers.

Support?

You need to assess the provider's ability to fix problems and how fast they respond to your needs. Try contacting their support line and see how long it takes to get through to someone and how customer focused that person is at being able to deal with your question.

Do they have enough people in their company to offer a high quality of service? Do they understand that you are trying to run a business?

Financial security?

This company will be maintaining your domain name and your company image in Cyberspace. Both of these are easily transferable technically but often cause administrative work and stress for you. So to avoid this, it is worth investigating how likely it is that your supplier will go out of business. How long have they been in business? Will they be in business in six month's time?

Do they have professional indemnity in case they make a mistake with your work and you run into a legal battle?

Next you need to decide how you are going to produce your web pages, please see Chapter 8.

3. Create your own web-site
This is where you create your own identity independent of your provider. This means that it can be invisible to your customers as to who is 'hosting' or publishing your materials. This is the preferred option if you are concerned about corporate image but want to keep your costs to a minimum.

In Cyberspace, you can have what is called a 'domain name'. This is like a name and address in the 'real' world. Like lots of things in Cyberspace, you are free from the physical limitations of the real world. Your domain name or address could be: the name of your company; the name of your product; the name of the service you provide; your product category or in fact anything you want.

In Cyberspace, all the domains are grouped together, so for example if you are an academic institute, your domain name has '.edu' added to the end. If you are an international commercial organisation or in the USA, you have '.com' added to the end.

Each domain name has to be unique. So the domains have been further grouped by country. Anyone in the UK can have '.uk' on the end of their domain name.

For a full glossary of international domain names and their meaning please see Appendix 6.

The Internet is pretty anarchic but it wouldn't work if anyone could just choose a domain name. So there is a central Network Information Centre (often called the NIC) which holds a master list of all the domain names and which computer they are to be found on. This non-profit-making organisation processes thousands of requests for domain names every day on a first come, first served basis. There is a huge queue of requests for new domain names, so even if choose a name that you know is not being used, it may be just your luck that someone in the queue has just requested it. It can take many weeks to get to the front of the queue. During this time, all you can do is cross your fingers and hope. (We explain how you can check whether your desired domain name is free later in this chapter.)

You do not personally apply for this registration, your provider will do this for you. You can include your full name, address and e:mail which will be held at the NIC so that people can look up your domain name at the NIC and can obtain your full name and address. This can be quite useful if you want to get in touch with someone and you only have their domain.

What domain name can I choose?

Your domain name becomes your address in Cyberspace.

'http://' is always the first part of your domain name because this indicates that you are on the world wide web. This stands for 'hypertext transfer protocol' and it indicates that it is a 'web page' rather than a file or a newsgroup etc. 'www' is not always necessary but is the syntax stating it is the world wide web. The next bit is where you need to make a decision.

Option 1

http://www.widget.co.uk/widget/

You would register 'widget.co.uk' as your domain name and decide on what you would like to call the sub-directory after this domain name, i.e. 'widget'. This indicates that you are a company based in the UK.

Option 2

http://www.widget.com/widget/

You would register widget.com as your domain name. This indicates that you are an international company and unless you state you are based in the UK on your pages, your customer has no idea where in the world you are based. This is great if you want to globalise your customer base or give the impression that you are bigger than you really are.

You will notice on these two options that there is a second reference to your company '/widget/' after your domain name. This is because you are being hosted on a provider's machine. You normally need to have your own dedicated server to have the luxury of Option 3 or 4.

Option 3 and 4

http://www.widget.co.uk
http://www.widget.com

Most companies want to have this format of address because it is easier for the customer to type in to return easily to the pages. Often customers will try typing in your company name to see if you are on-line and this is typically what they would type in.

However, you can usually only obtain this by having a dedicated machine to your company. Recently some providers are offering this option to companies that they are hosting but this is a premium priced service because they have to change their configuration for you (set up another IP address for the technical minded). It is also premium priced because it gives your customers the impression that you have your own server. Ask your provider whether they can offer this domain name option. It looks good if you can afford it!!

A little warning

Domain names are being registered by the thousands every hour and there is a likelihood that your desired company name has already been purchased. They are allocated by the NIC on a first come, first served basis. There are also some rather annoying gold-diggers buying up potentially lucrative domain names. You can easily check whether your desired domain name has been registered already by jumping from the accompanying web-site under this chapter heading under domain searching.

The two main options here are either outsourcing it completely or doing it in-house. This will obviously be dependent on how much internal resources and skills you have within your organisation

Working in partnership with a provider

This is the equivalent of having your own marketing agency. You brief the provider with your objectives and they create storyboards and creat design options for you. This is the most preferred route if you need a professional looking web-site and do not have the resources in-house to dedicate someone full-time on the project.

There are three types of companies in this arena.

1. Access providers

There are the access providers (list provided on the accompanying web-site referenced under this chapter) who are stereo-typically focused on the technical side. They often offer a one-stop shop but their designers are often Internet boffins rather than true marketing designers. It is a little like the early days of desktop publishing in the late 1980s where everyone thought that the software would turn them automatically into designers. The result was a proliferation of badly designed flyers with little marketing impact.

The difference between an Internet provider & an Internet marketing Co

2. Marketing companies

Then there are marketing companies (list provided on the accompanying web site referenced under this chapter) who are focused on the professional design, creative input and the marketing impact of their work for you. A true test of the difference between a technically focused and a marketing focused company is in the provision of story-boards with a series of options before moving to the programming stage of the project. Professional marketing companies will also spend time investigating your existing marketing materials, research your company, your company image and your success factors of Internet marketing. Another marked difference, using marketing companies is, of course, price. However, like most marketing projects, investment in planning, design and creative work usually pays off in the long-run. The big question here is do they understand your business?

'Don't ask what the internet can do for you, Sonny-boy, ask what you can do for the internet.'

We would recommend paying for a tender from a few of these marketing companies. State your objectives and include your marketing materials and pay on a time basis for the initial design phase separate from the Internet publishing. This means that you can assess the creative and technical skills of the marketing company and see if you can work creatively with them before you commit yourself to a long-term relationship.

There is much debate whether advertising agencies are better at producing pages than PR companies versus Internet marketing companies. Some marketers say that PR companies know how to make your web-site 'newsworthy'; others say that advertising agencies fail to appreciate the interactive nature of the Superhighway. It is not within the scope of this book to enter into this debate. It is hopefully sufficient to say that any marketing company who can appreciate your business and marketing objectives together with the nature and opportunity the Internet has to offer is likely to be the best choice.

3. Gold-diggers

Then there are the gold-diggers (which we cannot reference on our web-site for legal reasons). These are usually one-man bands who are capitalizing on customer naiveté and the Internet popularity. They will offer the same as the above on paper (or on Cyberspace) but are typically technically limited or creatively impaired, usually both. Beware of these.

Whichever of the above, please use our checklist for assessing a provider.

Renting some cyberspace and doing it all yourself
You can rent some 'web space' with a provider, ask them to register your domain name and write all your marketing materials yourself. This is ideal if you have an internal design and creative team who are also adept at HTML programming and understand the Internet culture.

Warning about internal resource needs

One word of warning here. To design and maintain your web-site yourself, your people must not only have an in-depth understanding of the Internet but enough time to continue to update themselves on this ever-changing new medium. We would recommend at least one full-time person on the project. They also need to have good analytical skills to build a structure to your site and your pages which is intuitive to your customers and will support your future innovations.

There are many products on the market to make the process of creating and maintaining your pages easily. One that is popular at this time is Lotus Web Publisher.

It is easy at this stage to jump into production rather than taking an analytical step back and involve a good creative team at the conception stage. We recommend you read Chapter 8 on how to produce your promotional materials in the most professional manner.

High budget promotional options

At this point, you will have appreciated the relevance of the Superhighway as being an effective and supportive medium to converse with your target market. This section describes how you may go further and really commit to promoting your company on the Superhighway. It assumes you can afford to have control of your own means of production, i.e. a Web-server – the computer that stores your promotional materials and enables your customers to access them 24 hours a day.

There are three choices here: rent a shared server; rent a dedicated server or have your own server in-house.

Rent a shared server

This is charged to you on an annual or monthly basis. The computer is located and maintained at the provider's premises. The provider bears all the set-up and administrative costs, together with paying for the telephone connection which provides 24 hour access for your customers.

This is the cheapest alternative but the downside is that at least one other organisation will be publishing their information on the same machine. Because the computer can only serve up one page at a time, your customers will have to compete to access your information. It is important to find out who you will be sharing with and set up some guaranteed service levels on access speed for your customers.

Likewise, because you are sharing, you are likely to have constraints put on you as to what services you are able to offer your customers. The more impressive and customer focused initiatives like response forms and customer database enquiries require extra computer processing and therefore may be restricted with this option.

You may not be able to have the one-word domain name like http://yourcompany.com here because you are sharing a server. Do enquire with your specific provider on whether this is possible.

Rent a dedicated server

Again this is charged to you on an annual or monthly basis and is located and maintained at the provider's. This is identical to having your own computer but it is maintained and checked for you by the provider. As before, the provider bears all the set-up and administrative costs, together with paying for the telephone connection which provides 24 hour access for your customers.

It is more expensive than a shared server but your customers do not have to compete with the customers of the other company you are sharing the server with. This option is essential if you want to take advantage of the more powerful features on the Internet like interrogating a customer database, lookup prices from a price database, downloading software, intelligent response forms etc. It also means that you can make the server more secure and give only selected customers access to information. For credit card payments, this is the minimum option that you need to consider. Although we would still recommend that you have an in-house server for high security payment systems.

The advantages of both the above options is that you can be closer to the core of the Internet. If you decide to select an American provider, you could even be on the 'backbone' of the Internet. This is the core structure which was historically based in the US and funded by the Government. The 'backbone' now spreads across the major countries of the world. In the last two years, global telecommunications companies like MCI and AT&T have started to replace the core structure and are investing heavily. These companies are using extremely high capacity networks. You cannot get a direct link to this core but an access provider may have such a direct link. It is the role of the access provider to concentrate all the small links to individual companies so that there is enough information traffic to justify a link on to the core. The closer you are to the core, the less links there are between you and your customer and this can improve the response rate of your information on-line.

Your own server located and maintained in-house
This is where you buy your own computer, load some software onto it, attach it to a 24 hour telephone link (usually a leased line connection) and away you go. We exaggerate about the simplicity but it is not as technically challenging as some of the access providers like you to think. It is often in their best interest not to encourage you to go this route. But once the initial headache of setting it up is all over, maintenance and upkeep is relatively simple.

One disadvantage of having your own server in-house rather than maintained for you by an access provider is that you are one stage removed from the Internet. In other words you are connected through a provider, which is one step away from having a machine maintained for you on the provider's premises. The speed differential does not have to be significant especially if you choose a provider who has a good response rate to start with.

For external marketing, this option gives you the most flexibility. Publish as much as your machine can store, use the most advanced functionality of the Internet to your heart's content and update your information easily at the touch of a button. You can set up as much or as little security as you feel fit. This option also means a fast acceleration up the Internet learning curve which will put you in good stead when you want to leverage it further for competitive advantage.

However, there are other two major benefits as to why you would select this option.

1. It enables you to provide Internet access for the whole of your organisation

You in effect act like an internal access provider.

You can provide e:mail for the whole organisation. Users' e:mail files are stored on this machine and forwarded onto the Internet or circulated internally where appropriate. If you already use some form of e:mail (Lotus Notes, cc:Mail, Microsoft Mail) you can link this system up with the Internet so that people can communicate both internally and externally.

You can provide every person inside your organisation access to the world wide web. They would have the software on their computer but your server would provide them with a route out to every web page in the world.

2. Internal communication system – Intranets

More and more companies are recognizing the power of this technology not only for gathering external information and promoting themselves to the world at large but also to communicate internally. (See Chapter 4 about this subject.)

The popularity of using the Internet for this purpose is growing. Individuals and teams create web pages and forums to disseminate information and collect response. They can even communicate with people that work from remote locations. This can make the whole process of 'buying in' key decision makers not only easy but fun. It also acts as a corporate receptacle so that information is spread uniformly across the organisation rather than being trapped in select areas. It also enables you to channel and target information by deciding who should see what information and in what format and when.

From a marketing perspective, you can use this server as the mechanism to promote what you are trying to achieve: to disseminate the marketing plan; set out the communications strategy; circulate PR articles; openly debate marketing issues; elicit response to support marketing tactical decisions; proof direct mail copy.... the list is endless. It can be used to transform the organisation's perspective of the marketing team and their work. Are you ready for notoriety? In some case studies that we have analysed, the benefits the server offers inside the organisation is even greater than the promotional benefits the Internet offers externally.

You need to have your own server if you are to offer on-line ordering and accept credit card payments for a number of different products. Using a mall is an option but this may be cheaper in the short-term and constraining to your business in the long-term.

You would also need this option if you want to set up levels of security where some customers receive services that others don't.

What do you need?

(a) IT skills to maintain the machine and provide technical support when needed. This person or team need to be knowledgeable about the Internet in order to be able to receive and send information to and from the provider's machine. They also need to be able to invest time in learning how the software on the server works and is configured. They will need this knowledge base if or when you decide to make use of the advanced functionality of the Internet like clickable maps, sound, video, response forms feeding direct into databases etc.

(b) A computer. The first decision you need to make is which operating system you wish to use. This will depend on what IT infrastructure and skill set you have existing in your organisation. This will then define which computer you need and how much you need to spend.

Windows 3.1, or Windows 95 do not make good Internet operating systems because they are not multi-user, not secure and are not robust enough to stand up to the pressure of 24 accessing day in, day out. There are ideal for web page creation but not for publishing these pages on the world wide web.

The options you have are: UNIX, Windows NT, Mac, AS400 or MVS.

The most popular operating system for use on the Internet is UNIX. This is because the Internet was built from a UNIX base. The benefits of UNIX for an Internet server is that it is very well tried and tested. All the software you will possibly need for the Internet is available on this operating system. The other attractive benefit is that UNIX scales up from small to very large computers easily. Smaller UNIX systems can be based on PCs but IBM, Hewlett Packard, Digital and Sun offer a range of UNIX machines from the small to the extremely large mainframe type systems. In general, UNIX compatible computers are available from a wide range of suppliers although because there are slight differences between each one, it is better to stick with a single supplier. The downside of UNIX is that it is a technically sophisticated and can be quite a challenge to set up and administrate.

Windows NT is becoming a popular alternative to UNIX because of its friendly administration and ease of installation. This is an ideal starting point for a quick and easy installation of a web-server. However, it is still relatively new and a number of companies we have worked with, have found that the performance has not been up to their expectations. The other downside is that it does not scale as far up into the large computers as UNIX.

Internet providers have recently started to sing the praises of Macintosh computers for Internet servers. If you currently use Apple equipment, this is most likely to be your best option, although much of the free software may not be available to you, so it may be slightly more expensive to set up. It is also not as flexible to cross platforms as Unix.

AS400 and MVS have not been widely used on the Internet at present but recent developments have made them an attractive option for those companies already using an AS400 or mainframe. IBM are going to be using a mainframe for the Olympic Games because of the huge number of people visiting their web-site.

The operating system will define the computer you need to buy. Obtain quotes from a variety of different vendors before you decide on the most suitable and ensure that you obtain reference sites of customers who have set up a web-server using the hardware platform that you have chosen.

(c) A provider to link your server with the Internet. Again you need to use the provider checklist outlined in the previous section. One other consideration here is how much the provider will support you in the early days of setting it up. Will they configure it for you and train your people? Will they give a good support response time if you run into difficulties?

(d) A telecommunication connection. There are two alternatives here: a leased line or an ISDN link. The leased line is the most expensive to set up but has the lowest running costs. This is provided by your telecommunications company or through your access provider who can arrange it more simply for you. A dedicated telephone line is then installed at your organisation where you may have a yearly cost (in the thousands) irrespective of how many telephone calls you make out or in using this line.

The alternative is an ISDN link which is less but you have to pay for the telephone calls in and out on it. This means that the more customers you attract to your web-site and the more people you have in your organisation using your web-server as a gateway to the Internet, the more you pay. You therefore have little control on the variable costs, so this makes this alternative quite unattractive.

You also need what is called a 'router'. This is a device which handles the dataflow to and from your Internet connection. Any messages that come from the Internet will be passed to you by your access provider. They will do this by sending the information down your link to the router which is located in your premises and is usually rented to you and maintained by the access provider. This is usually because the access providers needs to have the same make and configuration of routers.

Once the router receives the messages from the access provider, its task it to pass it on to the correct computer inside your organisation. Simply, there is a table of computer identities held within the router that allows it to decide whether to pass the data.

The router also has the ability to recognise any messages sent within the organisation which are destined for somewhere outside. When the router detects one of these, it passes it on to the access provider as the first step to reaching its destination somewhere in the world.

A router can be used to prevent outside access to your company's computers. But this alone is not adequate for complete security because it is quite possible for someone to falsify their 'sender's address'. This is where the router will think the message has come from a trustworthy source and do its job and pass it straight on. This brings us neatly to the bigger issue of security.

(e) A security system. The decisions involved in deciding the best security system are complex and really outside the scope of this book. There are whole books dedicated to this subject alone. There are also products coming on the market daily to make the complexity in this area easier to understand and act upon.

What we can explain in general terms is what security issues you need to be concerned with, so that you can professionally brief either your internal IT department, your access provider or your IT supplier as to your needs and your concerns.

I want to protect my web pages from being deleted or defaced?
You need to protect yourself from the hacker who may benignly or maliciously use your server and modify your setup and your web pages. You need to ensure that customers can read your web pages but not modify them.

> A funny case study about the web-site on the film 'Hacker' was benignly hacked by someone who drew moustaches on all the pictures and left some graffiti. This ironic turn of events was left on the web-site because it was such great PR!!

This basic security comes from within your web-server machine. Again, this is dependent on your IT people configuring your web pages securely. With any computer connected to the Internet, it is important to maintain high standards of administration. This includes mandating the use of passwords and keeping the software up to date because this ensures you get the most up-to-date security enhancements.

The best form of security is to have your dedicated web-server as a stand-alone system unconnected to any other computer in your building.

This by-passes the need for any further security beyond the router. However you do not get the benefits of offering the whole organisation Internet access.

I want to offer my company internet access but protect my company information from unwanted intrusion? And I want to restrict Internet services within the organisation?

Filters in

You need some sort of filter system on your server which enables your customers to get into your web pages but not go careering around areas that you don't wish them to access.

Filters out

You also need a mechanism to allow the people inside your organisation to access the world wide web and send their e:mail out. This may be used in addition to restrict times of people using the server; restrict pornographic areas of the Internet or restrict access to the Internet to certain types of use e.g. e:mail only, no downloading of software etc.

This filter mechanism for both internal and external data flow is constructed from either a software program, a router or a combination of the two. A filter looks at each packet of information as it passes through. Depending on the type of filter it will perform various checks, preventing unwanted access by removing packets that do not conform to the rules programmed.

It is worth paying extra for a good router because it will include the ability to filter. If you do not have one of these sophisticated routes, you will need additional filter software and probably an extra computer to run this software on. This extra computer will have to handle all the information in and out of your company. Therefore it will have to be a fast and expensive one.

If you are going to connect your web-server with any other computer in your organisation who must take security very seriously. This is critical especially if you wish to take on-line credit card orders because these need to be stored on a separate machine to your server. You need to investigate 'firewalls'. This is a conceptual term for a set of routers, computers and software which puts up a barrier between your web-server and your internal network. There are numerous configuration options here and we recommend that you read 'Firewalls and Internet Security' referenced at the end of this chapter.

A firewall works in both directions and is set to allow only 'safe' transactions across the wall. It acts a bit like a checkpoint where every request is carefully screened. You place this firewall between your web-server and your network. If correctly set up this will make it extremely difficult for external people to access your internal network.

(f) Server software. Once you have got your computer connected to the Internet securely. However you still have to make some more choices. You need to run a piece of software that will turn your computer into a web-server. In essence the software will sit and wait for your customers to make contact. It will take their requests for information, find it on the server and send it to them. It can send many different types of information: formatted text; graphics; sound, video and software programmes. Alone, all the web-server software does is find files and pass them back to the user.

For a more dynamic interaction with the customer, you need your web-server to play a more active role. It does this by taking the information from your customer. It then processes it and returns a response to the enquiry. The processing is done through a set of software programmes sitting on the web-server. Some of these programmes will come with your web-server, others you may need to source elsewhere.

There are two choices on web-server software. You either buy it packaged from a supplier or you obtain it direct from the Internet. Buying it provides you with manuals and technical support and a certain peace of mine. Unless you have advanced technical skills, this approach is strongly recommended.

Before you select which software to buy, you need to decide what facilities you will require:

I want response forms to ask for my customer's details, check if they are an existing customer, feed back answers to questions they may have and/or thank them for filling in the form.

Some web-server software has the ability to process forms built inside them. This is the most convenient because otherwise you will need to have programming skills within your organisation to offer this to your customers.

I want to have several addresses on the same server? (e.g. widget.com, widgetx.com, widgety.com)

Check that the web-server does this. You will still have to register these names with your provider.

I want to measure statistics of customers accessing your web pages.

This is the marketer's dream, you can see what pages of marketing material each customer looks at for how long and in what order. This information will help you improve your information and evolve your Internet site in tune with customer needs. Not all web-server software offers this – so do check.

I want to offer different information to different people?

For example, you may wish to offer different information to internal people and to subsets of customers. Flexible security systems with password protection is a key feature of some web-server software and this is definitely worth investigating.

(g) An uninterruptible power supply (UPS). A UPS box enables you to ensure that your server stays accessible 24 hours a day even if there is a power cut. You pay more depending on how long you want the UPS box to maintain the machine in the event of a power cut. Your choice will depend on how likely power cuts are to happen and how important the web-server will be to your business.

INTEGRATING YOUR ADVERTISING IN CYBERSPACE WITH THAT IN THE REAL WORLD

The theme of advertising helps to give the product a personality and character and helps communicate an understandable message. This can be very powerful when you have the same message from different medias, all reinforcing each other. Often the net result is more than the sum of the impact that the individual medias create. This synergy can be achieved when the advertising across medias reinforce, support and enhance each other. This was brought out in the recent Guinness success story where TV advertising, Internet promotion and magazine advertising supported a common campaign which was itself then given huge national and international press coverage. The recipe for good advertising has the following three ingredients:

Concentration

Many organisations make the mistake of excessive dispersal of the advertising budget by using too many different media. It is far better to opt for concentration, in terms of size and frequency, in a limited number of media, than to risk limited exposure to larger audience by advertising in many media. At the same time, it has been proved over and over again that the Superhighway does not work in isolation and you need an integrated approach if you are to attract people to your Internet site. You almost need an advertising budget to promote your Internet site. This may sound ludicrous – why advertise to attract people to your advertisement, but the Internet can be so much more than an advertisement and also when people do visit you in Cyberspace and you satisfy their needs they not only return but remain loyal to you.

Domination

Any advertising should dominate at least for some of the time and in relation to some of the target audience. In the long term, the budget available determines the amount of advertising that is possible, but to outspend competition is the only way to achieve domination of the selected media. In some cases, a different creative approach from the competition can achieve domination of the media for a short period of time. On the Superhighway, you can dominate more effectively and cheaper than on any other media. However, dominating an advertising media is only relevant if the whole of your target audience reads that media. Do not invest in domination of the Superhighway if your target audience is not present yet – learn, experiment and wait for the best time to invest heavily.

Repetition

Awareness and comprehension of product benefits and attributes can only be communicated to large target audiences by repetitive exposure to the advertisements. Research suggests that for advertising to be effective in achieving its stated objective, requires at least three exposures to its target audience. On the Internet this is also true, as you need to encourage your customers to come back three times before they will buy.

In order to reach a substantial number of your target audience, invest in repetitive advertising.

The considerations of repetition, domination and concentration will help you formulate an effective media schedule and costing for the overall advertising campaign for a product or service.

MERCHANDISING

The term merchandising is one of the most misused words in the marketing language. Many people working in the field of marketing management also confine it to point-of-sale display activities for consumer products. Merchandising is much more than that. It is an essential element in the marketing mix which can achieve communication objectives not possible by using other marketing methods. In essence, merchandising ranges from the total presentation of a product from initiation to the point of purchase. It starts at the point of manufacture when a product is given its identity and personality through the use of packaging and labelling. It continues to the stage when it is packed for transport (for example in containers which carry the name of the product and the company). When the product is in transit, merchandising is used on the vehicles, and finally it is displayed in an outlet for customers to purchase.

A simple definition of the term merchandising is that it is a non-personal, visual projection of the company and its products, which exerts influence within and outside the purchasing environment to:

- Attract customers
- Stimulate desire
- Convert desire into buying action.

Unlike sales promotion, merchandising does not rely on direct influences, or the promise of tangible reward to achieve its objectives. It is much more concerned with the use of indirect influences and is used to promote both products and companies. In the case of products it is concerned with the most effective method of presentation to encourage the maximum number of potential buyers to purchase them. Perhaps the most useful role of merchandising is in helping to establish, maintain and project a corporate identify to the company's publics. A company's publics consist not only of potential and existing customers, but also current and potential employees, suppliers, shareholders, government bodies and local authorities.

If you wish to use your web-site to merchandise your products and take orders directly off the Internet, you really need to have your own server. Once this is in place, you need to design your organisation's shop-window.

You can design it in many different ways:

1. Your company in Cyberspace

Many of the car companies make their Internet site feel like a physical location (e.g. Chrysler). In this way the customer feels that they are being invited around the organisation in a physical way. It can be a powerful way to project an organisation larger or more credible than it actually is. It can project any message that you wish to convey. For example in Chrysler's case, it wants to project the feeling of innovation and so has references to innovations departments, R & D etc.

The main advantage of this approach is that it gives the customer a visual, spatial model to remember you by. Because this is new, few sites use it and it ensures that customers remember and return to you. It also enables you to develop a corporate image and brand in a more subtle way than merely posting your logo on your site.

Remember that this is a visual projection of the company and its abilities and therefore professional design and image is critical. The heavy use of your company logo integrated with complementary colour, themes, backgrounds and other multi-media devices (like sound) can project the strongest visual messages about the company and its products.

2. Corporate identity

Every company has to present itself to its publics. It is important, therefore, that an organisation should present itself in a way which will create and maintain the most favourable impressions. The presentation of an organisation and its abilities involves almost everything it does, and in particular it includes any means of communicating with the market place. A strong corporate identity, established through its consistent and well co-ordinated use in all company advertising, product planning and packaging must be reinforced with any Cybermarketing approach that you use. Do not be tempted to redesign your corporate image in Cyperspace. This will confuse your customers and you will not benefit from the existing goodwill and reputation surrounding your image.

Whatever method is selected for projecting the image of an organisation, it must be used consistently and with strict regulations in terms of the logo design, colour, type face, positioning and size. It might be necessary to use the key graphical features of your corporate identity only on the Internet because of its technical limitations (graphic downloading is slow) but so you should not apply this rule too vigorously.

3. Product display and packaging

Product display and packaging are the aspects most people usually associate with the term merchandising. This is because manufacturers employ merchandisers to display their products in distribution outlets and also it is a stage when potential customers are physically confronted with the product. An effective product display is a means of encouraging customers to handle the product in order to understand it's benefits. However on the Internet, with only a few exceptions, you cannot handle the goods. However the same underlying theories and techniques are just as relevant.

The factors that constitute an effective display in traditional merchandising environments and the Internet include making:

Full use of customer traffic flow

Just as in a retail store it is possible to measure traffic flow on the Internet using hit rates.

In a retail environment you position the most commonly sought-after products in a way that maximises the number of products that a customer sees on route to those items (eggs, bread and milk are usually positioned at diametrically opposite corners of the shop).

Likewise on the Internet, you can define routes through your site using hypertext links. You place products on the route by putting them on pages which contain these links. You may encourage your customers to sample other products on route by providing good enticing copy for alternative links. For example, when you visit *CDNOW* you can search ᵈd and go direct to the CD that you are interested, at the top of the page describing the CD, there are links to other exciting offerings like Top 100 CDs, special offers and with the clever use of graphics it is difficult to resist the temptation of visiting these.

In the retail environment, the purpose is to prompt purchase through the physical presence of the product. Products are promoted by being at eye height. However, on the Superhighway it is not particularly the look of the product that is going to elicit purchase, it is often the information surrounding the product. Information includes specification, price, but probably more importantly, commendation or verification of the product. Here endorsement by recognised experts can be an important merchandising tool. Another approach is to create an on-line forum where contented customers discuss your company's products, enabling your potential customers to gain an insight into their relative competitive performance.

Because the customer on the Internet is interested in information about the product it is often important to offer them a quick and easy search tool to be able to access the desire product. There are three approaches:

Provide a search form on the front of your site

The first is to provide a keyword search where the customer types in a word or words and is then presented with any items that match or are close. The advantage of this approach is that it provides your customer with a single step straight to the product that they desire. The disadvantage of this approach is that it provides your customer with a single step straight to the product that they desire and not via all the other products that you want to sell them!! It is notoriously difficult for the customer to spontaneously think up the correct keyword to find the product. A word to a customer which clearly identifies a single product may not do so. You may have failed to assign their desired product to their commonly used word for it. This can make search engines very frustrating and you can risk losing a potential customer because you are making it too difficult for them to find what they want. Only use a search engine when the customer can clearly identify the product that they are interested in (e.g. CD).

Provide a decision tree for the customer to navigate through

The second approach is to produce a decision tree presenting broad categories for which the customer chooses to follow a number of steps leading them to a product or set of products which are suitable for them. This overcomes the disadvantages of the search engine because it enables the customer to select from a list selected. It also offers the advantage to you of being able to entertain and interest your customer longer on their trip around your site and therefore have a great chance of capturing their heart and mind!

This style has the disadvantage that it will take your customer a number of steps to get to the information they require. So decision trees should not be made too deep or this will frustrate your customer who is ultimately paying for the experience of shopping with you. This approach really appeals to the beachcomber who will enjoy the sense of discovery as well as take you up on your diversionary offers. If these people are your intended target audience, ensure that their trip is fun and contains some surprises.

Provide the option of (1) and (2)

Although more complex, this has the potential to combine the advantages of both of the above but is more complex to set up. The best example of the use of both is by search on the World wide web with Yahoo (see Appendix 7 on how to go about this).

Full use of product packaging

Packaging is an integral part of the product. Often it is the only method of communicating the promise and benefits of the product to potential customers. Although packaging decisions are included in the overall product planning aspects of the marketing mix, but because it also visually projects certain images and persuades potential customers to buy, it must be considered as an aspect of merchandising. The image of the product plays an important role in helping to differentiate 'me too' or homogeneous products in the market. For consumer durable and industrial products, the finish of the product represents the packaging. The design of the package or the container in essence is what the customer eventually buys. For example, a hi-fi product may have very similar features, technology and benefits compared to other competing brands, but a potential customer will consider the name (and reputation) of the company and the product design as important factors in making the final purchasing decision. A reputable name such as Technics, established over a long period of time through strong corporate identity and distinctive packaging of the hi-fi system, will have an immediate advantage in the upper end of the market. Packaging is not just a matter of making the product look pretty or eye-catching at the point of sale. It must be carefully planned and integrated to ensure that it is suitable for every aspect of that product's life from production, distribution, in-transit and marketing, to wholesaler, retailers, consumer and even the final disposal.

This is most relevant in a retail environment where the product that a customer buys can almost be just the packaging (e.g. Easter eggs). However, this is not so true on the Internet where the physical packaging arrives after the purchase has been made, if at all. However, the issue of on-line packaging is an interesting one.

Packaging is heavily dependent on the type of product that you are merchandising and it is not true to say that you necessarily have to show the product as it looks physically. You can for example have great Cyperpackaging which has the added advantages of being practically free, easily changeable where you can see how it appeals to your target audience through the comparative hit rate through your web-site. With the Internet you can use sound, video and animation as part of this packaging. This is the pioneering edge of merchandising on the Internet. If you can't pick it up and feel the quality – maybe you can make it sound like a quality product?

Price advantage clearly visible

For retail environments this is quite obvious but essential. On the Internet, showing your prices is an interesting dilemma which we cover well in Chapter 4. You do need to be careful of competitive price wars. You also need to be careful of the global shopping front where you stand next to shops who may have a better currency rate and therefore cheaper products. However, the underlying rule here is that no-one will buy without knowing the price. Employ all the usual tricks used in a retail environment like:

- Use .99 rather than 1.00
- Use the word 'Only' a great deal
- Have prices crossed out and reduced ones next to them
- Use special offer closing dates
- Compare your price with the RRP (Recommended Retail Price)

Product accessible to all potential customers

In a retail environment, this is about making sure that children's products are put at the correct height etc. On the Internet, this may be more of an issue enabling international customers to buy from you. Can you reduce the price of postage? Can you take international credit cards without having to absorb a huge credit risk etc.?

Available technical and other sales support

The best merchandising factor on the Internet is the amount of pre-sale and post-sale support you can offer. The customer has only got a screen to know and understand you. If you can offer a human interface built into the price, this is often the trigger for purchase.

Point-of-sale material

Point-of-sale (or purchase) material is an essential element of communicating particular benefits or incentives of buying the product. It is used in promoting new or modified products and is very useful in gaining shelf space in distribution outlets. The main aim of using point-of-sale material is to encourage customers to sample it for the first time. It is normally closely integrated with a company's advertising and sales promotion campaign and must be designed to complement the image of the product. The type of material used has to be designed with due regard to the target market and type of distribution outlet. Bright colours may be appropriate to promote household items, but much more subtle design is necessary for fashion, consumer durable and industrial products. Point-of-sales material is particularly useful when customers do not have a brand in mind, but are looking for a product to solve their problems. For example, a person looking for carpet may only have colour, size and

175

quality in mind when in an outlet. The use of point-of-sale material can influence the customer's brand choice by communicating benefits and or other incentives that can be derived from purchasing a particular brand. The same applies to many industrial purchases that take place in wholesaling or distribution outlets. For example, a customer wishing to purchase electrical cable for plant maintenance may not have a brand in mind but can be influenced by point-of-sale material in the outlet.

On the Internet, this is more difficult because of the limitations on not being able to have the physical characteristics to display to the consumer at point of purchase. However, brand information and credibility can be transferred from the Internet to the retail environment. The Internet is an ideal low-cost way to launch a new brand name which can stick in the minds of your customers when at a point-of-sale in a retail environment.

SALES PROMOTION

Advertising is concerned with creating an awareness of a product, service or an organisation. It is also used to help potential customers understand the benefits and other attributes of the product or service and move people towards buying action. Sales promotion aids the sale of a product or service by using direct influences within the product's immediate environment. It is a direct form of communication because it normally takes place on or with the product or service. For example, a product may have a special offer of 20p off recommended price. This is communicated on the product and encourages the potential customer to physically handle the product and compare it with competing brands. Sales promotion is concerned with achieving the following two main objectives.

- To encourage sampling of a product, service or an organisation (as a supplier).
- To encourage repeat purchase of a product or service.

The creation of awareness of a product's availability or its benefits cannot guarantee that customers will buy the product. New products, in particular, can only survive if potential customers can be encouraged to try or sample them and then buy them on a regular basis. Many companies set up shop on the Internet but offer no incentive to buy a given product once inside. This is a mistake. Just as in direct mail you need to give an incentive, so also on the Internet do you need to use a sales promotion.

In informal marketing terms, therefore, sales promotion can be defined as 'An incentive aimed directly at encouraging a target audience to move towards buying a product or service'.

Put simply, it is a method of persuading people to take a course of action which, without the incentive or persuasion, they may not normally take.

Sales promotion should be used as deliberate action to achieve defined objectives rather than as a response to follow competition or as an afterthought of a promotion effort. Sales promotion is an integral part of the promotional mix and therefore of the marketing mix. As such it requires considerable emphasis on planning and effective implementation. Sales promotion activity requires two types of planning:

1. Strategic sales promotion

Firstly sales promotion can be incorporated in your organisation's annual marketing plan to support planned new product launches, growth in distribution outlets, increase in branch use or simply to encourage sampling and changes in frequency of repeat purchase.

An example of this is the decision to adopt a two-tier pricing strategy: one for the Internet and/or mail order and one for retail or traditional distribution channels. Software companies often choose to have a different (reduced) pricing strategy for the Internet. This is because the Internet is a cheaper form of distribution, in other words you can download the software directly. But primarily they use this as a form of sales promotion, offering a stripped down version of the software at a much reduced cost which then encourages the customer to sample. It is low cost and low risk for the consumer and practically free to the supplier.

At this level the sales promotion is a strategic decision within the organisation and needs to be considered in the overall business and marketing planning within the organisation.

2. Tactical sales promotion

The second type of planning is concerned with short-term tactical sales promotion activity. This may be as a result of competitive activity or because of variations in forecasted consumer buying behaviour. Such tactical sales promotion is used to ensure that the firm continues to meet specific needs of the product in order to achieve the overall marketing objectives in terms of market share or sales turnover.

Encouraging sampling is the main sales promotion tool used on the Internet. The easier and quicker it is for a customer to sample your product live from the comfort of their home, the more likely they are to buy and return regularly. Examples of effective sales promotion to encourage sampling on the Internet are:

- Free chapters of books which you can download and read at your leisure which later you can then purchase directly from the Internet.
- Samples of music which, although not long in duration, can help you decide if this is the CD for you.
- Downloadable full working copies of a given piece of software. Here the software has a flashing message which constantly reminds you that you have not paid for it. If the message is extremely annoying and the benefits of the software can be appreciated quickly, conversion to purchase can be as high as 70 per cent of the people who download it.
- Market research reports where only the executive summary is given.
- Financial assessments or health checks can be automatically generated for you on-line where you can sample the expertise of the financial organisation you are thinking about doing business with.

Encouraging repeat purchases is easier and cheaper than ever before because you can talk to those customers who have bought from you through e:mail. Examples and suggestions of how to encourage repeat purchase on the Internet are:

- Ensure that when you do receive an order that you take your customer's e:mail account. In this way you can:
  (a) Thank them for purchasing from you and offer them an immediate incentive to re-order. You can even tailor this e:mail to look very personal. The best example of this we received was a message saying:
  'Thank you for buying "Elton John's Top Hits". We hoped it arrived safely on the 24 September. Remember, if you don't like it, you can return it within 20 days for your no-quibble money back guarantee ...'
  (b) Send direct mail to them on new products that you have and any special offers that you are carrying.

- Whenever they purchase from you, ensure that when the product arrives, either direct from the Internet or through traditional means, that it contains information on how to purchase again, plus an incentive to do so. The authors have purchased many items from the Internet and very few companies offer any incentive to repeat purchase.
- Ask the customer to create an account with your on-line shop. It is a simple way to obtain their credit card details without having to pay for a secure web-server. It is also a proven way to encourage repeat purchase. If your customer just has to remember an account name, password or number and select their products, they are more likely to purchase again. To encourage account opening, ensure that you offer an incentive and make it as easy as possible. Once they have opened an account with you and purchased, ensure that you send them a membership card which they will want to keep.
- Use a membership club concept so that once a member has purchased more than X amount of products from you, they are entitled to a free Y. The authors have purchased over 20 CDs from an on-line CD shop in America and were disappointed not to have received any incentive or recognition for doing so.

Sales promotion activity is also used to help an organisation to gain greater distribution of a product. Wholesalers and retailers are more likely to carry a product if the manufacturers can demonstrate that it will be given adequate support to help them to attract customers into the outlet. Sales promotion techniques are also used for the purposes of helping manufacturers to gain increased shelf and display facilities, launch new or re-defined products, attract new purchasers and obtain repeat purchases and customer loyalty. It is also used to help wholesalers and retailers to reduce stock and build store traffic through the outlet. Sales promotion techniques are equally applicable to the promotion of services and industrial products. An understanding of what consumer sales promotion techniques can achieve can help managers to adjust these techniques for use in promoting services and industrial products.

In summary, sales promotion is an integral part of your promotional mix and has to be formally planned and effectively implemented to achieve specific communication objectives geared towards moving potential customers towards buying action or to adjust the frequency of their purchasing. Sales promotion also helps firms to expand distribution of products by illustrating to retailers and wholesalers that the products will attract customers to the outlets and move quickly. Sales promotion techniques directed at buyers include competitions, coupons, premium offers, reduced price offers, special demonstrations, free samples and trade stamps. Each of these incentives is designed to achieve specific buyer actions such as to obtain customer loyalty, encourage sampling, reduce stock by increased turnover and gain repeat purchases. Sales promotion techniques should not be used in an ad hoc manner but should be linked with your advertising and merchandising activities.

PUBLICITY AND PR

So many companies publish their web pages and sit back and wait for the money to flow in. It doesn't and they become disillusioned. This is identical to the entrepreneur leaving a collection of brochures in the first class compartment of a train and then wondering why nothing has happened.

Having a web-server, a web-site or a web-page is conceptually like having an interactive brochure floating in Cyberspace. This is identical to having a billboard in the middle of a field surrounded by other fields for 200 miles. You now need to make this site easily accessible and attractive to your customers.

1. Firstly you need to ensure that your web-site is listed in all the search engines. There are various pages on the Internet to provide you with a one-stop to including your web-site in all the popular web-sites. We highlight some of these in the web-page accompanying this chapter.
2. Secondly you must ensure that all promotional and advertising copy contains your web-site address. This is how your customers will become interactively involved with you. More and more adverts contain web-site addresses and will become commonplace in a year from now. However this will take time to filter through to prospective customers so do not expect an instant response.
3. You need to attract people to visit your web-site. The best way of doing this is to publicise it nationally and internationally. There is already an existing international PR network which can do this for you at a price but there are some simple ways to get your web-site visited:
   • Make it newsworthy yourself. Guinness achieved this by giving away a wonderful screen saver. Others achieve it through offering a

new service: insurance quotes on-line; home shopping etc. Being the
first to do something will ensure publicity if it is of real value to the
general public.

- Have a sales promotion or competition contained within the site
  that is only available to the Internet community. Nothing works
  better than thinking you are in a privileged position. (See above
  under sales promotion.)
- Have your site endorsed by a major name with their picture
  contained within it.

  King of Shaves promoted an innovative shaving product and
  achieved national press by including a picture of Will Carling
  (then captain of the English Rugby Team); on their site. The *Sun* took
  the story with the caption 'Will power is a real turn on' and
  highlighted the fact that you could turn Will Carling on yourself at
  the touch of a button. It certainly attracted people to the web-site!

  People will then be attracted to your site in order to download
  the photograph of your celebrity.
- Give something away free. People love getting something for
  nothing. Many marketers frown at this but ensuring that the give-
  away is connected to your product means that you can gain national
  and local press coverage and improve brand awareness at the same
  time.
- Write personally to all the Internet magazines requesting a review.
  Alternatively pay for an advert in these magazines launching your
  site to the Internet community.
- Be controversial – be different – be attention-seeking but don't
  break the code of netiquette in the process because the short-term
  PR will soon be replaced by long-term disapproval to a growing
  and affluent Internet userbase.

DIRECT MARKETING

The Superhighway offers a marketer the most cost-effective route to
direct marketing. You can now send thousands of letters out at the touch
of a button. However, we must stress that you CANNOT send Direct
mail to every Internet user. This is a common misconception by
marketers. You need to know someone's e:mail address in order for you
to send them direct mail. This is not a major problem because there are
many ways you can entice them to reveal their identity and also means of

finding out their identity. Read on to find the most exciting benefits the Internet has to offer you.

How do I build up my direct marketing database?

There are seven ways of doing this.

1. Collect your customers' e:mail direct from your web-site

You must put a response mechanism on your web-site. We have stated this throughout the book and although obvious to every marketer, you would be amazed at the number of sites not offering this.

Preferably use a response or order form which then enables you to capture the respondent's full postal address, full name, company details (if appropriate) and other demographic and segmentation identifications. You may need to offer an incentive to obtain this information but a free report or bulletin can often be all that is needed.

If you don't put a response or order form on your site, be sure to have an e:mail address for your organisation which is checked and replied to at least twice a day.

2. Create a mailing list

You can create electronic lists where your prospects and customers can add and remove themselves to your database. They do this to receive useful information which you regularly send out. This is just like customers subscribing to your in-house magazine.

Case study: Bill Gates publishes a mailing list of customers using Windows 95. This mailing list gives subscriber hints and tips, updates on fixes, alerts for any problems and general news about the world of Windows 95. The copy is very punchy and full of important information for users of this product.

In order to subscribe, an interested customer sends a blank e:mail to win95@microsoft.com and they will then be added to the mailing list and start receiving the newsletter. Each newsletter sent out contains the instruction on how to unsubscribe. To unsubscribe, all the customer has to do is send a blank e:mail message to unsubscribe@microsoft.com.

The advantage to the marketer of this approach is that your customer can unsubscribe easily without becoming annoyed with your direct mail activities and you do not have the manual work of taking them off your mailing list because the technology handles the unsubscription as automatically as it handled the subscription. In this way, once this mailing list is set up, it is very easy and economical to maintain. You only challenge it to attract and maintain interest for your subscribers. Done well it is one of the most fantastic ways of creating a dialogue with your customer base and has been used especially well in regard to loyalty clubs. (N.B. It can also be an excellent way of informing people that your web-site has changed.)

News group comment: 'I am not a bug fan of unsolicited e:mail but it is so easy to delete; I absolutely hate unsolicited direct mail'.

3. Create an automatic responder

This is identical to the process outlined in (2) but rather than having a regular newsletter, your customer e:mails a certain address to receive a flyer about a product, some information etc. This is heavily used in America but not so much in Europe at present. Many authors of Internet books promote this technique as a good promotion tool. Alfred and Emily Glossbrenner (1995) comment 'Ladies and gentlemen, that is the way to market on the Internet. Set up an autoresponder so that only those users who want your information will see it – which is to say, you will not be forcing your information on someone via e:mail or news group'.

4. Look up people's e:mail accounts from news groups

This is a little on the edge of breaking etiquette, but so long as you use their names with discretion and tell them that this is where you obtained their name and offer them an easy way to disassociate themselves from you, you should get away with it. Not many companies use this promotion mechanism but so long as you are offering the respondent something which you believe will be of genuine value, it is an ideal way of building your database.

5. Mail to existing web-sites

Many individuals try to generate business by e:mailing the 'Webmaster', or contact point on an existing web-sites. Again you have to be very careful because this is cold calling, but with targeted mailings with a good benefits statement up front and a polite explanation of where you obtained the e:mail address, this can be an effective starting point.

6. Buy an e:mail list

Just as you can buy names and addresses of potential prospects, more and more companies are offering e:mail address lists. To all intents and purposes, it is identical to buying postal mailing lists. The e:mail list is usually seeded so that the provider of the list can police the number of times you use it.

7. Ask your customers

If you want to find someone's e:mail address, the quickest way will be to just to ask them. Ensure that all response forms issued in any promotion or advertising asks specifically for the e:mail address.

Although there are a variety of 'white pages' services available on the Internet, they are far from complete most people are simply not listed. Major e:mail providers are working on a universal directory system, but that could be some time away.

What do I do with my long list of e:mails now that I have collected them?

When you do receive their e:mail addresses you then transfer them into what is called a 'Listserver'. It is a piece of software very like a Cyberspace mailing house which then automatically sends a given e:mail message (your direct mailshot) to all the people on your database. This software can be downloaded free from the Internet if you have your own web-server or alternatively there are some commercial versions which you can purchase.

For more sophisticated targeted direct mail by product type, interest area or by customer type, work closely with an Internet marketing company. Most good Internet marketing companies will offer you the services of database classification, segmentation and targeted direct mail.

Carefully categorised enquiries with electronic follow-up can be extremely powerful. Recently one of the authors requested an evaluation copy of a piece of software. He did this by sending an e:mail to the software company in question. A reply was automatically generated which included instructions to get the software and a password to use it. After following the instructions, the author decided that the software was not relevant, deleted it from his computer and left it at that. Two weeks later the author received an e:mail from the software company who said 'Sorry to hear that you haven't registered our evaluation software. Would you be so kind as to help us find out why'. It then gave a list of possible reasons which could easily be ticked and sent back to the company. Although the author did not purchase this time, he was left feeling positive and excited about the company in question. The company also gained from the interaction because they know why the purchase wasn't made and have the author's e:mail address ready for when they announce a new improved version.

The major disadvantage of direct mail shots in the traditional world is that over 90 per cent of direct mail communications tends to be wasted or thrown away by the receiver. In Cyberspace, you as a recipient of direct mail can easily put up filters which stop unwanted e:mails from being downloaded onto your machine. This takes little effort and therefore you are much less likely to anger customers in the same way as direct postal mail can often do. Also, customers filtering off your direct mail shots does not cost you anything.

The overall aim of any direct mail campaign should be to encourage the receiver to take some immediate action, such as to return to the web-site for further information. All this can be measured by hit rates and just as there is almost a scientific formula now for effective direct in the traditional world, soon there will be a mirror of this in Cyberspace. However, learning what works and doesn't work on the Superhighway has just begun to be explored. Just like traditional marketing where in most instances the high wastage of direct mail effort can be explained by the lack of proper targeting of the receiver, so too is a great deal of e:mail being ignored for the same reasons.

Why use direct marketing on the Internet?

- Provides a direct contact between the company and individuals by name, status, job function and their role in the decision making unit.
- Can be personalised by pre-selection of the target audience.

- Allows considerable flexibility in presentation (with the aim of immediate action and filing), frequency and geographical distribution.
- Your message is not simultaneously competing for the reader's attention as in press advertising. Your reader reads the message when they have made a conscious decision to spend time doing it – therefore they are more receptive to the message.
- Helps to keep potential customers 'warm' and informed.
- Allows opportunities for use with other sales production and merchandising incentives.
- Commercial availability of lists of names and addresses of specific target audiences and availability of complete direct mail services, including preparation of lists, letter writing, brochure design, dispatch and response handling.
- Loyalty building especially through the circulation of a company magazine. This is widely used and extremely powerful when the magazine or newsletter gives the reader valuable information and the feeling of exclusivity.

PERSONAL SELLING

Personal selling can be defined as an interpersonal persuasive process designed to influence another person's decision. It is a direct form of communication that is used to inform, counter objections and collect information from existing and potential customers of the firm. In marketing orientated businesses its emphasis is on communicating the benefits of the product or service.

The Superhighway can be used for personal selling at a fraction of the cost of traditional communication. Newsgroups on the Internet, forums in CompuServe and Special Interest Groups (SIGs) in Delphi enable your sales people or yourself to:

1. **Find out about your customer's needs.** By simply listening, observing, and by asking right questions, you can cost effectively market research your customers' needs. Have a look back at Chapter 3 for more information on how to do this.
2. **Offer advice and consultancy in response to your customer's needs.** You can then help the customer decide on the combination of products and specifications that satisfy their needs. The role of the

salesperson, therefore, is that of an expert or a consultant – interested in solving the customer's problems.

3. **Identify new customers.** Some people attend conferences and exhibitions for the sole purpose of networking and building a prospect list. The Internet is another mechanism to do that with the enormous benefits that you can network from your office or home at a time to suit your work commitments.

4. **Sell your products and services.** Selling is about finding a need and proving that your product solves that need. The Superhighway collects together people with similar interests to enable a discussion to occur. By taking part in a conversation, you will be able to identify people's needs and then offer to solve them. This can only be an effective sales and marketing tool when you have a credible presence within the discussion group and are seen as an insider.

There is a significant difference between receiving a comment from someone in Cyberspace against meeting them and speaking to them face to face. This is particularly important to appreciate when selling on the Superhighway. Anyone can send a message in Cyberspace and when you receive it you need little additional information in order to assess its credibility. The mechanisms to gain credibility are:

- professional input or contribution to the discussions in the newsgroups
- invite people from the newsgroups to visit your web-site to provide customer testimonials, financial information and other credibility gaining information
- take care and attention when writing e:mails and newsgroup messages. Although the Internet has a very casual style, spelling mistakes and bad grammar indicate lack of professionalism.

The process by which someone uses newsgroups and forums for selling has to be very subtle. The analogy is that you can meet someone at a conference, take a business card and sell to them six months down the line. You meet people in forums where the conversation is broadcast to anyone who is interested. This is similar to a conversation over a large table at a conference. People who respond will give you their e:mail address just as they might give you their business card at the conference. You can then use private e:mail conversations to develop the personal relationship and the sales process further. It is as likely for you to able to do business directly within a newsgroup or forum, as it is to sell your products in the coffee break at a conference. It is much more likely that you invite them to visit your web-site which, whilst not trying to stretch the analogy too far, is like inviting them to visit your organisation on a sales appointment.

A typical sales process in Cyberspace

Sales Process	Mechanism	Example
Stage 1 – Enquiry	Newsgroup or forum	How do I get a really good frying pan, my problem is that size is a big problem in my small boat.
Stage 2 – Information provision	Combination of one or more of the following: Newsgroup or forum, visit to web-site or e:mail communication	My own company m ake a special range of pans just for small boat owners.
Stage 3 – Assessment of need compared to product benefits	E:mail or traditional communication	You can find out more on our web-site http://www.boatpans.com
Stage 4 – Objection handling	E:mail or traditional communication	'What did you think about our web-site? If price is an issue – we offer the best price in the industry and we can even improve on this if you buy in quantity!'
Stage 5 – Close of sale	Traditional means or on-line through web-site	'Can I take your order?'

This is the best way of building your customer database, selling on line and promoting your web-site and cannot be underestimated as a cost-effective promotion tool. Innovative sales managers insist on their sales people becoming well known and respected in appropriate forums for exactly this reason.

> A good case study of this approach is *Marketing Guild*, who proactively promoted their Internet marketing seminars in forums, sigs and newsgroups, inviting people to visit their web-site. As a result they obtain several bookings which generated £7000 of direct profit and relationships with new companies which has the potential of generating ten times this initial sale.

5. Gathering market intelligence. The other main attraction of putting your whole sales team on-line is the huge amount of market intelligence that you can gather about competitors, market demand and changes happening in the industry as a whole. Sales representatives are the people closest to the marketplace. They interact with existing and potential customers, come in contact with competitors' products and sales forces and can observe the changes in end user requirements. Information gathered by sales forces on such matters can be more reliable than marketing research data that relies on asking customers direct questions. Many new product ideas and recommendations for product line modifications come from sales force reports to a company's marketing information system.

6. Suppressing rumours. Some companies dedicate one person to scan all forums for potential rumours about their company and their products and services. The impact of bad PR can be very damaging for an organisation and being aware and able to suppress such negatively early on can save the organisation a great deal of money. Jokes about the Pentium chip having a mathematical error gave Intel some bad press for some time on the Internet.

7. Provide after-sales service. By creating a relationship inside a forum and being dominant over a significant time period will give members some reassurance that on purchasing from your web-site, they can easily obtain after-sales support. It would not be in your interest if they were to complain about your products and therefore you would be able to give them privileged support. This could act as a further guarantee or warranty on their purchase from you. For you, being able to demonstrate that you have sold only through the forum or newsgroup, but supported people who have bought, adds to your personal credibility and the brand awareness of your organisation.

CONCLUSION

Most of the books on the Internet focus on the promotion aspects of this new media. They focus on design, programming, style and creative issues. This is only one part of marketing. They are equivalent to books on brochure design. But marketing is not about designing a good brochure or a good web-site.

This chapter helps you evaluate the benefits of the Superhighway as a promotion vehicle for your organisation. It outlines where the Internet is today, what it is predicted to become and some case studies of successes. It then outlines your options

CHECKLIST

You now know:

What promotion is.	☐ Yes	☐ No
How the use of promotion can act as a differential advantage for you.	☐ Yes	☐ No
What makes up the tools and techniques within this element of the marketing mix.	☐ Yes	☐ No
Which tools and techniques are used to achieve your communication goals.	☐ Yes	☐ No
How to set advertising objectives.	☐ Yes	☐ No
How to decide which media to use.	☐ Yes	☐ No
How appropriate the Superhighway is as a media choice.	☐ Yes	☐ No
Where the Superhighway is today.	☐ Yes	☐ No
How it differs from traditional medias.	☐ Yes	☐ No
What choices there are for putting your organisation on the Superhighway.	☐ Yes	☐ No
How to merchandise your products and services on the Superhighway.	☐ Yes	☐ No
How you can use the Superhighway for direct marketing.	☐ Yes	☐ No
How you can use 'personal selling' on the Superhighway.	☐ Yes	☐ No
How promotion is not the only issue you need to consider when you think about 'marketing on the Superhighway'	☐ Yes	☐ No

WHAT NEXT?

Having appreciated the various communication goals and approaches to promotion, you may have decided to launch a presence on the world wide web. In this case, it is worth highlighting the various issues which are worth considering when you actually produce your materials in Cyberspace. The next chapter helps you produce a world class presence

REFERENCES

Cheswick, W. and Bellovin, S. (1994) *Firewalls and Internet Security: Repelling the Wily Hacker*, Addison-Wesley, London.

Glossbrenner, A. and Glossbrenner, E. (1995) *Making Money on the Internet*, McGraw-Hill Inc.

8 Producing your promotional materials in Cyberspace

The Internet is in flux, indeed it will always be in flux. It is about involving and entertaining your customer in the here and now; building relationships and changing people's perceptions of you. For you as a marketing or business professional, you can see the Internet as a dream come true. It provides additional functionality over and above traditional promotion mechanisms.

- It is a brochure that can be read in many different ways and can change at the touch of the button, incurring little costs.
- It is a camera feeding back to you which customers looked at your brochure and what interested them.
- It is a television advertisement that you can stop and replay.
- It is an eternal exhibition stand.
- It is a telephone conversation which does not cost you a telesales person.
- It is magazine article which has minimal publishing costs.
- It is a return coupon which is automatically fulfilled.
- It is self-filling customer database of potential customers.

For your customers, within a couple of hours of joining the Superhighway, they will have experienced these things. Just because your organisation has used some of the above functionality, this fails to impress. The key is deciding who your customers are and what will entertain and involve them. If you get this right they will come to you.

Don't do what so many organisations do, which is to try to involve and entertain 30 million people. The likelihood is you will fail to impress anyone including your existing customers. You may even damage your company image by bad reviews in the press.

The difference between an Internet magazine reviewer and your customer

The real test of a good web-site is when your intended target audience is prepared to spend time and money clicking around. You may still get some bad reviews because reviewers are global beachcombers with a different value set to your intended target audience. This is OK because you then have a valid come-back which is that it was intended to impress them!

The analogy is a bit like the options of building an exhibition stand which will attract every visitor to the exhibition. You put in great plants, free coffee and ice-cream. You give away free products, you entertain everyone. It costs you a fortune. You build up a database of everyone at the exhibition. You then spend another fortune after the exhibition trying to identify who is actually interested in your products and another fortune trying to convince them that you have the solution to their needs.

We recommend that you set up a totally targeted exhibition stand (in Cyberspace) which is geared around meeting the needs of your intended target audience. Taking the analogy a little further, you only offer free coffee if this is what your intended customers hanker for. You offer entertainment which only your customers will find entertaining. You give freebies that are only of interest to your target audience. Your stand only looks of interest to your intended audience. Then you wait. Yes, lots of people will look and walk on – but that's great, you haven't wasted money giving them your promotion material. At the end of the exhibition, you have only 200 names and addresses but these are people who are likely to buy.

This does seem so obvious to existing marketing managers and business professionals as it complies with traditional marketing think. But little of this knowledge and know-how is applied to the Superhighway. Hardened marketing people hanker after huge 'hit rates' (people accessing their pages), fail to offer response devices and fail to leverage the true business potential of the Internet.

HOW DO YOU GO ABOUT IT?

This book is not about how to produce interesting and exciting web pages. There is a plethora of books on the market doing exactly that. What you really need to know is that the secret of writing a good website is the same secret you already know about producing a good brochure, i.e. appealing to your target audience. The plethora of books about 'Marketing On The Internet' are often IT professionals helping other IT professionals understand what promotional devices work and which ones fail.

So what are the stages involved in making your Superhighway presence professional and leading edge and most importantly effective as a marketing device? We recommend that you plan for four distinct stages: a planning and preparation stage, a design stage, a launch stage and lastly a maintenance stage. So many companies jump straight into design and then spend little time launching effectively. Even if you are a relatively small company, spending time planning and launching effectively can double the effectiveness of your Cybermarketing. Equally, it is important to be aware of the maintenance costs of maintaining your site. So many companies put their presence up and forget it after two or three months – this communicates to your customers that you don't really care about them.

1. GETTING READY TO GO LIVE

Brainstorming and creative input

Involve people as early as possible in the project; they will feel more committed to making it a success. Involve people closest to your customer to ensure that the Internet site is most likely to win the hearts and minds of your target audience.

Involve front-line business people alongside the marketing team to brainstorm out all the possibilities. Capture them in any format that you desire but documentation is critical here because it sets the scene to your web-site and is a good reference to return to three or six months into the project or when you have sufficient resources to move onto other ideas.

Constrain the creative process as little as possible but do take some of the learning from the book to guide the creative input. Two of the most valuable inputs are: who are we targeting with this web-site and what value are we offering these people in exchange for reading our promotional materials.

Decide your objectives and your budget

Be realistic. In our experience, companies want to conquer the world for as little money as possible, as fast as possible. This is feasible but only with an extraordinary creative exchange between your target customer and yourself. A good example of this was Guinness:

> Guinness launched their Internet presence on national TV with a screen saver which was not only high value to the end customer (IT managers all over the country complained that they were inundated with requests for the Guinness screen saver) but was of immediate value to Guinness as free advertising. Approximately, 45,000 people downloaded this screen saver in the first two months.

As the Internet becomes more popular, the chances that you can come up with a unique creative concept like this becomes less – another good reason for going live sooner rather than later. At present the Internet is still in its infancy, so you may well be able to conquer the world for next to nothing – but the challenge is high.

We recommend that you focus on a phased implementation strategy. Here you would set up phased objectives:

Phase 1 – **Getting yourself known** – register your company and/or brand names; produce some initial promotional materials using existing proven concepts.

Phase 2 – **Start to interact with customers** – create an interactive dialogue with your target audience to test various concepts

Phase 3 – **Start to experiment** – take orders off the Internet to create a revenue stream; use it as a sales promotion tool etc.

The main reason we recommend this approach is that Internet customers like to be wooed. Evolving your site over time, adding value as you go, leaving on-line ordering until later, will create a certain amount of goodwill. Typically a user needs to visit a site three times before they buy anything, so you need to create good reasons for them to come back again and again.

Internal 'buy-in'

The sooner you can involve key decision makers, product managers and sales people the better. They will be critical to the success or failure of your Internet promotion. A good communications strategy upfront will save a huge amount of time and effort justifying your pages after you go live.

Financial commitment

Don't attempt an Internet site on a shoestring if you need a credible and professional presence. Obtain quotes from Internet marketing companies and ensure that you have the financial commitment to this level of investment. The Internet is packed with half-baked Internet sites which could have been the success stories of the 1990s with the correct level of investment. The question you need to ask is 'Are we serious?' I would suggest that if money is a major constraint, you need to rethink the objectives.

2. DESIGNING YOUR SITE

The three rules to web-site design is:

1. Understand your target audience
2. Understand your target audience
3. Understand your target audience

We cannot stress this enough and the ONLY difference between a good site and a bad site is in their understanding of their target audience.

Your target audience are Internet users, so you do need to see the Internet from their perspective. Never think of becoming involved in the design phase unless you have visited at least twenty sites. We make this easy by offering you a list of sites to visit in the web page that accompanies this chapter.

In general your target audience has similar needs to every Internet user so there are some basic rules that you need to abide by:

GENERAL RULES FOR ALL INTERNET SITES

2.1 Use graphics to give your reader something

We know that you are proud of your logo and you want it big and bold but your user has to pay for it to be downloaded and they are going to have a negative feeling towards your corporate image if they have wasted their time and money on it. Use graphics when they give the customer something. It could be argued that the user can choose to take off the option to display graphics but then you subject them into a boring visit to your site.

However, a strong visual idea can often communicate more convincingly than half a page of factual information. So the best compromise is to use graphics when they give something to the reader: a picture of your product, the packaging etc.

Alternatively, design your web-site such that they can read some great benefits statements about what you are just about to offer or show them – while they are waiting for the graphic to be downloaded. One example of this is the recipe pages within *J Sainsbury Plc*. You can read all the ingredients and instructions for cooking and just as you finish you are rewarded with a wonderful picture of the dish.

The best way to reduce the problem of graphics is to reduce the number of colours used. You will see on the accompanying web-site a number of line art graphics which download fast and conveniently.

Most browsers keep the picture stored in memory for a certain amount of time after it has been viewed. So if you have a graphic on the home page and your reader has downloaded it fully, on all subsequent pages that displays the same graphics, it appears almost instantly. Therefore re-use graphics to make your site appear even faster than it is.

This all sounds so obvious but so many sites that you go to force you to wait for their graphics before you can see anything or make any decision about whether it holds any information of value for you.

2.2 Use exciting copy

You have less than four seconds to attract, captivate and absorb your Internet reader. So do remember the two models, AIDA and DAGMAR, covered in the previous chapter. Use all the traditional techniques that you use in direct mail, PR, advertising and promotional literature. Tell them what is of interest for them, not about you. If you excite them, interest them about what your products or services can do to make them happy, rich or successful – don't worry, they'll find out more about you!! They'll respond immediately.

> 'A bore is someone who talks more about themselves than they do about you' – the same goes for a web-site.

The exception to this rule is approximately the first 26 words on your home page. The robot search engines (e.g. Infoseek – see Appendix 5) will only display these initial words when customers search to find you. It is therfore imperative that the first 26 words of your site achieve the following objectives:

- Describe your organisation and what you offer.
- Describe what value your pages are offering.
- Make it attractive for the person seeing your listing in a search engine to investigate your sight further.
- Declare your geographic boundaries if you only want to attract customers inside them.

We recommend that even if you are not using a professional copy writer for the rest of the web-site that you use one to design these 26 words. It can mean the difference between your customers finding you and not finding you. Words that you think your customers will type in the search engine to find you, may not be how they think of you. If you want to test this, it may mean returning to the marketing research in Chapter 3 to use observational techniques. This is the only way to ensure that customers wanting your products and services will be able to locate you. In our experience this word crafting becomes a strategic marketing issue and must not be underestimated.

The other area of strategic importance is the style of copy will differ greatly on the Internet because it is a less formal medium to talk to your customers. Some companies fail to appreciate this and alienate their customers by making it appear too much like their corporate brochure. This is similar to turning up on your first date with your best work suit on! So many sites make simple mistakes like having an icon saying 'Our products and services'. Innovative sites use less formal language and more of a direct marketing approach such 'Find out how to increase your productivity by 20 per cent'; 'Special offer ONLY to Internet readers'. 'Discover what we can offer you'.

Hot copy tips:
- Make it 'Newsy'. People love to feel they have privileged, state of the art information, so make it like a news bulletin. This will appeal to the global workers, the knowledge traders and the get-aheads (Chapter 5) who are trying to keep their fingers on the pulse.
- Make it 'Verby'. To convey an interactive and dynamic feel to the web-site use verbs to indicate what action you wish the reader to perform: 'Read our exciting newsletter'; 'fill in our response form to receive our free report'. This will appeal to the global surfer but also maintain the attention of your reader whichever target audience you are appealing to. Remember you are trying to persuade them to explore your site as much as possible.
- Make it short. Don't use large sentences or long paragraphs – people tire and frustrate easily. Convey your message as quickly as possible in the most exciting way.
- Make it intimate. You can afford to be more personal with this new medium. Use the word 'you' more than you would in a brochure. If you fail to convey an intimacy, people will think that you are stand-offish and using the Internet purely as an advertising medium, not as an opportunity to talk to the 'common person'. Even if you are a blue-chip multinational company – this is your chance to present yourself as a caring, interested and real entity. Body Shop in the UK has gone so far as not to promote their products and services but to sponsor and publicise ethically sound projects, inviting their customers to become involved. Here their customers can join them in a common project and in doing so become intimate with the organisation.
- Make it memorable. Your readers will read so many sales messages that you need to differentiate yourself. Good copy can and is worth paying for.
- Give them the option to read it off-line. It seems that people don't find it easy to read off a computer screen – so offer the option of sending printed copy by direct mail or autoresponding to their e:mail

(see previous chapter on Direct Marketing). Another option is have the whole web-site as a downloadable file which they can save onto their computer and read off-line. This saves their telephone bill and shows that you understand their needs. It also means that when they do read it, they are likely to be more relaxed and interested in what you have to offer. A product called 'Acrobat', widely distributed on the Internet, overcomes some of these problems. What you put on an Acrobat document appears exactly the same including fonts, columns, layouts etc. Your customer downloads this file saved in Acrobat onto their hard disk (this can take some time, so it does cost your customer) and works across all Internet compatible machines (PC, Mac and Unix).

2.3 Enable people to respond and interact with you

Rather than displaying every product and service your company provides, use forms or clickable graphics to enable the Internet reader to choose what interests them. Enabling your customer to see the benefits and giving them options of what most appeals to them means that you are creating an interactive conversation with them. The more like a conversation you make it, the more response and information you will elicit. You then create a dialogue which is documented in the hit rate comparison of your pages. You will be able to find out how many people see your home page and then as a response what percentage decided to take the various paths forward that you offer. For example, how many take you up on your special offers (page 2) or look at your special marketing report (page 3). If you find that people are not attracted to your page 4, which is all about Product X, you can conclude that either your copy about product X is not exciting enough or that this product does not appeal to your target audience. In order to assess this, change the copy for the link into these pages: make it look more appealing and see if this affects the hit rate. In this way you are truly interacting with your customer because you are evolving your web-site in tune with their response. Those companies that monitor hit rates and redesign accordingly are fine tuning their Internet offering light years ahead of their competitors. As soon as your customers appreciate the dynamic nature of your web-site, they will return to regularly (e.g. they bookmark you).

2.4 Prove your credibility

An Internet site is as easy to produce as a business card. Just as you would not think to invest in someone based purely on the fact that they had a business card, neither can you expect customers who don't know you to invest in you based solely on the fact that you have a web-site. The question is how do you prove credibility on a web-site? Client lists, company financial information, PR articles are used frequently. Having a secure web-site (i.e. Netscape's Security feature) helps because it proves that you have afforded this option and therefore are unlikely to be a gold-digger. However, people will still be reluctant to part with their money unless you can demonstrate your credibility in real terms. We would recommend that you publish basic information to make this as easy as possible. Your address, your telephone number and your company registration number. This is especially important for any web-site where you are asking the Internet reader to purchase anything.

Offer guarantees and warranties with any product you sell on line, ensuring that you explain your ordering and refund policy clearly.

2.5 Don't expect too much from your Internet reader

Just as we highlighted in the preface to our book. The Internet is a courting tool allowing you to woo your customers to build a lasting relationship. We argue that this will help you understand your market well enough to adapt to its needs in order to achieve business profit. Our advice is to ensure that your site conveys the courting ritual approach rather than the one-night stand. Yes, you want the business so it is very tempting to publish a glorified order form. Unfortunately, this is a little bit like going on a first date with a tooth-brush sticking out of your pocket. Some sites offer a list of products which, when you click to find out more, takes you straight into an enquiry form, e.g *Lawnet*. Whilst it is good that they offer you a means of communicating and responding with them, it fails to convey that they are interested in a dialogue or a relationship with you.

The classic example of expecting too much from their readers is companies asking for orders of high priced products. It is too much of a high risk for a user to pay serious amounts of money direct on the Internet to a company that they may not even know. Instead, entice your reader to buy a small item of reasonably low value from you. Deliver it efficiently and then the next higher value sell will be easier.

2.6 Enable your customer to respond to you

So many sites offer no way of responding for their customers. Sometimes they have a bizarre reference to their 'webmaster' at the bottom of the screen but this is not designed to elicit customer feedback. It is usually intended for the customer to comment on the design of the Internet site.

Response from your customers must be one of your main driving forces behind having a web-site. Just posting a web-site with no response mechanism is similar to a sales call where you do not ask for the customer's opinion of your products.

So why doesn't every Internet site offer a response mechanism?
Some companies misunderstand the Internet and see it purely as an advertising medium. They are wasting their time on the Internet. It damages their brand image as it reinforces the point that they are not a responsive organisation. It may even convey the impression that they are not a caring organisation. Large accountancy companies are the worst culprits of this approach.

Most commonly, the lack of a response mechanism is due to the fear of the amount of work needed to respond to the variety of questions a customer may ask, or worry about the number of brochures or information packs that may be requested. Our answer to this is to offer a tailored response form which helps the customer identify their interest area and what information they need and then provide 'autoresponders' (see the direct marketing section in the previous chapter). Alternatively, if you are looking to send information packs, why not use a fulfilment, response handling agency who will collect your responses directly from the Internet and dispatch them for you immediately, *Merit Direct* was the first major player to offer this in the UK and highlights this on their web-site.

2.7 Ensure the consistent quality of your web-site

It is not possible for you to control exactly what your web page looks like. The world wide web is based on a page layout system called HTML

(Hypertext Mark-up Language). The basic concept is that this language provides a set of formatting commands such as bold, italic, heading and flashing, to name but a few. These describe your intention as to what the format of the text and graphics should look like. The actual display of these instructions will be dependent on the decisions made by your customers and the browser that they use. You usually have little control of the font that is displayed as the user can define this in their browser options. The user can also define how small or large they like the browser window to appear and this will mean that large blocks of text will automatically position itself to fit the window. They may have a different browser or an old-fashioned browser that does not enable the design flexibility that the one you use enables you to make use of. This language is evolving rapidly with new features being added all the time. Eventually there will be a much more consistent platform to develop your web-site on, but at present you do need to be aware of these problems. To solve these temporary issues with respect to consistency, you can adopt one of the following three key strategies:

(1) Stick rigidly to the core of formatting commands supported by every browser on the market. You can find a copy of what these core formatting standards are on the web page that accompanies this chapter. The net result will be that your page looks very similar irrespective of which browser your customer is using. Whilst this is good, it does mean that you cannot use some of the most exciting design options that the leading browsers give you, like an exciting background to your pages, exciting use of clickable graphics or specially designed forms etc.

(2) Choose to exploit the features of a particular browser. It is clear that Netscape provide at least 70 per cent of all the browsers used on the Internet and this would make a good choice. As a courtesy, here you should offer the Internet reader the option of changing their browser to the one you are using. To do this merely provides a convenient link to the browser's web-site where your customer can download the software free of charge.

(3) Provide several alternatives. Use a simple home page which works with every browser (option 1), then ask your customer to click on the browser that they are using, which then moves them onto a page which is specifically designed for their browser. By far the most customer friendly approach, this is unfortunately the most expensive. You need to develop at least twice as many web pages and therefore this at least doubles the development and maintenance costs.

Browsers will lay out the page based on the customer's screen. It is therefore not possible to control accurately where the text will appear on the page. Therefore, because many of your customers choose to have their browser at a reduced screen size, you should not use very large graphics which scan the whole screen but instead use smaller ones that can be adapted to a smaller screen size.

Also, most computers display only 256 colours, and what may look wonderful on your desktop publishing system can look coarse and grainy on your customer's computer.

The best advice we can give you is:
Always test your pages on a cheap computer, with a cheap monitor with a cheap modem with a non-standard browser, with the window reduced in size. Most good Internet marketing companies will provide this testing service for you free of charge if they are designing your web pages.

Some companies attempt to get around all the problems highlighted above by producing their whole pages as graphics where they can decide which font, which colour, and which size themselves. Although this does give you total control, it is disastrous. It will totally frustrate, anger and annoy your customers, negating all the benefits you are trying to communicate. Don't do it until the speed of the Internet has increased!

Look at products like Acrobat™ by Adobe which enable you to send your customer a file which displays exactly how you have formatted it: fonts, columns and graphics, irrespective of the computer make they have. This costs the customer in the time it takes to download but is a cost-effective and suitable medium to issue magazines and newsletters.

2.8 Guide your reader around the site

Your customer is not in your mind and although it may be obvious to you that they must scroll down the page, it may not be obvious to them. It may be obvious to experienced Internet users that they can click on graphics, but it may not be obvious to all. Helping people navigate around your site with instructions may ruin the design of your site – we have some ideas.

A common mistake is to fill the top of the home page (your first page) with lovely graphics and lots of copy – leaving all the links to other pages until further down. This will result in customers reading your home page, thinking you only have one page and moving on. Instead, use graphics that lead the reader's eyes down to the second page or put the links on the first screen of the home page.

Another common mistake is to make the home page say it all. It is a misconception that you have to show everything you have got to offer on the first page. The home page should be the invitation in to your web-site. Give the reader the benefits of reading on; tell them what you have to offer them; excite them about wanting to know more; then invite them into the core of your web-site. Make it inviting and your customer will make a decision to come into your further pages. Once they have made the decision to find out more, they have demonstrated an interest and are more likely to be receptive to your messages. Cognitive dissonance takes over and they may even actively search to find something of value to them – making your job easier.

If you are appealing to different target audiences, the home page is the ideal switching device that enables you to cater for their differing needs. Enable the customer to select what kind of person they are or what kind of product that they are interested in and from then on you can design and target the further pages to suit the style and appearance which will most attract them.

Manchester Business School are a fine example of this. The home page gives a list of a variety of different products: MBA, executive programmes, doctoral programmes. As you select each, the design, graphics and copy style changes dramatically. The MBA programme page is fun and innovative with a conversation style of copy. The executive programmes show a much more serious granite background with a cleaner use of design with a dramatic change in copy style.

Provide obvious navigation buttons to help your customer return to where they have gone and progress forward easily. If your pages are long (and each web page can scroll almost infinitely down the page) ensure that you give the reader the ability to return to the top of the page, and provide an index of headers at the start so that the reader can choose which place to start reading from.

2.9 Provide added value to your reader by providing links

Most web-sites provide links to other sites which their target audience would be interested in. This is a convention but is also very important for two reasons.

(1) It is an essential part of the Internet. It is how the Internet has grown as popular as it has in a relatively short period of time. It is critical to its long-term success. Its success is also the success of your web-site, so do follow this convention by enabling your reader to travel from you to another web-site which complements yours.

(2) It provides a free-of-charge service which adds value to your end customer. Your customer knows this and will be disappointed if you don't offer this service.

To provide a link to another web-site is very easy and also free. All you need to do is to programme the URL into your web page. You do not need to gain the permission of the web-site owner but it is great netiquette if you do. However, there is a protocol which is that if someone references your web-site, you will return the gesture and reference theirs. To do this all you have to do is to e:mail the web-site owner stating that you wish them to reference you, stating why you have referenced them on your web-site; request that they follow suit and leave your URL. This joint bundling can add value to both parties and is practically free.

You do need to publish a disclaimer if you are to offer these links. This will protect to you to some degree if any of your hyperlinks act in an offensive manner but ...

A word of warning. There have been cases in America where web-sites providing hyperlinks to disreputable web-sites have been incriminated. No real precedent has been set in European law but our advice to you would be to only reference highly credible sites which you would be happy to have your organisation associated with. We would not advise you to link to personal web pages unless you really have to. Lastly, always check your links regularly and keep them up to date. URLs change and it is frustrating for your customers if you lead them up a blind alleyway.

2.10 Provide the customer with some other helpful information

Internet users love 'FAQs' or frequently asked questions. These are in effect like 'problem pages' but enable customers to sift through what questions other customers have asked before posting their own. People love to eavesdrop and it is basically a little like this. You create a page with some customers' questions and answer them in a friendly, informative way. Ensure that you date the questions to give the feel of how dynamic the interaction is. Encourage your customers to post you new questions by providing an e:mail address at the bottom and top of the FAQ page. Be sure to update the page regularly. Done well this provides a customer forum for your customers and will add great value to your site – it might even be the highest value part of it. It also prevents you from having to answer the same questions over and over again.

Do be a little careful with this. An FAQ full of acknowledged problems with your products can give a very negative image.

Other information of interest to your customers is:

* Date of last update.
* Count of people who have visited the site since it was launched.

2.11 Market test, market test and last of all market test

The true test of a good design is that it has been market tested. No company would even contemplate selling a product which was not been tested, yet very few companies really market test the acceptability of their web-site.

Invite a selection of your customers to visit a URL, which you have not published on any of the search engines, but published just to elicit feedback. Make it worth their while with a free prize for the most useful feedback and ask them what they liked and didn't like. Be open to suggestions because many people will only visit your site the first time it is launched and you need to get it memorable from the start.

3. LAUNCHING YOUR SITE

So you have tested your pages, adapted accordingly and you are now ready to launch. The steps we recommend that you take are:

1. List on all search engines – we reference a one-stop site to do this on the web page that accompanies this chapter.
2. Announce it in mailing lists (see Chapter 7 under Direct Marketing).

3. Announce it in all newsgroups that would find it of interest and abide by the specific etiquette of that particular newsgroup.
4. Promote with classified adds inside the Internet and printed materials.
5. Press release it to journalists worldwide ensuring that all Internet magazines and publications are aware of the site (see the PR Planner reference in Chapter 3).
6. Ensure that your web-site is referenced on all your own advertising and promotion materials, especially free product giveaways, e.g. pencils and pens advertise web-sites well.
7. Get your salespeople to mention it at every sales appointment and within every telephone conversation. Ensure that salespeople use newsgroups to attract people to your web-site.
8. Show your web-site at every exhibition and in your customer reception area (running off the computer rather than permanently connected to the Internet).

4. KEEPING IT GOING

This is the hardest stage. The bright lights have faded. The initial inertia is over and you now have to think about how to improve it. It feels like you have just finished decorating your whole house and you are asked to completely redecorate it. However, this is the bit which ensures a long-term dialogue with your customers. Fail here and you fail your customers forever and the whole process has been a total waste of time.

This is in fact the main reason why companies choose Internet marketing companies to work with. They can often provide the inspiration and ideas that will keep the momentum going when your organisation has moved on to the next exciting project or campaign.

To monitor the effectiveness of your web-site you need to compare two ratios of information provided by your web-server or the company who is hosting your web pages.

1. **Enquiry/Hit conversion ratio.**
The number of enquiries are the number of actual names of people who have approached you as a result of your Internet presence. Typically this is the number of people who have responded electronically through your response or e:mail form but you may need to include here telephone enquiries if you have promoted telephone access on your web page.

The hit rate is a very loose term for the number of visitors you have had to your site. We say that it is loose because it actually refers to the number of requests users have made whilst on your pages. If they click on a graphic, this is also considered to be a hit, so it is not an accurate number but does give you an indication of the activity inspired by your pages.

Again do not get obsessed by a low hit rate of say 300 per week. This may mean that you have hit your target audience effectively and you have 300 potential buyers looking at your site per week. What is important is how effective your pages are at pulling in your enquiries: No enquiries in your first month after a good launch means that your pages need redesigning.

2. **Order/Enquiry conversion.**
This is the true test of how effective your web-site is but only if it has been designed with this sole purpose in mind. Many sites are after brand awareness and so this may not be applicable.

If these ratios indicate a redesign return to the drawing board, conduct some market research to find out why they were a disaster and follow all the steps from stage 1, paying particular attention to market testing and the launch initiative; this was obviously not done thoroughly enough.

When you do launch again, make sure you present the world with your web-site just as though it was a new one, re-registering it as a new entry with different text in all the search engines. You may even want to reference that it has been redesigned.

The real test of an effective web-site is that it meets with your marketing objective. If brand awareness has been your desired intention then a good hit rate will be your primary concern.

CONCLUSION

Our last words are good luck. It is a bit like trying to pass your driving test – it all seems so daunting and frightening at first but once you pick it up, it all seems so obvious! Unlike producing a corporate brochure, making a mistake is an essential part of learning about this new medium and will not result in a stock room tragedy!

CHECKLIST

You now know:

Why knowledge about the target audience is essential to web page design.	☐ Yes	☐ No
How to go about producing your Superhighway materials.	☐ Yes	☐ No
How to design your site.	☐ Yes	☐ No
How to launch your site.	☐ Yes	☐ No
How to keep it going.	☐ Yes	☐ No
How to measure if it is working.	☐ Yes	☐ No
The importance of experimentation.	☐ Yes	☐ No

WHAT NEXT?

Having launched a site and kept it going, you now need to integrate the Superhighway into your everyday marketing activities. It is only by using it yourself can you truly appreciate your customers' use of it. It also has some huge benefits to offer you as a professional wishing to develop yourself, your team and your organisation. Read on for some ideas of how it can help.

9 Integrating the Superhighway into everyday marketing

Whether you are trying to find a new marketing agency, a new team member or innovative new ways of doing your job, the Internet is the place to search. It can provide you with a directory of suppliers, on-line recruitment and access to leading articles about how to improve your productivity. This chapter is about how you can use the Superhighway in your everyday activities at work and at home.

1. SOURCING YOUR SUPPLIERS

The decision-making process by which an organisation selects suppliers is often ad hoc, based on lack of information of alternatives, for convenience and even random. This results in a supplier relationship which is not maximising your business resources. There are two ways the Superhighway can help you improve your supplier selection process to optimise your budget within given quality constraints:

1.1 Using the Superhighway for supplier tendering

To do this write the tender document in your wordprocessor and e:mail it to all suppliers that you are already in contact with. In addition post a request on your web presence that you are looking for a tender response from a given type of supplier and instruct interested parties to contact you via e:mail. This can be a highly efficient way of attracting new suppliers to you, speeding up the process of tendering and generally lighten the burden of paperwork. The Government uses this approach widely for tendering.

1.2 Using the Superhighway to find a selection of suppliers

The growth of businesses using the Superhighway to promote themselves makes giving a list of suppliers virtually impossible. We recommend that you conduct on-line searching first to obtain an overview of potential suppliers. To do this either go to http://www.marketinget.com/cybermarketing/search.html or alternatively look at Appendix 5.

We also list a good starting point for looking for suppliers within the web pages that accompanies this chapter. These include a site which references all the *advertising agencies in London*, marketing research companies and PR companies for example. This is kept dynamically updated and if you find a site which has proved useful to you which, for some reason, has not been included in our site – please do e:mail us and we will add it immediately.

2. DEVELOPING YOURSELF AND YOUR TEAM

The Internet is growing at 10 per cent per month and those that succeed in promoting their companies are those that give value to the end user. This is normally given by providing information about products, management know-how and even case studies. Just as you aim to attract people to your site by giving them free information, so too will you and your team benefit from sites doing exactly the same. In this way the Internet is slowly becoming a learning tool as well as a communication medium.

At present you can obtain the complete works of Shakespeare, information on all major films, access countless libraries, and this is only the start of things to come. This is not new to the IT community because they have been using the Internet to access information, software and suppliers and achieved a vast improvement in knowledge sharing as a result. There are 'knowledge traders' described in Chapter 3, who use the information on the Internet to leverage higher salaries, status and power. You can do the same thing for yourself and your team by integrating the Internet into your daily or weekly routine.

The best example of the power of using the Internet in this way is a demonstration of the quality of free information published on the

Internet. It is reproduced here with the kind permission of *Peter Thomson*, the originator of the model. The exact site can be found on the accompanying web pages to this chapter.

The model is called Windows of Opportunity and can equally be applied to business or team development. It describes the use of a grid as in Figure 8.1 below, where you type your customers' names where the table has letters and then your range of product where it shows numbers.

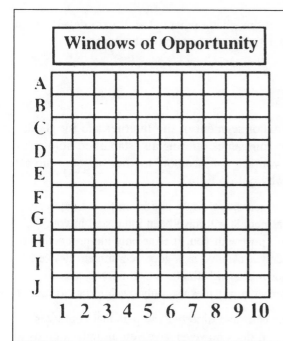

Windows of Opportunity

The Windows of Opportunity form can be used to improve your penetration rate of product/servicto customers. Customers A–J Products 1–10. The 100 windows above represent each hundred windows in your business. If your business has 200 customers and 10 products then you have 2,000 windows of opportunity, or 20 times the above form. Start by looking at your 10 biggest customers. Find out from your records which products/services each of those customers currently buy from you. Colour in the matching square of customer to product or service purchased. The 'holes' that are left are your **Windows of Opportunity.** The % of coloured windows to total windows is the current penetration rate of your business.

Figure 8.1
Windows of Opportunity by Peter Thomson

You colour in the top of the box when you have told the customer about that particular products and then you colour in the bottom half of the box when you have sold it to them. The last column is left for referrals where you ask your customer who else would benefit from your products or services. In this way, you can easily spot business development opportunities where you can cross-sell across your product range.

The same model can be applied to team development, where you list your team members on the y axis and the skill set they need across the x-axis. This time the split colour implies 'taught' them the skill and 'caught' them demonstrating it.

It is exactly these types of tools and techniques that are readily available. They are, of course, intended for you to buy the products and seminars that accompany them but if you have found it valuable, this will be the route you then pursue.

A full list of training organisations giving personal and team development information is provided under the accompanying web chapter.

3. EXPANDING YOUR TEAM

Recruitment is becoming a major segment of the Internet and for good reason. Without recruitment companies offering an established hold on the market, companies like yourself can promote to your target group at almost negligible costs. So why not do both?

Many companies include 'Now recruiting' as an option on their home page and the advantage here is that people will have been interested in your company before applying for a post with you. It costs only the production of a web page and has been widely acclaimed as a good recruitment device if the person you are looking for meets with the target group you wish to attract to your site. Most Internet companies use only the Internet to recruit.

Using recruitment companies can save time but the personal contact is still needed most of the time. It does however give you an indication as to which recruitment companies are innovative and ahead of the game. One company said that they used an on-line recruitment company because they wanted good IT people, and the supplier being on-line demonstrated their understanding of this market. A sample of European recruitment companies are offered at the web page which accompanies this chapter.

4. IMPROVING YOUR PERSONAL AND TEAM'S COMMUNICATION

Whatever your business, the quality of service to your customers defines your success. These customers are not just those people who buy your products but your internal customers within your organisation. The faster and more effectively you can communicate with both, the better your perceived standard of service is to them. The Internet is a critical tool to enhance this perceived service level. A good example of this was a PR director who informed me that she faxed and e:mailed 18 people the minutes of a client briefing that she had conducted only half an hour previously. This was done through the luxury of a train carriage, a mobile phone, a portable computer and the fax/e:mail services offered by CompuServe. This not only gave the client good service but also her internal colleagues who were servicing the account. This may sound leading edge but will be the normal way of conducting business in a relatively short period of time. Those that leverage the understanding of this way of working early will be able to differentiate themselves from their competitors and obtain strategic advantage.

5. KEEPING AHEAD OF THE GAME

The only way you can keep one step in front of your competitors is to integrate the Internet into the everyday activities of your team. In this way, what appears new or radical here will appear normal and everyday. Demanding that your team and your new recruits are Internet aware, and users will provide the mechanism of market intelligence built in at source within your organisation. Gone are the days that you commission someone to investigate your market once a year, typically just before the business planning cycle. If your team are in touch with the marketplace on a day in, day out basis, you merge with and work in partnership with your target market and this is primarily what this book has been about.

6. IMPLEMENTING REMOTE WORKING TO IMPROVE TEAM PRODUCTIVITY AND CUSTOMER SERVICE

The Internet can be the network that enables you to implement remote working. Using the e:mail and dial-up access to internal and external web pages enables your team to contribute and access corporate data wherever they may be in the world.

Remote working can improve team productivity if managed well. It can also empower your team to be more creative and imaginative in their work. On a more bottom-line basis, it can be used to:

- Give the sales team information for pre-sales visits
- Provide on-line access to product availability
- Obtain customer feedback
- Obtain sales people's feedback about competitors
- Obtain sales information for central update in your customer database
- Collect orders
- Query stock levels remotely
- Disseminate information quickly throughout the organisation from a remote site
- Gain overview of the state of play of budgets where all expenditure is captured on-line (e.g. sales people expenses, purchase orders etc.).

CONCLUSION

The Internet is the tool to educate your customers, your team and your marketplace. It can help you personally, professionally and operationally to achieve success. This can only be achieved once it is integrated into your thinking, your everyday activities and your marketing plan. Seeing it as an isolated promotion tool is what your competitors are doing. This book is pointing you in the direction of using it for long-term competitive advantage.

CHECKLIST

You now know:

How the Superhighway can be used in your everyday activities.	☐ Yes	☐ No
How the Superhighway can be used to find new suppliers.	☐ Yes	☐ No
How the Superhighway can be used to develop and expand your team.	☐ Yes	☐ No
How the Superhighway can be used to improve team communications and productivity.	☐ Yes	☐ No
How the Superhighway can keep you ahead of the game.	☐ Yes	☐ No

How the Superhighway can be used to enable you
to free yourself and your team from your
organisational boundaries.   ☐ Yes   ☐ No

WHAT NEXT?

The last chapter of this book is the excuse for the authors to pontificate
on the future of this new technology. They may be wrong but they
welcome feedback and actively encourage you to comment about what
you think the future holds – read on to see if you agree with their
predictions.

10 Where is this all taking us?

'The Internet is a wonderful, critical development and a very clear element of the final system (the Information Highway) but it will change significantly in the years ahead... Much of the Internet culture will seem as quaint to future users of the Information Highway as stories of wagon trains and pioneers on the Oregon Trail do to us today'

Bill Gates, *The Road Ahead*, 1995.

We are at the pioneering stage of this technology and any book that even attempts to describe this new phenomena is out of date as soon as it is published. What we have given you in this book is a model of how to apply traditional marketing thinking and concepts to your use of this ever-changing media. This will not date. Supported by a dynamically updated web-site it will become the essential starting point for any serious professional wishing to 'market' using the Superhighway.

You are in the privileged position of being at the pioneering stage of the Internet where relatively speaking it is practically empty. You have the potential to use it in the most creative way and by doing so going down in history for it. You have the potential of being the next Guinness success story. You can be the creative genius of tomorrow where books and magazines will reference you in a God-like fashion. You are only constrained in this endeavour by your imagination. And your imagination will be fuelled by technical and creative developments that take place almost every day. You have the advantage that you are not looking at this innovation from a technical perspective and therefore your innovations are marketing focused and by implication more likely to succeed.

Likewise, we have tried to make this book as practical and as low-stress as possible. We purposefully didn't use screen shots and resisted the temptation of covering the book with URL references. The reason is that it is stressful for marketers and senior managers to read books of this nature. It either frustrates, alienates or leaves you feeling that you are missing the boat. The stress factor then takes over and the messages of the book are lost.

We would like to reinforce this in our parting message to you. The Internet and other on-line services contain a great deal of corporate dribble. A great deal of it is media hype propagated by people with vested interests. It is also heavily dominated by IT people who are not adept at marketing and merchandising. This is, as we said, a temporary transition stage and it will develop into a very powerful new medium. However, we are still in the early stages and there is absolutely no need to rush into designing a web-site overnight in your anxiety to get on-line. Adopting the methodology suggested in the book and using a good creative team or agency can mean the difference between an overnight wonder and a lasting success. It also takes a brave organisation to say that they do not see the Superhighway as fitting in with their marketing strategy and choosing to wait for the market to mature. It may not be relevant for you right now and we commend your decision to pull back and review its relevance over time.

Whatever you decide to do, we hope that you have appreciated the core message of the book, which is that although the technology is new, your approach to it does not have to be. Using traditional marketing concepts will ensure that your message is communicated to your target audience in a meaningful and powerful way. Implementing your Cybermarketing in this structured way will put you years ahead of your competition, who may have rushed in on the rather wobbly bandwagon.

WHAT WILL HAPPEN NEXT?

Producing web-sites and web pages will become easier and easier. The tools used today to produce printed material are all being upgraded to produce web-ready information. Tomorrow you will be able to produce a web-site as easily as you produce material for a brochure.

However, the Internet technology is moving on in several important ways:

1. **It is getting easier.** At present, the technology can be often frustrating and difficult to use unless you are technically confident. PC software

is becoming more integrated with this technology. You can send a mail message from within your wordprocessor, you just write and send without having to load another piece of software. If you select the help option within your wordprocessor, it will connect you direct to their on-line support team via the Internet.

2. **It is defining the way to communicate.** People will use the Internet to send information just as they use the fax today. It will become commonplace.

3. **Improving the content of your presentation in Cyberspace.** It is going from a simple page of graphics and text to a full multi-media experience – embedding video clips, live video and audio broadcasts, sound, animation, virtual reality etc

4. **The level of interactivity is become very powerful.** For example, Hot Java allows you to make use of the customer's own computer to run more powerful and complex computer programmes. This frees the world wide web from the electronic magazine model and opens up endless possibilities for genuine interaction between your customer and yourself.

5. **The Internet is coming into the home.** At present you need a computer to get onto the Internet, tomorrow your TV will be your gateway. You buy a black box, plug it in and start using the Internet. This will be as cheap as satellite and provide education, entertainment and information. Home shopping and home banking will become commonplace. Home education will also become very lucrative where opportunities for personal development through interactive learning becomes more accessible.

6. **It is getting faster and cheaper.** With the prospect of using ISDN as it becomes cheaper, and the major support of this technology by the leaders in IT, e.g. Microsoft, this technology can only get cheaper and faster.

7. **It is becoming more global.** At present it is still very American but the growth rate in the Europe, Asia and Australia is changing the balance significantly over time. At the moment the Internet language is English but it will become multi-lingual over time. This is an issue which you may be wise to consider sooner rather than later. At present, very few web-sites offer multi-lingual translations and this would be innovative if you adopted this approach now. Building in cultural sensitivity even at this stage is essential.

8. **It is becoming more professionally used.** At present a comment from one user group was 'Creating web-sites has come to mean that people

have climbed on the preverbal technology bandwagon. It doesn't persuade me that there's a lot of understanding of what it means to market in a computer mediated environment'. This will change and creative marketers around the world will be tapping into your customer base and your market. It is a race against the imagination of your competitors, not just in your national market, but across the world.

9. **It is becoming more secure.** Soon people will have no qualms about typing in their credit card numbers. Global shopping will be commonplace and physical buying constraints will be eroded away. Some fear that we will sit at home and lose the personal interaction with shopping, others argue that the tedious repetitious shopping will merely be stripped away, to be replaced by luxury goods shopping. No-one can predict accurately the way this will affect the social and economic behaviour of our society. All that we can say is that it will.

CONCLUSION

Mary Cronin (1995) completes her book with the statement: 'The electronic highway is not merely open for business; it is relocating, restructuring and literally redefining business in America'. This book has been intended for a European audience, attempting to give an understanding and an appreciation of how the Superhighway affects the process of marketing as a discipline and how it can be integrated into an organisation's overall marketing effort. Almost without exception, those companies who have been successful in their use of the Internet have been those who have integrated it fully into their marketing and business strategy rather than just simply using it as another advertising medium.

This is such a new area, we have looked at the marketing processes and attempted to illustrate how the Internet can and could be used to support such activities. However, as the Internet develops over the next few years, its use as an additional marketing tool is discussed in this book. The analogy is similar to the invention of a printing press where marketers ask 'to what business benefit can this technology be used?' The only answer is 'what do you do, what do you want to do and what are you trying to achieve?' Imaginative and integrated marketing is the only answer. The book can only outline concepts and ideas which can act as a framework within this creative process.

We welcome your feedback about any issue discussed in this chapter and indeed this book. We are contactable from the web-site that accompanies this book. We look forward to hearing from you.

REFERENCES

Bill Gates with Nathan Myhrvold and Peter Rinearson (1995) *The Road Ahead*, Viking.

Mary Cronin (1995) *Doing More Business On The Internet*, Van Nostrand Reinhold, New York.

Appendix 1
What is the Superhighway
– give me the background

1956   Sputnik launched by the USSR. The US forms the Advanced Research Projects Agency (ARPA) to gain competitive advantage in science and technology for the military.

1965   Ted Nelson coins the word hypertext.

1967   Andy Van Dam and others build Hypertext Editing System - the core of HTML which is the layout language used on the Internet.

1968   Doug Engelbart demonstrates NLS, a hypertext system.

1969   ARPANET group set up by the DoD for research 'networking'. First ever Internode set up at UCLA. First manned moon landing.

1972   First International Conference on computer communications. ARPANET was demonstrated on 40 machines. E:mail was invented and demonstrated to work where users collected their messages remote from the network.

1973   First international link up. England and Norway connect up and HM the Queen sends her first e:mail message.

1977   THEORYNET created at the University of Wisconsin providing electronic mall to over 100 researchers in computer science.

1978   The Aspen Movie map, the first hypermedia videodisc, shown at MIT.

1979   USENET established, which enables and lists newsgroups. Prestel and MicroNet established in UK. The personal computer is born.

1981   Minitel (Teletel) is established in France by French Telecom. This is then used to organise strikes and blockades in the late 1980s.
Ted Nelson conceptualises 'Xandu' a hypertext database encompassing all written information.

1982   First definition of an 'internet' as a connected set of networks. This comes from INWG establishing TCP (Transmission Control Protocol) and IP (Internet Protocol) the core communication of the Internet.

1983   ARPANET split into ARPANET and MILNET. Personal computers become popular as desktop workstations.

1984   Over 1000 host computers. JANET (Joint Application Network) established in UK. Number of computers breaks 1000.

1986   ARPANET bureaucracy prevent it from being used to interconnect centres. NSFNET established by NASA and DoE. This enables connections to grow, especially between universities. MS-DOS 3.0 becomes networkable.

1987   Over 10,000 host computers. Office-based IT revolution comes about. Windows Version 1. released by Microsoft. Apple Computers introduces Hypercard, the first widely available personal hypermedia authoring system.

1989   Over 100,000 host computers. Electronic mail provider CompuServe links up with the Internet through Ohio State University.

1990   ARPANET ceases to exist. Electronic mail provider MCI links up with the Internet.

1991   Commerical Internet Exchange (CIX) Association Inc. formed. WAIS released from Thinking Machines Corporation. Gopher released by University of Minnesota.

1992   Over 1,000,000 host computers - growing exponentially. Internet Society is chartered. World wide web released by CERN. First audio multicast and video multicast. Local area networks are common. Modems fall dramatically in price

1993   US White House, UK Government, United Nations and the World Bank go on-line. Internet Talk Radio begins broadcasting. Businesses and media start to take notice of the Internet. Mosaic takes the Internet by storm; WWW proliferates at a 341,634 per cent annual growth.

1994   Communities begin to be connected though local suppliers. Interflora takes flower orders. Shopping malls and mass marketing grows. Mass e:mailing take place and are correspondingly censored.

1995   Many millions of host computers are now established. Netscape takes the Internet market by storm and gains 80-90 per cent market share of the 'browser' market (i.e. software interface to the WWW). 10,000 businesses go on-line. Electronic payments systems become practical and widespread, supported by Barclaycard. TV programmes encourage readers to write in using e:mail. Increased interest in the Internet by the general population. More than 30 providers in the UK. Local Points of Presence (PoP) covers 90 per cent of the UK population. Microsoft release Windows '95 and MSN. MSN will enable every Windows '95 user to access the Internet for a monthly subscription.

Appendix 2
Get me onto the Superhighway

'I want to go on-line'

Before you can travel the Superhighway, you need to get connected. To do this, you need to have your own identity as an individual on the Superhighway – your own e:mail address where people can write to you. This is not difficult but it can seem like it because of the new language and communication issues. All you need is a reasonable (less than two years old) PC or Mac and a modem and a telephone socket.

A modem translates the output from the computer into a signal for the phone. The faster your modem is at translating and sending the data, the faster your Superhighway access is going to be. If you are paying for your telephone calls, this can save you money because you can obtain information quicker. It is measured in bits per second, this is called the baud rate. The range is 1200 baud (don't buy one like this) to 33,600 (the latest). The average modem is 28,800 now but this is changing monthly!

You need to be technically quite knowledgeable to add a modem to your computer. So either buy a machine which is pre-configured or make sure your supplier is willing to set it up for you. Alternatively contact your IT department if you have one in your organisation.

Next you need the software to get connected. You will get this when you subscribe to an Internet Provider. Some of the software that is commonly used with the Internet is free to download once you are connected. On the books companion web-site under this chapter, you will find links to various software which will be useful additions or substitutions to the software provided by your Internet provider.

A few things you need to consider when selecting an Internet provider.

1. Do you want just the Internet or do you want to buy additional commercial on-line services?

There are two basic types of access provider. The first (Internet Providers) simply sell you a connection to the Internet. The second (Commercial On-line Services) provides information and may also give you an Internet connection as part of the service but their main focus is to sell you information and other services. Some of these services will include discussion groups and access to companies and support groups which are not on the Internet. These commercial on-line service providers charge not only for their information but also for accessing the Internet. So if you just want to access the Internet this may be a very expensive way to do it.

Before making your decision, we will outline some examples of what each of the Commerical On-Line Service providers can offer.

CompuServe
This is the father of on-line services. It has one of the most easy to use interfaces. It is a collection of everything from train timetables to software support in hundreds of conferences. This is the provider if you want to make friends and influence people!

There are phone numbers for CompuServe in London and other major cities; this means that you may only need to pay local phone rates to use their services. However, their baud rates of connection are not always at the latest speeds, and therefore, what you might save by dialling locally you may spend longer on-line.

But the services are paid for by you according to how long you are on-line. This is on top of your telephone costs. If your objectives are to abstract information from the Internet rather than converse in forums or use CompuServe's information databases, this could be the most expensive provider. However, it may not be cheap but it does have 2 million members and an easy-to-use interface. It also offers Internet mail and newsgroups. Tel: 0800 289 378.

MSN™

Microsoft's Network (MSN™) had much speculation in the press. Initially people thought that it would be a closed network competing with the Internet. It is in fact a route to the Internet accessing it through Microsoft's set of information services. As a commercial services provider, you may pay as you use their information databases, but you will be able to access the Internet in addition.

At the time of printing of this book, MSN is not operable and the media is filled with speculation about the prospect of Microsoft offering on-line charging for areas of information. What is promised is that Microsoft will offer Internet access, and to do this, you only have to buy Windows 95™ and click on the icon MSN™. It will then take your credit card details to subscribe.

Compulink Information Exchange (CIX)

One of the best known on-line conferencing systems in the UK. This is established and user-friendly. It specialises in providing a group of forums for users to talk amongst themselves. There is an extremely wide range of topics. The whole of CIX is pervaded with a clubby atmosphere and the people who run the system moderates the conferences. This means that you don't waste your time wading through lots of irrelevant and obscure messages.

It offers an excellent off-line reader to keep the cost low. An off-line reader allows you to collect information onto your PC and read it later when not connected on the phone – this is one of the disadvantages of the very popular world wide web where you cannot read off-line. (A word of warning, this off-line reader was developed at the University of

Guelph and so it can be a bit imposing to use if you are not technically minded).

It offers Internet access and mail and unlimited newsgroup access. However, using the Internet access requires a extra degree of technical competence and is not recommended for those who fight shy of the technology. Tel: 0181 390 8446.

Delphi

Delphi is a US derived service provider and is owned by the Murdoch Group. It is very US focused but offers a variety of membership schemes and good access to US discussions. At present it has a rather old fashioned interface but is extremely simple for new users to get to grips with. It has an off-line reader for PCs, not for the Mac. Tel: 0171 757 7080.

If you decide on any of the above, merely phone the numbers given and they will send you a disk with instructions. If at this point you have decided that you want just Internet access, read on to decide which Internet provider you choose.

2. Which Internet provider do I choose?

An Internet provider is the cheapest way to access the Internet. They do not charge as you use it, you subscribe to their services on a monthly or yearly basis. This market is changing extremely rapidly; it will probably have changed by the time that you have finished reading this chapter. Therefore, we have not given you an exhaustive list of providers or prices.

We recommend that you buy an Internet magazine to review prices and services about providers. Currently the 'Internet' magazine (published by Emap Business Communications) regularly test the service and quality of access providers and publish the results by way of a guide.

There is one overriding principle, stick with the bigger and more mature access providers. Others may seem to be a bargain but the consistent and fast service they offer today will attract many customers, and if the access provider fails to invest in the technology, their service will degrade very rapidly. You may then have a year's subscription to a service that you don't use.

We have given you a free month's subscription to Pipex via the card enclosed in this book. Pipex has provided commercial access for many of the well-known companies in the UK and it offers a high quality reliable service. 80 per cent of companies in the UK connect through Pipex and so do many of the smaller access providers. They also work closely with Microsoft and are likely to be a market leader for some timw. A recent innovation enables Pipex to offer 80 per cent of the UK to access the Internet via a local rate phone call.

To contact them call: +44 (0) 1223 250100.

Other providers you may wish to consider are:

Cityscape	Tel: +44 (0) 1223 566 950	Fax: +44 (0) 1223 566953
BBC	Tel: +44 (0) 181 576 7799	Fax: +44 (0) 181 576 1130
Demon	Tel: +44 (0) 181 371 1234	Fax: +44 (0) 181 371 1150
Eunet	Tel: +44 (0) 1227 266466	Fax: +44 (0) 1227 266477

Once you have received your disk it is easy to install. If you are using a Mac or Unix computer, this disc won't work so phone Pipex on the above number for a replacement disk. If you are using a PC with a modem, the following instructions apply:

1 Ensure that your modem is connected and that you know which type of modem it is and how it connects to your PC (i.e. which port it is connected to: com1, com2, com3 etc.).

2. Insert the disk in your computer and run the programme 'Setup' through Windows.

3. It will ask you what modem it is and how it is connected to your machine. Answer these questions and it will automatically set your computer up to connect with the Internet and allow you to use Netscape as your software for browsing the world wide web.

4. To get to the web-site which accompanies this book, put your cursor in the box at the first box on the top of the screen and type this: http://www.marketingnet.com.cybermarketing

Appendix 3
Tell me about e:mail
accounts

What do you call yourself in Cyberspace?

Your access provider will issue you with an e:mail account. Depending on the supplier, you may have the option to choose your name in Cyberspace. All e:mail addresses are of a similar structure:

yourname@domain

yourname

Your access provider may give you free choice for the 'yourname' part of the e:mail address. It's popular to use your surname and initials joined together to make one word, e.g. bickertonmj. Another form is to put the '_' as a space between your initials and your name, e.g. bickerton_mj. Any characters can be used with the exception of spaces and punctuation. At present, CompuServe issue you with a number of the form 12345,678.

domain

This is made of two sections: the first is defined by your access provider, the second is fixed by the Internet standards. The first part could be the name of your access provider. Some providers actually allow you to use your own company name. This is usually an additional expense. The second part is one of two types: the original Internet classification '.com'; or alternatively it will be of the form '.co.uk'.

The format of e:mail accounts differ per provider and here are some examples:

Examples of e:mail formats by provider

CIX users	bloggs@cix.compulink.co.uk
CompuServe	12345,678@CompuServe.com
Pipex	bloggs@dial.pipex.com
Demon	bloggs@demon.co.uk
or	bloggs@mycompany.demon.co.uk
BBC Networking club	bloggs@bbcnc.org.uk

Companies who have their own Internet connection (see Chapter 7) may have e:mails of the following form:

bloggs@company.co.uk

or   bloggs@company.com

You might also have customer service lines, or help desks as the following:

moreinfo@company.co.uk

helpdesk@company.com

One consideration is the company image of your provider, especially if it is going to appear on your business card. Because you are aligning your company and yourself with a supplier, it is best to ensure they too have an image which is of high quality. Another reason why we recommend choosing an established and high quality supplier as your provider.

When do I get my e:mails?

The way that e:mail works is that messages sent to you will be stored by your access provider, waiting for your collection. When you connect to the Internet and start your e:mail software it will collect your messages, moving them from the access provider's machine onto yours. If you get a lot, you might want to disconnect and read and reply whilst not taking up time on the phone. Then re-connect later to dispatch the messages in one go. It is very difficult for us to give you a step by step guide because every mail software works in a slightly different way.

If you would like to test whether your e:mail is working – we guarantee to reply to you, simply address your e:mail to pb@marketingnet.com

How do people know my e:mail address?

They don't unless you tell them. There are directories of e:mail names but these are usually so user-hostile, time consuming and incomplete, that it is best to assume that there aren't any.

Don't worry about the fact that you have to remember people's e:mail addresses because as soon as you have written to someone once or they have written to you, you can store that message and re-use it at a future time.

How do I manage my e:mail system?

The key to managing your e:mail is to create a structure of folders as soon as possible. Most e:mail systems support this in various ways. We suggest:

> Prospects or Enquiries
> Int_Boss
> Int_Companymemos
> Ext_Customer1
> Ext_Customer2
> Ext_Supplier1
> Ext_Supplier1
> Know_Articles
> Know_Info
> Projects_Campaigns

Where **Int** implies internal to your organisation; **Ext** implies from an external source; **Know** implies knowledge and information (typically from news groups etc.).

Used well, e:mail can be an incredibly efficient way of communicating and increasing your productivity by degrees of magnitude. Your correspondent does not need to be there when you wish to communicate. They are more receptive when they read your message because they have chosen a time to collect their communication. You can be shorter and less formal than in conventional communications and people respond faster because it is easier to do.

Warning: e:mails are not secure. People can read your e:mail as it is being passed to the intended recipient – use conventional communication if this is an issue. Encrypted e:mail will be widely supported in the near future which will reduce this problem.

How often should I check for new e:mail?

People expect you to read your e:mail once a day and reply immediately. This is etiquette and if you do not wish to follow this – we would suggest you tell people how frequently you pick up your messages at the first point of contact (e.g. when you give them your business card) so that you do not disappoint or insult them.

What if I am inundated with e:mail?

Good e:mail packages will allow you to set up rules which act as filters. You can decide that you want to delete every e:mail from a given source automatically. You can decide automatically to store all e:mail from a given source in certain folder for reading at another point in time. You can also use 'auto-responders'. Here a customer may send a message with a prescribed (by you either on your web page or promotion materials) subject heading or contents. When this messages reaches your access provider, it can be automatically replied to with a reply which you have written. Talk to your access provider about setting this up. Auto-responders can be built into your web-site (see Chapter 8).

Finding someone's e:mail address

If you want to find out what someone's e:mail address is, the quickest way will be to just pick up the phone, call and ask them! Although there are a variety of 'white pages' services available on the Internet, they are far from complete – but most people are simply not listed. Major e:mail providers are working on a universal directory system, but that could be some time away.

Some 'white pages' services might give you some leads but not much more. If you want to have a go at finding someone on the Superhighway, then use one of the following:
ns for finding out more.

Four11.com

> Four11 is a commercial online directory service with over 1.1 million listings (as of June 1995). All Internet users are provided free basic access, which includes a free listing and free searching. To try the service out, send mail to info@four11.com or browse http://www.four11.com/.

Lookup.com

> LookUP! at http://www.lookup.com/ is an online directory service with hundreds of thousands of listings as of June 1995. Basic searching is available to anyone with a web browser. Members get more features.

Usenet-addresses server

> If you think the person you are interested in may have posted a message to the Usenet. You may be able to find their address in the Usenet address database on the machine rtfm.mit.edu. To query the database, send an e:mail message to mail-server@rtfm.mit.edu with 'send addresses/name' in the body of the message. The 'name' should be one or more space-separated words for which you want to search; you should list all of the words you think might appear in the address, including first and last name, username, and the host name (e.g. 'marketingnet' for a person who you think is at MarketingNet). For more details about how to use the database, send the command 'send Usenet-addresses/help'.

Searching Listserver mailing lists

> You can ask a Listserver to send you a membership list. To do this, send mail to listserv@host. In the body of your message, include the command 'review list-name', where 'list-name' is the name of the mailing list you wish to search.

E:mail the postmaster

> Most sites have an individual responsible for network and mail operations at the site, usually with the user ID of 'postmaster'. Many postmasters will refuse to answer questions about user identification, for reasons of privacy, though they may be willing to forward your address so your intended recipient can write to you.

Appendix 4
Tell me things I need to know – *Netiquette*

The Internet has a culture of its own and when in Rome, do what the Romans do is definitely important. Because you are talking across country, organisation and cultural boundaries, there are rules which prevent you for unconsciously insulting people.

When you are writing e:mails, the style is informal. So you are lulled into the sense that you having a conversation but it is not face to face. A comment face to face comes with a smile, a wink or anger but the same words in an e:mail leave no clue. It is very easy to cause offence.

Emotions

:-)	Smile	:-D	Big Smile	>:)	Evil grin
;-)	Wink	:-))	Very happy	>:-)	Evil smile
:-X	I'm not telling	}:-)	Devilish	:^)	Tonge in cheek
0:-)	Saint	:-)8	Wearing a bow tie	8:-)	Happy with glasses
%-)	Drunk	:-0	Shocked	:-l	Indecision
:'(	Crying	:-(	Sad	:-{	Sad
>:-(	Very sad	:-###..	Being sick	[:-)	Wearing headphones

You are more informal using e:mail than in a fax or letter. In fact if you do not make the style of your e:mails like this, you can easily appear pompous. At the other extreme, if you use expressions like 'lots of love', this can also be misinterpreted and you can appear too familiar. Never use the word 'love' unless you are talking to your partner or someone you wish to be your partner.

Never use capital letters in e:mails, (e.g. PLEASE REPLY TO MY MESSAGE) this is very rude on the Superhighway as it implies shouting. If you want to emphasise something, use * around the word you wish to stress, e.g. *Please* reply to my message. This takes the place of using bold or italic.

When you construct your e:mail message try not to exceed more than 60 characters across because it makes it hard for your correspondent to read it.

When replying to someone, another netiquette rule is never change or delete words within a line of their original message. You can delete lines but not delete or add words into their lines. This means that when you are asking someone a question, it is best to put each question on a separate line so that the responder can just insert an answer.

Appendix 5
How do I search for things?

COMPUSERVE

At the general level within CompuServe, click on the magnifying class on the command line and this enables the command FIND. This will find any database which has your word in the keyword criteria. Once you find one that you are interested in, simply click on the traffic lights to initiate the command GO.

The tips for beginners that CompuServe promote in their magazine are as follows:

⇒ Start by accessing the basic services (GO BASIC). This electronic suburb is a microcosm of the service where you can learn how to use CompuServe before moving on to explore extended services.

⇒ Look in on the Member Support features (GO HELP). One of them is the CompuServe Help Forum (GO HELPFORUM).

⇒ Browse the CompuServe Directory included in the centre of this guide to find services that interest you.

⇒ Once you have charted your course for further exploration, locate forums and drop in for a visit. CompuServe is at its best as a person-to-person medium and questions and answers are its lifeblood.

⇒ When you find forums that serve your interests, leave messages introducing yourself and strike up a conversation. Remember: fellow visitors can tell you about other features you might be interested in. After all, no-one knows all of the features of CompuServe (just as no-one has visited all there is to see in New York, London or Tokyo) but people of like interests do share valuable pointers with each other.

THE INTERNET

The Internet is like a library of books, articles, flyers and waster paper, dropped from 1/2 mile up and left in a huge pile. Therefore, the secret to mastering the Internet is to make use of 'search engines' and other guides. We have given you the easiest way of searching by providing a web page with all the search engine entry forms on one page. Here you can enter your key search word in a selection of search facilities and we deal with all the different commands that you would otherwise have to learn. This is the most valuable thing the accompanying web-site offers you and we recommend that bookmarking this site is the first thing you do when you visit this book on-line. Go to:

http://www.marketingnet.com/cybermarketing/search.html

Even if you get nothing else from the accompany web-site – this will provide you with an easy starting point to explore the world wide web for yourself.

The main ways of searching for things on the Internet are:

Your own bookmarks

Whenever you go to a site that it interesting and you are likely to return to again, all you have to go is 'bookmark' it. This is supported by most Internet software and you usually just make a menu selection when you are on the page that you wish to bookmark. We would recommend that you immediately bookmark:

www.marketingnet.com so you can return to us at any point.

As you become more experienced on the Internet, the fuller this bookmark list becomes, and it then becomes your starting point for searching. We recommend that you follow a structured approach to bookmarking with a hierarchy at the top level similar to the following:

Search tools
Your company web-site (if you have one)
Competitors
Professional interest
Personal interest
Fun and entertainment
News and general information
Needs sorting out

Magazines

The most popular way to find out what is new on the Internet is to read Internet magazines. They are becoming more and more targeted towards a certain age and interest area so you need to decide the one most suited for your needs. They typically review new and popular web-sites by subject area and are good for giving you an overview of what is available on line.

After you have whetted your appetite with these magazines, you may now want to conduct some searches of your own on a specific subject. Because there is not one centralised search facility on the Internet, we have provided you with a list of search facilities under this chapter on our accompanying web-site. Below, we explain what the differences are between these and recommend some good starting points.

Robots

There are computers connected to the Internet which spend all of their time following links from web page to web page. As they go, they collect information about each page. They are continuously searching and some of the more established machines have absolutely enormous databases containing extracts from a high percentage of all web pages. They allow you to enter keywords and return lists of possible sites of interest. It is important to remember that the searching is automatic and so you have to accept lots of inappropriate recommendations. For example if you want to understand the concept of the 'world wide web' and you type this in as your search criteria, you will receive a huge list of almost every site as often web pages say 'on our world wide web page, we can ......'.

Lycos is one of the most popular robots on the Internet and with a well designed interface is a good starting point. The search results displays the first set of words which appear on that particular page.

Categorised lists

These computers are connected to the Internet but are not actively searching around the Internet but are databases which people submit information. People add entries describing their web-site which is then updated to appear in a classified list. It is up to the person publishing their pages to define where their entry appears. The extracts held in the database are also specifically defined for entry into this database and as such make for much better reading when you have completed a search.

Again, you can enter keywords and receive lists but the descriptions are usually more intelligible. However, the real strength of this approach is that you can start with a broad category, e.g. travel, and then explore down a decision tree to narrow your search. This is a very good way of assessing how much other related information exists for a particular topic and therefore how popular this topic is.

Yahoo (shortly to change its name) is one of the most popular categorised lists. It is free to make an entry and its free to search. They sell advertising space to make their money. When you get the results of your search, you will get a panel enticing you to click on it and move to a company's web-site. Because this service is so popular, they provide the opportunity for advertisers to gain access to a large number of users.

Infoseek is free to add an entry into the database and also free for users to search on a limited basis. For full search functionally they make a small charge. You set up an account giving your credit card number over the phone and then they deduct payments as you use this service. One nice feature is the ability to store your search criteria and return to them at a later point. This is an excellent way of tracking competitors outlined in Chapter 2.

Haystack is free to search but you have to pay to have your web-site as an entry. There are various levels of charges depending on how much information you want displayed on the search results for your customers to look at.

News group searches

Although news groups are classified into subject areas, it is sometimes difficult to guess where a particular issue will be discussed. Therefore, an excellent way of finding the right way to talk is to use one of the news group search engines.

http://www.altavista.com is a good example where you can define your search to news groups, type in a key word and it will report a list of news groups containing that word.

The best of....

Particularly loved by the 'global beachcombers' (see Chapter 7), these give you a chef's tour of interesting or new sites to review. The Top 5 per cent is an example of one where sites are nominated by anyone who cares to express an opinion and the top five each year are given a Top 5 per cent Award – this is the equivalent to the Oscars and is a very sought-after award. For the ultimate beachcombing experience there are several sites which will randomly choose a site for you. It is quite incredible what you can see using this approach. We recommend that you do this just to soak up the atmosphere of the Internet.

Links off other sites

If you know of a site which is related to an area of your interest, visit it
and it is a common feature of a web-site to offer links to other relevant
web-sites. What usually happens is that web publishers agree to cross-link
their pages in this way.

Advertisements

It is becoming more and more popular to include a web-site in all your
promotional literature. Look out for this in papers, magazines and TV.

Asking people on forums

It is quite acceptable to find the right news group and post a question
asking for recommendations. 'Do you know of any web-sites that do . .
.?' Many news groups would appreciate if you posted back a summary of
your findings for use by other people. This is an extremely good way of
coming in on a news group and also of publicising your web-site if it is of
relevance to your particular news group.

Guessing URLs

This is very desperate, it is a last ditch attempt but quite common. This is
where you type in a likely company URL at the bar at the top of screen.
It is very hit-and-miss but try several combinations as follows:

http://www.companyname.co.uk
http://www.companyname.com
http://companyname.co.uk
http://companyname.com

Also try product names in the same way.

This Appendix has given you the basics for searching. Please remember
that you are unlikely to find all your needs satisfied by only one search
mechanism and it is the combination of the above which can make you a
true Cyberspace professional.

Appendix 6
Technical information you might want/need to know about the Superhighway

Browser   This is the name given to the software that runs on your PC that displays web pages. There are many makes of this software. The market leader at present is the Netscape Navigator which has 70 per cent of the marketplace.

FAQ   Stands for Frequently Asked Questions and is a popular inclusion in many web-sites. It enables the customer to identify if their problem has been expressed and solved through a previous customer's enquiry.

HTML   Stands for Hypertext Markup Language. This is the programming commands that define how your pages look when your customer sees them. Some examples of this language are:

<h1> = start of a heading
</h1>   = end of heading
<b> = start bold
<i> = italic

HTTP   Stands for Hypertext Transfer Protocol. This is a set of computer standards that are used to make the world wide web work. You always see it as the prefix to a URL

URL   This stands for a Universal Resource Locator. This is like the address for a piece of information on the Internet. Each page on a web-site has a unique URL. This is how your customers can access your pages as discreet entities in Cyperspace. A URL is constructed from three parts:

Part 1: The type of item. It can be 'http://' for a web page; 'ftp://' for a computer file; 'gopher://' for a text based information system; 'telnet:// for an on-line computer; 'news://' for a news group.

Part 2: The name of the machine where the information is stored. For a web-site, it is common to call the machine 'www', therefore you will often see the second part like 'www.marketingnet.com'.

Part 3: The directory and name of the file. This describes the actual item stored on the computer that you are reading. For example: '/cybermarketing/appendix/search.html'

Modem   This is a device used to convert digital computer information into sounds that can be passed over a telephone line. The speed at which a modem can transfer information is measured in bits per second or baud rate. 33,600 bit per second is the maximum speed currently available, although using special compression techniques (this is called V34 or V34bis) it is possible to get higher speeds. However, much of the information on the Internet, especially graphics, is already compressed so these modems will not increase the speed by as much as you expect.

Direct Access   This is a term commonly used to describe a PC that is connected to the Internet permanently. This is achieved by a permanent 'line' between the PC and the Internet provider, who in turn has a permanent connection to another Internet provider and so on. Direct access is required if you wish to publish information on the Superhighway.

Downloading   This is the process of copying information and files from the Internet on to your own computer.

Uploading   This is the process of copying a file from your computer on to some machine connected to the Superhighway.

SLIP and PPP   These are two types of communication standard, with a dial-up account, one of these protocols will be used to connect your PC to your access provider. If you have got someone else to set up your PC for the Internet, or you have easy-to-use Internet access software, you will not even be aware of this. For the non-technically minded, if you find yourself dealing with SLIP or PPP it's time to get some different access software.

FTP

File-transfer protocol – this allows you to up- and down-load files to and from your computer. On all good Internet software packages you will find an FTP facility, the better ones show two windows, one lists the files on your PC, the other shows the files on a remote computer connected to the Superhighway, and you can move files between the two computers.

There are a large number of public file libraries on the Superhighway, these can provide PC applications, FAQ files, fonts, documents, image libraries and almost anything else as well. The distribution of files in this way can be used to provide your customers with updates to software, screen savers with your message built in, documents or multi-media presentations that they can down-load and use on their own PC.

If you want to set up a system to allow people to pick up files you have left you will need to set up an FTP server. This is similar technology to a web server and the reader is referred to Chapter xx).

There is another popular method of sending someone a file, most mail reader programs allow you to 'attach' a file to an e:mail. When received at the other end the file can be unattached and saved on the receiver's PC. This is most appropriate if you want to send a file to a single person. The FTP method is much more convenient if you want to leave a file for many to pick up.

Telnet

This allows you to log-on to a remote computer connected to the Superhighway. Logging on means you will be able to enter commands and run programs just as if you were using the remote computer from its own keyboard and screen. This type of service is particularly useful for searching databases, computerised library card catalogues and live interactive games. However, with the advent of the world wide web many of these telnet services have been replaced by an interactive web page offering the same service.

WAIS

Wide-Area Information Server – This tool will allow for searching across many databases at the same time. You are unlikely to use this tool directly, but you may see reference to 'WAIS' with no other clue as to its use. Usually you simply enter keywords of interest and wait for it to return the matching results.

Gopher	is a program that most good Internet access packages will provide, most of the world wide web browsers can be used to access Gopher. Gopher provides a menu system that will give you access to a huge variety of online databases.
IRC channel	Internet Relay Chat – this simulates CB radio over the Internet. With this you are able to 'tune in' to an IRC channel and then 'broadcast' and 'listen' by using your keyboard to chat. Conversation takes place as each person enters lines of text.
Bang	An exclamation mark !
UNIX	This is the generic name for a large number of computer operating systems (its equivalent on your PC is MS-DOS or System 7). The UNIX is the dominant operating system for all the servers and information providers on the Internet. You may find at times you are confronted with UNIX, this is particularly likely if you use Telnet or FTP. Here are some of the very basic commands that you may need to type in to get going with UNIX (UNIX is case sensitive so always use lowercase for everything):
Crash	The computer fails to work suddenly. It is virtually impossible for the entire Superhighway to crash at once even if one computer shuts down, the rest of the network stays up. You can no more break the Superhighway than you can the phone system. If something goes wrong, try again. If nothing at all happens, you can always disconnect. If the worst comes to worst, you can turn off your computer.
E:mail	This stands for electronic mail: the passing of messages from one person to another. The advantages of it are: speed, the ability to access databases, convenience, sending electronic files/programmes and it is very cheap. You need a computer programme on your PC to use it – this is usually provided with all the other Internet software you require by your provider.
POP	Point of Presence. The telephone number through which an Internet provider can be reached. This is the number you use to connect to the Internet. Internet providers aim to have many POPs in order to enable their customers to benefit from local rather than national telephone costs.

Domains	These are equivalent to area codes in a telephone system. In general, American addresses end in an organisational suffix, such as '.edu' (which means the site is at a college or university). Other American suffixes include:

> .com for businesses
> .org for non-profit organisations
> .gov and .mil for government and military agencies
> .net for companies or organisations that run large networks.

Sites in the rest of the world tend to use a two-letter code that represents their country. For example: .ca for Canadian sites; .ch for Swiss sites; .za for South Africa.

News groups	See Appendix 7
Finger	This is a utility that will allow you to get some more information about someone. If all you have is their e:mail address you can run the finger utility and assuming the owner of the e:mail address has enabled these requests you will receive back some information about them.
IRC	This stands for Internet Relay Chat, it is a program that lets you hold live keyboard conversations with people around the world. It's a lot like an international CB radio. When you type something on your computer and it is instantly sent around the world to whoever happens to be on the same channel with you.
MUD	This stands for Multiple-User Dimensions or Dungeons (MUDs) they are live, role-playing games where many people join from all over the world to play at the same time.
Viruses	By downloading files into your computer you are open to catching a computer virus. The best form of defence is never to connect to the Internet. The second best is to use, regularly, a virus checking program on your PC. This will scan through your PC files looking for evidence of files with viruses in them. If one is found the program will attempt to remove the problem files and minimise the damage to your system. A virus is a small program concealed inside a computer file, and once activated the consequences can range from nothing, to producing unexpected messages on the screen, right through to completely destroying all the information on your PC.

Appendix 7
News groups

News groups are an essential tool for the marketer. They represent discussions on particular topics and as such are a vital market segmentation tool. Used effectively they provide an ideal communication channel with your target audience.

News groups on the Internet are provided by the Usenet system. Unlike e:mail, which is usually 'one-to-one,' Usenet is 'many-to-many.' To many people, Usenet IS the Superhighway where over 100 million characters a day are entered into the system – nearly an encyclopedia's worth of writing. These are like conversations with a group of like minded individuals. It is similar to e:mail in style but, unlike e:mail which is one-to-one, it is one-to-many. Anyone can 'listen in' on the conversation and then make a comment. The comment is composed just like an e:mail and is 'posted' to the news group. The comment is then copied around the world, allowing everyone who is looking at the group to see your comment. A reply can either be sent privately to you via e:mail or publicly by adding a comment to the news group. The news group builds up to be a list of messages and by reading through them it allows you to follow a discussion made up from people posing a sequence of comments on the same subject.

Each group will have a style and culture of its own. Some are open to new comments, others it can be difficult to make a comment without eliciting a rude reply. The best way to understand the culture of a group is to spend some time acclimatising to the news group before making your first comments. If you see others asking seemingly well intentioned comments and getting a negative response adjust your comments to fit. However, the majority of busy groups welcome new contributors and it can be a very rewarding use of the Internet (see Chapter xx).

Usenet is made up of over 9,000 news groups (on other networks these are called conferences or forums). Each one is dedicated to a particular subject. The news groups distributed worldwide are divided into eight broad classifications. These are:

bionet	Research biology.
humanities	Professional and amateur topics in the arts and humanities.
bit.listserv	Conferences originating as Bitnet mailing lists.
biz	Business products and services.
comp	Topics of interest to both computer professionals and hobbyists, including topics in computer science, software source, and information on hardware and software systems.
misc	Groups addressing themes not easily classified under any of the other headings or which incorporate themes from multiple categories.
news	News about Usenet itself.
rec	Groups oriented towards the arts, hobbies and recreational activities.
sci	Science other than research biology. These discussions are meant to be marked by special and usually practical knowledge, relating to research in or application of the established sciences.
soc	Groups primarily addressing social issues and socializing, often ethnically related.
talk	Politics and related topics. These groups are largely debate-oriented and tend to feature long discussions without resolution and without appreciable amounts of generally useful information.
alt	Controversial or unusual topics; not carried by all sites.

In addition there may be local news groups such as:

uk	UK related topics.
pipex	Pipex (the access provided) related topics.

Clarinet

Usenet 'news groups' is not really the correct name, they are often not news but provide for discussions and questions. However there are several sources of news and sports on the Superhighway.

One of the largest is Clarinet, a company in Cupertino, Calf., that distributes wire-service news and columns.

249

Because Clarinet charges for its service, not all host systems carry its articles. Those that do carry them as Usenet groups starting with 'clari.'. Some of the areas covered include business news (clari.biz); general national and foreign news, politics (clari.news), sports (clari.sports); columns by Mike Royko, Miss Manners, and others (clari.feature); and NewsBytes computer and telecommunications reports (clari.nb). Clari news groups feature stories updated around the clock. There are even a couple of 'bulletin' news groups for breaking stories: clari.news.bulletin and clari.news.urgent. Clarinet also sets up new news groups for breaking stories such as major natural disasters and the like.

NEWS GROUP NETIQUETTE

This section[1] describes the Usenet culture and customs that have developed over time. The key to successful marketing with the Usenet news groups is to become adept at becoming 'part of the conversation'. The role you wish to play is up to you but here are some basic rules which will help you improve your performance.

Select your news groups carefully
When you post an article, think about the people you are trying to reach. Try to get the most appropriate audience for your message, not the widest.

Be familiar with the group you are posting to before you post! You shouldn't post to groups you do not read, or post to groups you've only read a few articles from – you may not be familiar with the on-going conventions and themes of the group. One normally does not join a conversation by just walking up and talking. Instead, you listen first and then join in if you have something pertinent to contribute.

Remember that the Usenet news group system is designed to allow readers to choose which messages they see, not to allow posters to choose sets of readers to target. When choosing which news group(s) to post in, ask yourself, 'Which news groups contain readers who would want to read my message' rather than 'Which news groups have readers to whom I want to send my message?'

---

[1]Based on the FAQ 'A Primer on How to Work With the Usenet Community' by Chuq Von Rospach

If your message is of interest to a limited geographic area (apartments, car sales, meetings, concerts, etc.), restrict the distribution of the message to your local area. Some areas have special news groups with geographical limitations, and the recent versions of the news software allow you to limit the distribution of material sent to world-wide news groups. Check with your system administrator to see what news groups are available and how to use them.

When you decide to post a message you will need to specify the news group in which it should be sent. However, sometimes you will feel the item should be discussed in more than one group. For example you may feel a question about vegetarian restaurants would be best discussed by participants in both rec.restaurants and rec.vegetarian. Cross-posting is a mechanism within the Usenet that allows this to be done. By sending one message but marking it for both groups you will be able to attract both audiences. The undesirable alternative would be to send two messages, one to each news group, this would result in someone who is registered to both groups seeing your message twice, using the cross posting they will only see it once.

Sending a message that is of no relevance to a news group will cause a lot of consternation. For example posting an advertisement for your services in an unrelated discussion group will do you more harm than good, even if your service is good your audience will see your act as destructive. The Usenet is a workable system only because people attempt to make it work. This is a central tenet of the majority who use the news groups to attempt to subvert the news classification scheme and filling up people's computers with your unwanted advertising is extremely anti-social.

Avoid spamming
Spamming, is the great news group 'crime'. Here you will send a message, of no direct relevance, to many news groups. The aim is to shove your message in front of as many people as possible, the result will be a PR disaster. Although there may seem no problem attracting the wrath of Usenet users, unfortunately the most zealous network of Usenet defenders are the systems operation personnel who manage the underlying computer systems. There is a well practised procedure that has been developed which can result in your connection to the Internet being ruined or cut off. The typical action taken is to send you so many e:mails your e:mail system fills up and you start to miss messages or your web-server is overloaded with automatic requests for information.

Never forget that the person on the other side is human

Because your interaction with the network is through a computer it is easy to forget that there are people 'out there'. Situations arise where emotions erupt into a verbal free-for-all that can lead to hurt feelings.

People all over the world are reading your words. Do not attack people if you cannot persuade them with your presentation of the facts. Screaming, cursing, and abusing others only serves to make people think less of you and less willing to help you when you need it.

If you are upset at something or someone, wait until you have had a chance to calm down and think about it. Hasty words create more problems than they solve. Try not to say anything to others you would not say to them in person in a room full of people.

Don't blame system administrator for their users' behaviour

Sometimes, you may find it necessary to write to a system administrator about something concerning their site or one of their users. No matter how steamed up you may be, be polite to the system administrator, he or she may not have any idea of what you are going to say, and may not have any part in the incidents involved. By being civil and temperate, you are more likely to obtain their courteous attention and assistance.

Never assume that a person is speaking for their organisation

Many people who post to Usenet do so from machines at their place of work. Despite that, never assume that the person is speaking for the organisation that they are posting their articles from (unless the person explicitly says so). Some people put explicit disclaimers to this effect in their messages, but this is a good general rule. If you find an article offensive, consider taking it up with the person directly, or ignoring it. Learn about 'kill files' in your news reader software, and other techniques for ignoring people whose postings you find offensive.

Be careful what you say about others

Please remember – you read netnews; so do as many as 3,000,000 other people. This group quite possibly includes your boss, your friend's boss and your girl friend's brother. Information posted on the net can come back to haunt you or the person you are talking about. Think twice before you post personal information about yourself or others.

Be brief

Say it succinctly and it will have a greater impact. Remember that the longer you make your article, the fewer people will bother to read it.

Your postings reflect upon you – be proud of them

Most people on Usenet will know you only by what you say and how well you say it. They may someday be your customers, co-workers or friends. Take some time to make sure each posting is something that will not embarrass you later. Minimise your spelling errors and make sure that the article is easy to read and understand. Much of how people judge you on the net is based on your writing.

Use descriptive titles

The subject line of an article is there to enable a person with a limited amount of time to decide whether or not to read your article. Tell people what the article is about before they read it. A title like 'Car for Sale' to rec.autos does not help as much as '66 MG Midget for sale: Beaverton OR.' Don't expect people to read your article to find out what it is about because many of them won't bother. Some sites truncate the length of the subject line to 40 characters so keep your subjects short and to the point.

Be careful with humour and sarcasm

Without the voice inflections and body language of personal communications, it is easy for a remark meant to be funny to be misinterpreted. Subtle humour tends to get lost, so take steps to make sure that people realise you are trying to be funny. Use smileys. No matter how broad the humour or satire, it is safer to remind people that you are being funny. But also be aware that quite frequently satire is posted without any explicit indications. If an article outrages you strongly, you should ask yourself if it just may have been unmarked satire. Several self-proclaimed connoisseurs refuse to use smiley faces, so take heed or you may make a temporary fool of yourself.

Please rotate messages with questionable content

You may see reference to 'rot13' and a very garbled looking message. This is an indication that the person sending the message has included something they think may offend. If you want to unscramble the message after reading the warnings about its contents your PC mail reader software should offer you the option to unscramble it. These can be quite effective at encouraging people to spend the time reading your message, just like the intriguing 'Don't press this' button.

Summarise what you are following up
When you are following up someone's article, please summarise the parts of the article to which you are responding. This allows readers to appreciate your comments rather than trying to remember what the original article said. It is also possible for your response to get to some sites before the original article. Summarisation is best done by including appropriate quotes from the original article. For example:

```
Yes I can help:

> How do I get a really good frying pan, my problem is the
>size is a big problem in my small boat.

My own company make a special range of pans just for small
boat owners. You can find out more on our web-site
http://www.boatpans.com …
```

The convention is to mark with a > quotes from the message you are replying to.

Do not include the entire article since it will irritate the people who have already seen it. Even if you are responding to the entire article, summarise only the major points you are discussing.

When summarising, summarise!
When you request information from the network, it is common courtesy to report your findings so that others can benefit as well. So if you asked a question and you got lots of personal replies, post a quick summary back to the news group. This is one of the best ways to get on the 'in-crowd'. The best way of doing this is to take all the responses that you received and edit them into a single article that is posted to the places where you originally posted your question. Take the time to strip headers, combine duplicate information, and write a short summary. Try to credit the information to the people that sent it to you, where possible.

Use mail, don't post a follow-up
One of the biggest problems we have on the network is that when someone asks a question, many people send out identical answers. When this happens, dozens of identical answers pour through the net. Mail your answer to the person and suggest that they summarise to the network.

This way the net will only see a single copy of the answers, no matter how many people answer the question. If you post a question, please remind people to send you the answers by mail and at least offer to summarize them to the network.

Read all follow-ups and don't repeat what has already been said
Before you submit a follow-up to a message, read the rest of the messages in the news group to see whether someone has already said what you want to say. If someone has, don't repeat it.

Be careful about copyrights and licenses
Once something is posted onto the network, it is in the public domain unless you own the appropriate rights (most notably, if you wrote the thing yourself) and you post it with a valid copyright notice; a court would have to decide the specifics and there are arguments for both sides of the issue. For all practical purposes, assume that you effectively give up the copyright if you don't put in a notice. When posting material to the network, keep in mind that if you post any material published under a copyright this could cause you or your company to be held liable for damages.

Cite appropriate references
If you are using facts to support a cause, state where they came from. Don't take someone else's ideas and use them as your own. You don't want someone pretending that your ideas are theirs; show them the same respect.

Don't overdo signatures
Signatures are nice, and many people can have a signature added to their postings automatically by placing it in a file call '.signature'. Don't overdo it. Signatures can tell the world something about you, but keep them short. A signature that is longer than the message itself is considered to be in bad taste. The main purpose of a signature is to help people locate you, not to tell your life story.

Limit line length and avoid control characters
Try to keep your text in a generic format. Many (if not most) of the people reading Usenet do so from 80 column terminals or from workstations with 80 column terminal windows. Try to keep your lines of text to less than 80 characters for optimal readability. If people quote

part of your article in a follow-up, short lines will probably show up better, too. You should also try to avoid the use of tabs, too, since they may also be interpreted differently on terminals other than your own.

Do not use Usenet as an advertising medium
Advertisements on Usenet are rarely appreciated. In general, the louder or more inappropriate the ad is, the more antagonism it will stir up. The accompanying posting 'Rules for posting to Usenet' has more on this in the section about 'Announcement of professional products or services'. Try the biz.* hierarchies instead.

HOW TO CREATE A NEW USENET NEWS GROUP

This section outlines how to create a new news group in the comp, news, sci, misc, soc, talk, rec areas. The alt area has a considerable less formal process but follows similar lines. The process will require help and there is a body of volunteers who can be contacted on group-mentors@amdahl.com They assist people who want to propose new groups with the formation and submission of a good proposal.

The basic process is as follows:

Step 1
A request for discussion on creation of a new news group should be posted to news.announce.newgroups, and all related groups.

Step 2
The name and charter of the proposed group and whether it will be moderated and by whom, will be determined during the discussion period. If there is no general agreement after 30 days, the discussion will stop. In order to proceed a new proposal must be submitted as Step 1.

Step 3 – The vote
The Usenet Volunteer Votetakers (UVV) are a group of neutral third-party vote-takers who currently handle vote gathering and counting for all news group proposals. The co-ordinators of the group can be reached

at uvv-contact@amdahl.com; contact them to arrange the handling of the vote.

The vote involves sending out a call for votes and for at least 21 days those who read the call will be able to vote. It is normal to set up two e:mail addresses – one for 'yes' and one for 'no' votes.

Step 4 – The result
After the voting is complete the results must be posted to news.announce.newgroups and any other relevant groups or mailing lists to which the original call for votes was posted. The tally should include a statement of which way each voter voted so that the results can be verified. Next you must wait five days and if there are no serious objections that might invalidate the vote, the results can be calculated.

A news group can be created if 100 more valid 'yes' votes are received than 'no' and at least two thirds of the total number of valid votes received are in favour of creation. The special control message can then be sent and the group started.

A proposal that fails should not then be discussed again for six months.

THE NEWS GROUPS

The categorisation is somewhat chaotic so you have to resort to scanning through all the groups in order to decide where you might find something of relevance. We have included a list of news groups that are circulated globally. We have only included the comp, news, sci, misc, soc, talk and rec groups. The other main group alt is considerably less formal although some of the groups are very busy and important there are far too many to list here. You will need to explore the alt group on-line in order to assess the worth of contributing to one of its groups. For a fuller list, see the web pages which accompany this Appendix.

An [M] indicates the group is moderated by someone.

News group	Description
alt.building.architecture	Building industry architecture.
alt.building.engineering	Building industry engineering.
alt.building.jobs	Building industry jobs.
alt.building.manufacturing	Building industry manufacturing.
alt.building.realestate	Real estate and the building industry.
alt.business.misc	All aspects of commerce
alt.business.accountability	Corporate accountability.
alt.business.franchise	Franchising discussions
alt.business.home.pc	For displaying PC home business plans and services.
alt.business.hospitality	Hotel, resort, tour and restaurant businesses.
alt.business.import-export	Business aspects of international trade.
alt.business.import-export.consumables	Import and export of consumable products
alt.business.internal-audit	Discussion of internal auditing.
alt.business.multi-level	Multi-Level Marketing is NOT Pyramid Sales, honest!...
alt.business.seminars	Discussion and announcements of business seminars.
alt.cad	Computer Aided Design.
alt.cad.cadkey	Cadkey, Datacad, and other Cadkey, Inc. products.
alt.calc-reform	Making hardened calcium a productive member of society.
alt.california	The state and the state of mind.
alt.christnet	Equal time.
alt.co-ops	Discussion about co-operatives.
alt.cooking-chat	Food, wine and recipe discussions
comp.admin.policy	Discussions of site administration policies.
comp.ai	Artificial intelligence discussions.
comp.ai.alife	Research about artificial life.
comp.ai.doc-analysis.misc	General document understanding technologies.
comp.ai.doc-analysis.ocr	OCR research, algorithms and software.
comp.ai.fuzzy	Fuzzy set theory, aka fuzzy logic.
comp.ai.games	Artificial intelligence in games and game-playing.
comp.ai.genetic	Genetic algorithms in computing.
comp.ai.jair.announce	Announcements and abstracts of the Journal of AI Research. M
comp.ai.jair.papers	Papers published by the Journal of AI Research. M
comp.ai.nat-lang	Natural language processing by computers.
comp.ai.neural-nets	All aspects of neural networks.
comp.ai.nlang-know-rep	Natural Language and Knowledge Representation. M
comp.ai.philosophy	Philosophical aspects of Artificial Intelligence.
comp.ai.shells	Expert systems and other artificial intelligence shells.

comp.answers	Repository for periodic USENET articles. M
comp.apps.spreadsheets	Spreadsheets on various platforms.
comp.arch	Computer architecture.
comp.arch.arithmetic	Implementing arithmetic on computers/digital systems.
comp.arch.bus.vmebus	Hardware and software for VMEbus Systems.
comp.arch.embedded	Embedded computer systems topics.
comp.arch.fpga	Field Programmable Gate Array based computing systems.
comp.arch.storage	Storage system issues, both hardware and software.
comp.archives	Descriptions of public access archives. M
comp.archives.admin	Issues relating to computer archive administration.
comp.archives.msdos.announce	Announcements about MSDOS archives. M
comp.archives.msdos.d	Discussion of materials available in MSDOS archives.
comp.bbs.majorbbs	Support and discussion of The Major BBS from Galacticomm.
comp.bbs.misc	All aspects of computer bulletin board systems.
comp.bbs.tbbs	The Bread Board System bulletin board software.
comp.bbs.waffle	The Waffle BBS and USENET system on all platforms.
comp.benchmarks	Discussion of benchmarking techniques and results.
comp.binaries.acorn	Binary-only postings for Acorn machines. M
comp.binaries.amiga	Encoded public domain programs in binary. M
comp.binaries.apple2	Binary-only postings for the Apple II computer.
comp.binaries.atari.st	Binary-only postings for the Atari ST. M
comp.binaries.cbm	For the transfer of 8bit Commodore binaries. M
comp.binaries.geos	Binaries for the GEOS operating system. M
comp.binaries.ibm.pc	Binary-only postings for IBM PC/MS-DOS. M
comp.binaries.ibm.pc.d	Discussions about IBM/PC binary postings.
comp.binaries.ibm.pc.wanted	Requests for IBM PC and compatible programs.
comp.binaries.mac	Encoded Macintosh programs in binary. M
comp.binaries.ms-windows	Binary programs for Microsoft Windows. M
comp.binaries.newton	Apple Newton binaries, sources, books, etc. M
comp.binaries.os2	Binaries for use under the OS/2 ABI. M
comp.binaries.psion	Binaries for the range of Psion computers. M
comp.bugs.2bsd	Reports of UNIX* version 2BSD related bugs.
comp.bugs.4bsd	Reports of UNIX version 4BSD related bugs.
comp.bugs.4bsd.ucb-fixes	Bug reports/fixes for BSD Unix. M
comp.bugs.misc	General UNIX bug reports and fixes (incl V7, uucp).
comp.bugs.sys5	Reports of USG (System III, V, etc.) bugs.
comp.cad.autocad	AutoDesk's AutoCAD software.

comp.cad.cadence	Users of Cadence Design Systems products.
comp.cad.compass	Compass Design Automation EDA tools.
comp.cad.i-deas	SDRC I-DEAS Masters Series software.
comp.cad.microstation	MicroStation CAD software and related products.
comp.cad.pro-engineer	Parametric Technology's Pro/Engineer design package.
comp.cad.synthesis	Research and production in the field of logic synthesis.
comp.client-server	Topics relating to client/server technology.
comp.cog-eng	Cognitive engineering.
comp.compilers	Compiler construction, theory, etc. M
comp.compilers.tools.pccts	Construction of compilers and tools with PCCTS.
comp.compression	Data compression algorithms and theory.
comp.compression.research	Discussions about data compression research. M
comp.constraints	Constraint processing and related topics.
comp.databases	Database and data management issues and theory.
comp.databases.gupta	Gupta SQLWindows client-server development.
comp.databases.ibm-db2	Problem resolution with DB2 database products.
comp.databases.informix	Informix database management software discussions.
comp.databases.ingres	Issues relating to INGRES products.
comp.databases.ms-access	MS Windows' relational database system, Access.
comp.databases.object	Object-oriented paradigms in database systems.
comp.databases.olap	Analytical Processing, Multidimensional DBMS, EIS, DSS.
comp.databases.oracle	The SQL database products of the Oracle Corporation.
comp.databases.paradox	Borland's database for DOS and MS Windows.
comp.databases.pick	Pick-like, post-relational, database systems.
comp.databases.progress	The Progress 4GL and RDBMS.
comp.databases.rdb	The relational database engine RDB from DEC.
comp.databases.sybase	Implementations of the SQL Server.
comp.databases.theory	Discussing advances in database technology.
comp.databases.xbase.fox	Fox Software's xBase system and compatibles.
comp.databases.xbase.misc	Discussion of xBase (dBASE-like) products.
comp.dcom.cabling	Cabling selection, installation and use.
comp.dcom.cell-relay	Forum for discussion of Cell Relay-based products.
comp.dcom.fax	Fax hardware, software, and protocols.
comp.dcom.frame-relay	Technology and issues regarding frame relay networks.
comp.dcom.isdn	The Integrated Services Digital Network (ISDN).
comp.dcom.lans.ethernet	Discussions of the Ethernet/IEEE 802.3 protocols.

comp.dcom.lans.fddi	Discussions of the FDDI protocol suite.
comp.dcom.lans.misc	Local area network hardware and software.
comp.dcom.lans.token-ring	Installing and using token ring networks.
comp.dcom.modems	Data communications hardware and software.
comp.dcom.net-management	Network management methods and applications.
comp.dcom.servers	Selecting and operating data communications servers.
comp.dcom.sys.cisco	Info on Cisco routers and bridges.
comp.dcom.sys.wellfleet	Wellfleet bridge and router systems hardware and software.
comp.dcom.telecom	Telecommunications digest. M
comp.dcom.telecom.tech	Discussion of technical aspects of telephony.
comp.dcom.videoconf	Video conference technology and applications.
comp.doc	Archived public-domain documentation. M
comp.doc.techreports	Lists of technical reports. M
comp.dsp	Digital Signal Processing using computers.
comp.edu	Computer science education.
comp.edu.languages.natural	Computer assisted languages instruction issues.
comp.emacs	EMACS editors of different flavours.
comp.emacs.xemacs	Bug reports, questions and answers about XEmacs.
comp.emulators.announce	Emulator news, FAQs, announcements. M
comp.emulators.apple2	Emulators of Apple // systems.
comp.emulators.cbm	Emulators of C-64, C-128, PET, and VIC-20 systems.
comp.emulators.misc	Emulators of miscellaneous computer systems.
comp.emulators.ms-windows.wine	A free MS-Windows emulator under X.
comp.fonts	Typefonts – design, conversion, use, etc.
comp.graphics.algorithms	Algorithms used in producing computer graphics.
comp.graphics.animation	Technical aspects of computer animation.
comp.graphics.api.inventor	Object-oriented 3D graphics in Inventor.
comp.graphics.api.misc	Application Programmer Interface issues, methods.
comp.graphics.api.opengl	The OpenGL 3D application programming interface.
comp.graphics.api.pexlib	The PEXlib application programming interface.
comp.graphics.apps.alias	3-D graphics software from Alias Research.
comp.graphics.apps.avs	The Application Visualization System.
comp.graphics.apps.data-explorer	IBM's Visualization Data Explorer (DX).
comp.graphics.apps.gnuplot	The gnuplot interactive function plotter.
comp.graphics.apps.iris-explorer	The IRIS Explorer, aka MVE.
comp.graphics.apps.lightwave	NewTek's Lightwave3D and related topics.
comp.graphics.apps.pagemaker	Question, answers, tips and suggestions.
comp.graphics.apps.photoshop	Adobe Photoshop techniques and help.
comp.graphics.apps.softimage	Softimage applications and products.
comp.graphics.apps.wavefront	Wavefront software products, problems, etc.
comp.graphics.misc	Computer graphics miscellany.

comp.graphics.packages.3dstudio	Autodesk's 3D Studio software.
comp.graphics.rendering.misc	Rendering comparisons, approaches, methods.
comp.graphics.rendering.raytracing	Raytracing software, tools and methods.
comp.graphics.rendering.renderman	RenderMan interface and shading language.
comp.graphics.visualization	Info on scientific visualization.
comp.groupware	Software and hardware for shared interactive environments.
comp.groupware.lotus-notes.misc	Lotus Notes related discussions.
comp.home.automation	Home automation devices, setup, sources, etc.
comp.home.misc	Media, technology and information in domestic spaces. M
comp.human-factors	Issues related to human-computer interaction (HCI).
comp.infosystems	Any discussion about information systems.
comp.infosystems.announce	Announcements of internet information services. M
comp.infosystems.gis	All aspects of Geographic Information Systems.
comp.infosystems.gopher	Discussion of the Gopher information service.
comp.infosystems.harvest	Harvest information discovery and access system.
comp.infosystems.interpedia	The Internet Encyclopedia.
comp.infosystems.kiosks	Informational and transactional kiosks. M
comp.infosystems.wais	The Z39.50-based WAIS full-text search system.
comp.infosystems.www.advocacy	Comments and arguments over the best and worst.
comp.infosystems.www.announce	World-Wide Web announcements. M
comp.infosystems.www.authoring.cgi	Writing CGI scripts for the Web.
comp.infosystems.www.authoring.html	Writing HTML for the Web.
comp.infosystems.www.authoring.images	Using images, imagemaps on the Web.
comp.infosystems.www.authoring.misc	Miscellaneous Web authoring issues.
comp.infosystems.www.browsers.mac	Web browsers for the Macintosh platform.
comp.infosystems.www.browsers.misc	Web browsers for other platforms.
comp.infosystems.www.browsers.ms-windows	Web browsers for MS Windows.
comp.infosystems.www.browsers.x	Web browsers for the X-Window system.
comp.infosystems.www.misc	Miscellaneous World wide web discussion.
comp.infosystems.www.servers.mac	Web-servers for the Macintosh platform.
comp.infosystems.www.servers.misc	Web-servers for other platforms.
comp.infosystems.www.servers.ms-windows	Web-servers for MS Windows and NT.
comp.infosystems.www.servers.unix	Web-servers for UNIX platforms.
comp.internet.library	Discussing electronic libraries. M
comp.internet.net-happenings	Announcements of network happenings. M

comp.ivideodisc	Interactive videodiscs – uses, potential, etc.
comp.lang.ada	Discussion about Ada*.
comp.lang.apl	Discussion about APL.
comp.lang.asm.x86	General 80x86 assembly language programming.
comp.lang.awk	The AWK programming language.
comp.lang.basic.misc	Other dialects and aspects of BASIC.
comp.lang.basic.visual	3rd party Add-ins for Visual Basic.
comp.lang.basic.visual.announce	Official information on Visual Basic. M
comp.lang.basic.visual.database	Database aspects of Visual Basic.
comp.lang.basic.visual.misc	Visual Basic in general.
comp.lang.beta	The object-oriented programming language BETA.
comp.lang.c	Discussion about C.
comp.lang.c++	The object-oriented C++ language.
comp.lang.c++.leda	All aspects of the LEDA library.
comp.lang.c.moderated	The C programming language. M
comp.lang.clipper	Clipper and Visual Objects programming languages.
comp.lang.clos	Common Lisp Object System discussions.
comp.lang.cobol	The COBOL language and software.
comp.lang.dylan	For discussion of the Dylan language.
comp.lang.eiffel	The object-oriented Eiffel language.
comp.lang.forth	Discussion about Forth.
comp.lang.fortran	Discussion about FORTRAN.
comp.lang.functional	Discussion about functional languages.
comp.lang.hermes	The Hermes language for distributed applications.
comp.lang.idl-pvwave	IDL and PV-Wave language discussions.
comp.lang.lisp	Discussion about LISP.
comp.lang.lisp.mcl	Discussing Apple Macintosh Common Lisp.
comp.lang.logo	The Logo teaching and learning language.
comp.lang.misc	Different computer languages not specifically listed.
comp.lang.ml	ML languages including Standard ML, CAML, Lazy ML, etc. M
comp.lang.modula2	Discussion about Modula-2.
comp.lang.modula3	Discussion about the Modula-3 language.
comp.lang.mumps	The M (MUMPS) language and technology, in general.
comp.lang.oberon	The Oberon language and system.
comp.lang.objective-c	The Objective-C language and environment.
comp.lang.pascal.ansi-iso	Pascal according to ANSI and ISO standards.
comp.lang.pascal.borland	Borland's Pascal.
comp.lang.pascal.delphi.components	Writing components in Borland Delphi.
comp.lang.pascal.delphi.databases	Database aspects of Borland Delphi.
comp.lang.pascal.delphi.misc	General issues with Borland Delphi.
comp.lang.pascal.mac	Macintosh based Pascals.

comp.lang.pascal.misc	Pascal in general and ungrouped Pascals.
comp.lang.perl.announce	Announcements about Perl. M
comp.lang.perl.misc	The Perl language in general.
comp.lang.pop	Pop11 and the Plug user group.
comp.lang.postscript	The PostScript Page Description Language.
comp.lang.prograph	Prograph, a visual object-oriented dataflow language.
comp.lang.prolog	Discussion about PROLOG.
comp.lang.python	The Python computer language.
comp.lang.sather	The object-oriented computer language Sather.
comp.lang.scheme	The Scheme Programming language.
comp.lang.sigplan	Info and announcements from ACM SIGPLAN. M
comp.lang.smalltalk	Discussion about Smalltalk 80.
comp.lang.tcl	The Tcl programming language and related tools.
comp.lang.verilog	Discussing Verilog and PLI.
comp.lang.vhdl	VHSIC Hardware Description Language, IEEE 1076/87.
comp.lang.visual	General discussion of visual programming languages. M
comp.laser-printers	Laser printers, hardware and software. M
comp.lsi	Large scale integrated circuits.
comp.lsi.testing	Testing of electronic circuits.
comp.mail.elm	Discussion and fixes for the ELM mail system.
comp.mail.headers	Gatewayed from the Internet header-people list.
comp.mail.list-admin.policy	Policy issues in running mailing lists.
comp.mail.list-admin.software	Software used in the running of mailing lists.
comp.mail.maps	Various maps, including UUCP maps. M
comp.mail.mh	The UCI version of the Rand Message Handling system.
comp.mail.mime	Multipurpose Internet Mail Extensions of RFC 1341.
comp.mail.misc	General discussions about computer mail.
comp.mail.mush	The Mail User's Shell (MUSuperhighway).
comp.mail.pine	The PINE mail user agent.
comp.mail.sendmail	Configuring and using the BSD sendmail agent.
comp.mail.smail	Administering and using the smail email transport system.
comp.mail.uucp	Mail in the uucp network environment.
comp.mail.zmail	The various Z-Mail products and their configurability.
comp.misc	General topics about computers not covered elsewhere.
comp.multimedia	Interactive multimedia technologies of all kinds.
comp.newprod	Announcements of new products of interest. M
comp.object	Object-oriented programming and languages.

comp.object.logic	Integrating object-oriented and logic programming.
comp.org.acm	Topics about the Association for Computing Machinery.
comp.org.cpsr.announce	Computer Professionals for Social Responsibility.
comp.org.cpsr.talk	Issues of computing and social responsibility. M
comp.org.decus	Digital Equipment Computer Users' Society news group.
comp.org.eff.news	News from the Electronic Frontier Foundation. M
comp.org.eff.talk	Discussion of EFF goals, strategies, etc.
comp.org.fidonet	FidoNews digest, official news of FidoNet Assoc. M
comp.org.ieee	Issues and announcements about the IEEE and its members.
comp.org.issnnet	The International Student Society for Neural Networks.
comp.org.lisp-users	Association of Lisp Users related discussions.
comp.org.sug	Talk about/for the The Sun User's Group.
comp.org.uniforum	UniForum Association activities.
comp.org.usenix	USENIX Association events and announcements.
comp.org.usenix.roomshare	Finding lodging during Usenix conferences.
comp.os.chorus	CHORUS microkernel issues, research and developments.
comp.os.coherent	Discussion and support of the Coherent operating system.
comp.os.cpm	Discussion about the CP/M operating system.
comp.os.geos	The GEOS operating system by GeoWorks for PC clones.
comp.os.linux.advocacy	Benefits of Linux compared to other operating systems.
comp.os.linux.announce	Announcements important to the Linux community. M
comp.os.linux.answers	FAQs, How-To's, READMEs, etc. about Linux. M
comp.os.linux.development.apps	Writing Linux applications, porting to Linux.
comp.os.linux.development.system	Linux kernels, device drivers, modules.
comp.os.linux.hardware	Hardware compatibility with the Linux operating system.
comp.os.linux.misc	Linux-specific topics not covered by other groups.
comp.os.linux.networking	Networking and communications under Linux.
comp.os.linux.setup	Linux installation and system administration.
comp.os.linux.x	Linux X Window System servers, clients, libs and fonts.
comp.os.lynx	Discussion of LynxOS and Lynx Real-Time Systems.

comp.os.mach	The MACH OS from CMU and other places.
comp.os.magic-cap	Everything about General Magic's Magic Cap OS.
comp.os.minix	Discussion of Tanenbaum's MINIX system.
comp.os.misc	General OS-oriented discussion not carried elsewhere.
comp.os.ms-windows.advocacy	Speculation and debate about Microsoft Windows.
comp.os.ms-windows.announce	Announcements relating to Windows. M
comp.os.ms-windows.apps.comm	MS-Windows communication applications.
comp.os.ms-windows.apps.financial	MS-Windows financial and tax software.
comp.os.ms-windows.apps.misc	MS-Windows applications.
comp.os.ms-windows.apps.utilities	MS-Windows utilities.
comp.os.ms-windows.apps.winsock.mail	Winsock e:mail applications.
comp.os.ms-windows.apps.winsock.misc	Other Winsock applications.
comp.os.ms-windows.apps.winsock.news	Winsock news applications.
comp.os.ms-windows.apps.word-proc	MS-Windows word-processing applications.
comp.os.ms-windows.misc	General discussions about Windows issues.
comp.os.ms-windows.networking.misc	Windows and other networks.
comp.os.ms-windows.networking.ras	Windows RAS networking.
comp.os.ms-windows.networking.tcp-ip	Windows and TCP/IP networking.
comp.os.ms-windows.networking.windows	Windows' built-in networking.
comp.os.ms-windows.nt.admin.misc	Windows NT system administration.
comp.os.ms-windows.nt.admin.networking	Windows NT network administration.
comp.os.ms-windows.nt.advocacy	Windows NT advocacy arguments.
comp.os.ms-windows.nt.misc	General discussion about Windows NT.
comp.os.ms-windows.nt.pre-release	Unreleased and beta Windows NT versions.
comp.os.ms-windows.nt.setup	Configuring Windows NT systems.
comp.os.ms-windows.nt.setup.hardware	Windows NT hardware setup.
comp.os.ms-windows.nt.setup.misc	Windows NT software setup.
comp.os.ms-windows.nt.software.backoffice	Windows NT BackOffice.
comp.os.ms-windows.nt.software.compatibility	Win NT software compatibility.
comp.os.ms-windows.nt.software.services	Windows NT system services software.
comp.os.ms-windows.pre-release	Pre-release/beta versions of Windows.
comp.os.ms-windows.programmer.controls	Controls, dialogs and VBXs.
comp.os.ms-windows.programmer.drivers	Drivers and VxDs – no driver requests!
comp.os.ms-windows.programmer.graphics	GDI, graphics and printing.
comp.os.ms-windows.programmer.memory	Memory management issues.
comp.os.ms-windows.programmer.misc	Programming Microsoft Windows.
comp.os.ms-windows.programmer.multimedia	Multimedia programming.
comp.os.ms-windows.programmer.networks	Network programming.

comp.os.ms-windows.programmer.nt.kernel-mode	Windows NT driver development.
comp.os.ms-windows.programmer.ole	OLE2, COM and DDE programming.
comp.os.ms-windows.programmer.tools	Development tools in Windows.
comp.os.ms-windows.programmer.tools.mfc	MFC-based development for Windows.
comp.os.ms-windows.programmer.tools.misc	Windows Development tools.
comp.os.ms-windows.programmer.tools.owl	OWL-based development for Windows.
comp.os.ms-windows.programmer.tools.winsock	Winsock programming.
comp.os.ms-windows.programmer.vxd	Windows VxD and driver development.
comp.os.ms-windows.programmer.win32	32-bit Windows programming interfaces.
comp.os.ms-windows.programmer.winhelp	WinHelp/Multimedia Viewer development.
comp.os.ms-windows.setup	Installing and configuring Microsoft Windows.
comp.os.ms-windows.video	Video adapters and drivers for Windows.
comp.os.ms-windows.win95.misc	Miscellaneous Topics about Windows 95.
comp.os.ms-windows.win95.setup	Setup and Configuration of Windows 95.
comp.os.msdos.apps	Discussion of applications that run under MS-DOS.
comp.os.msdos.desqview	QuarterDeck's Desqview and related products.
comp.os.msdos.djgpp	DOS GNU C/C++ applications and programming environment.
comp.os.msdos.mail-news	Administering mail and network news systems under MS-DOS.
comp.os.msdos.misc	Miscellaneous topics about MS-DOS machines.
comp.os.msdos.pcgeos	GeoWorks PC/GEOS and PC/GEOS-based packages.
comp.os.msdos.programmer	Programming MS-DOS machines.
comp.os.msdos.programmer.turbovision	Borland's text application libraries.
comp.os.netware.announce	Netware announcements. ᴹ
comp.os.netware.connectivity	Connectivity products (TCP/IP, SAA, NFS, MAC).
comp.os.netware.misc	General Netware topics.
comp.os.netware.security	Netware Security issues.
comp.os.os2.advocacy	Supporting and flaming OS/2.
comp.os.os2.announce	Notable news and announcements related to OS/2. ᴹ
comp.os.os2.apps	Discussions of applications under OS/2.
comp.os.os2.beta	All aspects of beta releases of OS/2 systems software.
comp.os.os2.bugs	OS/2 system bug reports, fixes and work-arounds.
comp.os.os2.comm	Modem/Fax hardware/drivers/apps/utils under OS/2.
comp.os.os2.games	Running games under OS/2.
comp.os.os2.mail-news	Mail and news apps/utils (on- and off-line) under OS/2.

comp.os.os2.marketplace	For sale/wanted; shopping; commercial ads; job postings.
comp.os.os2.misc	Miscellaneous topics about the OS/2 system.
comp.os.os2.multimedia	Multi-media on OS/2 systems.
comp.os.os2.networking.misc	Miscellaneous networking issues of OS/2.
comp.os.os2.networking.tcp-ip	TCP/IP under OS/2.
comp.os.os2.networking.www	World wide web (WWW) apps/utils under OS/2.
comp.os.os2.programmer.misc	Programming OS/2 machines.
comp.os.os2.programmer.oop	Programming system objects (SOM, WPS, etc).
comp.os.os2.programmer.porting	Porting software to OS/2 machines.
comp.os.os2.programmer.tools	Compilers, assemblers, interpreters under OS/2.
comp.os.os2.setup.misc	Installing/configuring OS/2; misc. hardware/drivers.
comp.os.os2.setup.storage	Disk/Tape/CD-ROM hardware/drivers under OS/2.
comp.os.os2.setup.video	Base video hardware/drivers under OS/2.
comp.os.os2.utilities	General purpose utils (shells/backup/compression/etc).
comp.os.os9	Discussions about the os9 operating system.
comp.os.parix	Forum for users of the parallel operating system PARIX.
comp.os.plan9	Plan 9 from Bell Labs. [M]
comp.os.qnx	Using and developing under the QNX operating system.
comp.os.research	Operating systems and related areas. [M]
comp.os.vms	DEC's VAX* line of computers and VMS.
comp.os.vxworks	The VxWorks real-time operating system.
comp.os.xinu	The XINU operating system from Purdue (D. Comer).
comp.parallel	Massively parallel hardware/software. [M]
comp.parallel.mpi	Message Passing Interface (MPI).
comp.parallel.pvm	The PVM system of multi-computer parallelisation.
comp.patents	Discussing patents of computer technology. [M]
comp.periphs	Peripheral devices.
comp.periphs.scsi	Discussion of SCSI-based peripheral devices.
comp.programming	Programming issues that transcend languages and OSs.
comp.programming.contests	Announcements and results of programming contests.
comp.programming.literate	Knuth's 'literate programming' method and tools.
comp.protocols.appletalk	Applebus hardware and software.
comp.protocols.dicom	Digital Imaging and Communications in Medicine.
comp.protocols.ibm	Networking with IBM mainframes.
comp.protocols.iso	The ISO protocol stack.

comp.protocols.kerberos	The Kerberos authentication server.
comp.protocols.kermit.announce	Kermit announcements. M
comp.protocols.kermit.misc	Kermit protocol and software.
comp.protocols.misc	Various forms and types of protocol.
comp.protocols.nfs	Discussion about the Network File System protocol.
comp.protocols.ppp	Discussion of the Internet Point to Point Protocol.
comp.protocols.smb	SMB file sharing protocol and Samba SMB server/client.
comp.protocols.tcp-ip	TCP and IP network protocols.
comp.protocols.tcp-ip.ibmpc	TCP/IP for IBM(-like) personal computers.
comp.publish.cdrom.hardware	Hardware used in publishing with CD-ROM.
comp.publish.cdrom.multimedia	Software for multimedia authoring and publishing.
comp.publish.cdrom.software	Software used in publishing with CD-ROM.
comp.publish.electronic.developer	Electronic publishing developer tools.
comp.publish.electronic.end-user	Electronic publishing end-user tools.
comp.publish.electronic.misc	General electronic publishing issues.
comp.publish.prepress	Electronic prepress.
comp.realtime	Issues related to real-time computing.
comp.research.japan	The nature of research in Japan. M
comp.risks	Risks to the public from computers and users. M
comp.robotics.misc	All aspects of robots and their applications.
comp.robotics.research	Academic, government and industry research in robotics. M
comp.security.firewalls	Anything pertaining to network firewall security.
comp.security.misc	Security issues of computers and networks.
comp.security.unix	Discussion of Unix security.
comp.simulation	Simulation methods, problems, uses. M
comp.society	The impact of technology on society. M
comp.society.cu-digest	The Computer Underground Digest. M
comp.society.development	Computer technology in developing countries.
comp.society.folklore	Computer folklore and culture, past and present. M
comp.society.futures	Events in technology affecting future computing.
comp.society.privacy	Effects of technology on privacy. M
comp.soft-sys.app-builder.appware	Novell's visual development environment.
comp.soft-sys.app-builder.uniface	Uniface Client/Server App Development.
comp.soft-sys.dce	The Distributed Computing Environment (DCE).
comp.soft-sys.khoros	The Khoros X11 visualisation system.
comp.soft-sys.math.mathematica	Mathematical discussion group. M
comp.soft-sys.matlab	The MathWorks calculation and visualization package.
comp.soft-sys.powerbuilder	Application development tools from PowerSoft.
comp.soft-sys.ptolemy	The Ptolemy simulation/code generation environment.

comp.soft-sys.sas	The SAS statistics package.
comp.soft-sys.shazam	The SuperhighwayAZAM econometrics computer program.
comp.soft-sys.spss	The SPSS statistics package.
comp.software-eng	Software Engineering and related topics.
comp.software.config-mgmt	Configuration management, tools and procedures.
comp.software.international	Finding, using, and writing non-English software.
comp.software.licensing	Software licensing technology.
comp.software.testing	All aspects of testing computer systems.
comp.sources.3b1	Source code-only postings for the ATandT 3b1. M
comp.sources.acorn	Source code-only postings for the Acorn. M
comp.sources.amiga	Source code-only postings for the Amiga. M
comp.sources.apple2	Source code and discussion for the Apple2. M
comp.sources.atari.st	Source code-only postings for the Atari ST. M
comp.sources.bugs	Bug reports, fixes, discussion for posted sources.
comp.sources.d	For any discussion of source postings.
comp.sources.games	Postings of recreational software. M
comp.sources.games.bugs	Bug reports and fixes for posted game software.
comp.sources.hp48	Programs for the HP48 and HP28 calculators. M
comp.sources.mac	Software for the Apple Macintosh. M
comp.sources.misc	Posting of software. M
comp.sources.postscript	Source code for programs written in PostScript. M
comp.sources.reviewed	Source code evaluated by peer review. M
comp.sources.sun	Software for Sun workstations. M
comp.sources.testers	Finding people to test software.
comp.sources.unix	Postings of complete, UNIX-oriented sources. M
comp.sources.wanted	Requests for software and fixes.
comp.sources.x	Software for the X Window System. M
comp.specification.larch	Larch family of formal specification languages.
comp.specification.misc	Formal specification methods in general.
comp.specification.z	Discussion about the formal specification notation Z.
comp.speech	Research and applications in speech science and technology.
comp.std.c	Discussion about C language standards.
comp.std.c++	Discussion about C++ language, library, standards. M
comp.std.internat	Discussion about international standards.
comp.std.lisp	User group (ALU) supported standards. M
comp.std.misc	Discussion about various standards.
comp.std.mumps	Discussions about Mumps standards. M
comp.std.unix	Discussion for the P1003 committee on UNIX. M
comp.std.wireless	Examining standards for wireless network technology. M
comp.sw.components	Software components and related technology.
comp.sys.3b1	Discussion and support of ATandT 7300/3B1/UnixPC.

comp.sys.acorn.advocacy	Why Acorn computers and programs are better.
comp.sys.acorn.announce	Announcements for Acorn and ARM users. M
comp.sys.acorn.apps	Acorn software applications.
comp.sys.acorn.games	Discussion of games for Acorn machines.
comp.sys.acorn.hardware	Acorn hardware.
comp.sys.acorn.misc	Acorn computing in general.
comp.sys.acorn.networking	Networking of Acorn computers.
comp.sys.acorn.programmer	Programming of Acorn computers.
comp.sys.alliant	Info and discussion about Alliant computers.
comp.sys.amiga.advocacy	Why an Amiga is better than XYZ.
comp.sys.amiga.announce	Announcements about the Amiga. M
comp.sys.amiga.applications	Miscellaneous applications.
comp.sys.amiga.audio	Music, MIDI, speech synthesis, other sounds.
comp.sys.amiga.cd32	Technical and computing talk for Commodore Amiga CD32.
comp.sys.amiga.datacomm	Methods of getting bytes in and out.
comp.sys.amiga.emulations	Various hardware and software emulators.
comp.sys.amiga.games	Discussion of games for the Commodore Amiga.
comp.sys.amiga.graphics	Charts, graphs, pictures, etc.
comp.sys.amiga.hardware	Amiga computer hardware, QandA, reviews, etc.
comp.sys.amiga.introduction	Group for newcomers to Amigas.
comp.sys.amiga.marketplace	Where to find it, prices, etc.
comp.sys.amiga.misc	Discussions not falling in another Amiga group.
comp.sys.amiga.multimedia	Animations, video, and multimedia.
comp.sys.amiga.networking	Amiga networking software/hardware.
comp.sys.amiga.programmer	Developers and hobbyists discuss code.
comp.sys.amiga.reviews	Reviews of Amiga software, hardware. M
comp.sys.amiga.uucp	Amiga UUCP packages.
comp.sys.amstrad.8bit	Amstrad CPC/PcW/GX4000 software/hardware.
comp.sys.apollo	Apollo computer systems.
comp.sys.apple2	Discussion about Apple II micros.
comp.sys.apple2.comm	Apple II data communications.
comp.sys.apple2.gno	The AppleIIgs GNO multitasking environment.
comp.sys.apple2.marketplace	Buying, selling and trading Apple II equipment.
comp.sys.apple2.programmer	Programming on the Apple II.
comp.sys.apple2.usergroups	All about Apple II user groups.
comp.sys.arm	The ARM processor architecture and support chips.
comp.sys.atari.8bit	Discussion about 8 bit Atari micros.
comp.sys.atari.advocacy	Attacking and defending Atari computers.
comp.sys.atari.announce	Atari related hard/software announcements. M
comp.sys.atari.programmer	Programming on the Atari computer.
comp.sys.atari.st	Discussion about 16 bit Atari micros.
comp.sys.atari.st.tech	Technical discussions of Atari ST hard/software.
comp.sys.att	Discussions about ATandT microcomputers.
comp.sys.cbm	Discussion about Commodore micros.
comp.sys.concurrent	The Concurrent/Masscomp line of computers. M

comp.sys.convex	Convex computer systems hardware and software.
comp.sys.dec	Discussions about DEC computer systems.
comp.sys.dec.micro	DEC Micros (Rainbow, Professional 350/380).
comp.sys.encore	Encore's MultiMax computers.
comp.sys.harris	Harris computer systems, especially real-time systems.
comp.sys.hp.apps	Discussion of software and apps on all HP platforms.
comp.sys.hp.hardware	Discussion of Hewlett Packard system hardware.
comp.sys.hp.hpux	Issues pertaining to HP-UX and 9000 series computers.
comp.sys.hp.misc	Issues not covered in any other comp.sys.hp.* group.
comp.sys.hp.mpe	Issues pertaining to MPE and 3000 series computers.
comp.sys.hp48	Hewlett-Packard's HP48 and HP28 calculators.
comp.sys.ibm.pc.demos	Demonstration programs which showcase programmer skill.
comp.sys.ibm.pc.digest	The IBM PC, PC-XT, and PC-AT. ᴹ
comp.sys.ibm.pc.games.action	Arcade-style games on PCs.
comp.sys.ibm.pc.games.adventure	Adventure (non-rpg) games on PCs.
comp.sys.ibm.pc.games.announce	Announcements for all PC gamers. ᴹ
comp.sys.ibm.pc.games.flight-sim	Flight simulators on PCs.
comp.sys.ibm.pc.games.marketplace	PC clone games wanted and for sale.
comp.sys.ibm.pc.games.misc	Games not covered by other PC groups.
comp.sys.ibm.pc.games.rpg	Role-playing games on the PC.
comp.sys.ibm.pc.games.strategic	Strategy/planning games on PCs.
comp.sys.ibm.pc.hardware.cd-rom	CD-ROM drives and interfaces for the PC.
comp.sys.ibm.pc.hardware.chips	Processor, cache, memory chips, etc.
comp.sys.ibm.pc.hardware.comm	Modems and communication cards for the PC.
comp.sys.ibm.pc.hardware.misc	Miscellaneous PC hardware topics.
comp.sys.ibm.pc.hardware.networking	Network hardware and equipment for the PC.
comp.sys.ibm.pc.hardware.storage	Hard drives and other PC storage devices.
comp.sys.ibm.pc.hardware.systems	Whole IBM PC computer and clone systems.
comp.sys.ibm.pc.hardware.video	Video cards and monitors for the PC.
comp.sys.ibm.pc.misc	Discussion about IBM personal computers.
comp.sys.ibm.pc.rt	Topics related to IBM's RT computer.
comp.sys.ibm.pc.soundcard.advocacy	Advocacy for a particular soundcard.
comp.sys.ibm.pc.soundcard.games	Questions about using soundcards with games.
comp.sys.ibm.pc.soundcard.misc	Soundcards in general.
comp.sys.ibm.pc.soundcard.music	Music and sound questions using soundcards.
comp.sys.ibm.pc.soundcard.tech	Technical questions about pc soundcards.
comp.sys.ibm.ps2.hardware	Microchannel hardware, any vendor.
comp.sys.intel	Discussions about Intel systems and parts.
comp.sys.isis	The ISIS distributed system from Cornell.
comp.sys.laptops	Laptop (portable) computers.

comp.sys.m6809	Discussion about 6809s.
comp.sys.m68k	Discussion about 68ks.
comp.sys.m68k.pc	Discussion about 68k-based PCs. M
comp.sys.m88k	Discussion about 88k-based computers.
comp.sys.mac.advocacy	The Macintosh computer family compared to others.
comp.sys.mac.announce	Important notices for Macintosh users. M
comp.sys.mac.apps	Discussions of Macintosh applications.
comp.sys.mac.comm	Discussion of Macintosh communications.
comp.sys.mac.databases	Database systems for the Apple Macintosh.
comp.sys.mac.digest	Apple Macintosh: info and uses, but no programs.
comp.sys.mac.games.action	Action games for the Macintosh.
comp.sys.mac.games.adventure	Adventure games for the Macintosh.
comp.sys.mac.games.announce	Announcements for Mac gamers. M
comp.sys.mac.games.flight-sim	Flight simulator gameplay on the Mac.
comp.sys.mac.games.marketplace	Macintosh games for sale and trade.
comp.sys.mac.games.misc	Macintosh games not covered in other groups.
comp.sys.mac.games.strategic	Strategy/planning games on the Macintosh.
comp.sys.mac.graphics	Macintosh graphics: paint, draw, 3D, CAD, animation.
comp.sys.mac.hardware.misc	General Mac hardware topics not already covered.
comp.sys.mac.hardware.storage	All forms of Mac storage hardware and media.
comp.sys.mac.hardware.video	Video input and output hardware on the Mac.
comp.sys.mac.hypercard	The Macintosh Hypercard: info and uses.
comp.sys.mac.misc	General discussions about the Apple Macintosh.
comp.sys.mac.oop.macapp3	Version 3 of the MacApp object oriented system.
comp.sys.mac.oop.misc	Object oriented programming issues on the Mac.
comp.sys.mac.oop.tcl	Symantec's THINK Class Library for object programming.
comp.sys.mac.portables	Discussion particular to laptop Macintoshes.
comp.sys.mac.printing	All about printing hardware and software on the Mac.
comp.sys.mac.programmer.codewarrior	Macintosh programming using CodeWarrior.
comp.sys.mac.programmer.help	Help with Macintosh programming.
comp.sys.mac.programmer.info	Frequently requested information. M
comp.sys.mac.programmer.misc	Other issues of Macintosh programming.
comp.sys.mac.programmer.tools	Macintosh programming tools.
comp.sys.mac.scitech	Using the Macintosh in scientific and technological work.
comp.sys.mac.system	Discussions of Macintosh system software.
comp.sys.mac.wanted	Postings of 'I want XYZ for my Mac.'
comp.sys.mentor	Mentor Graphics products and the Silicon Compiler System.
comp.sys.mips	Systems based on MIPS chips.

comp.sys.misc	Discussion about computers of all kinds.
comp.sys.msx	The MSX home computer system.
comp.sys.ncr	Discussion about NCR computers.
comp.sys.newton.announce	Newton information posts. M
comp.sys.newton.misc	Miscellaneous discussion about Newton systems.
comp.sys.newton.programmer	Discussion of Newton software development.
comp.sys.next.advocacy	The NeXT religion.
comp.sys.next.announce	Announcements related to the NeXT computer system. M
comp.sys.next.bugs	Discussion and solutions for known NeXT bugs.
comp.sys.next.hardware	Discussing the physical aspects of NeXT computers.
comp.sys.next.marketplace	NeXT hardware, software and jobs.
comp.sys.next.misc	General discussion about the NeXT computer system.
comp.sys.next.programmer	NeXT related programming issues.
comp.sys.next.software	Function, use and availability of NeXT programs.
comp.sys.next.sysadmin	Discussions related to NeXT system administration.
comp.sys.nsc.32k	National Semiconductor 32000 series chips.
comp.sys.palmtops	Super-powered calculators in the palm of your hand.
comp.sys.pen	Interacting with computers through pen gestures.
comp.sys.powerpc	General PowerPC Discussion.
comp.sys.prime	Prime Computer products.
comp.sys.proteon	Proteon gateway products.
comp.sys.psion	Discussion about PSION Personal Computers and Organisers.
comp.sys.pyramid	Pyramid 90x computers.
comp.sys.ridge	Ridge 32 computers and ROS.
comp.sys.sequent	Sequent systems, (Balance and Symmetry).
comp.sys.sgi.admin	System administration on Silicon Graphics' Irises.
comp.sys.sgi.announce	Announcements for the SGI community. M
comp.sys.sgi.apps	Applications which run on the Iris.
comp.sys.sgi.audio	Audio on SGI systems.
comp.sys.sgi.bugs	Bugs found in the IRIX operating system.
comp.sys.sgi.graphics	Graphics packages and issues on SGI machines.
comp.sys.sgi.hardware	Base systems and peripherals for Iris computers.
comp.sys.sgi.misc	General discussion about Silicon Graphics's machines.
comp.sys.sinclair	Sinclair computers, eg. the ZX81, Spectrum and QL.
comp.sys.stratus	Stratus products, incl. System/88, CPS-32, VOS and FTX.
comp.sys.sun.admin	Sun system administration issues and questions.

comp.sys.sun.announce	Sun announcements and Sunergy mailings. M
comp.sys.sun.apps	Software applications for Sun computer systems.
comp.sys.sun.hardware	Sun Microsystems hardware.
comp.sys.sun.misc	Miscellaneous discussions about Sun products.
comp.sys.sun.wanted	People looking for Sun products and support.
comp.sys.tahoe	CCI 6/32, Harris HCX/7, and Sperry 7000 computers.
comp.sys.tandy	Discussion about Tandy computers: new and old.
comp.sys.ti	Discussion about Texas Instruments.
comp.sys.transputer	The Transputer computer and OCCAM language.
comp.sys.unisys	Sperry, Burroughs, Convergent and Unisys* systems.
comp.sys.xerox	Xerox 1100 workstations and protocols.
comp.sys.zenith.z100	The Zenith Z-100 (Heath H-100) family of computers.
comp.terminals	All sorts of terminals.
comp.text	Text processing issues and methods.
comp.text.desktop	Technology and techniques of desktop publishing.
comp.text.frame	Desktop publishing with FrameMaker.
comp.text.interleaf	Applications and use of Interleaf software.
comp.text.pdf	Adobe Acrobat and Portable Document Format technology.
comp.text.sgml	ISO 8879 SGML, structured documents, markup languages.
comp.text.tex	Discussion about the TeX and LaTeX systems and macros.
comp.theory.info-retrieval	Information Retrieval topics. M
comp.unix.admin	Administering a Unix-based system.
comp.unix.advocacy	Arguments for and against Unix and Unix versions.
comp.unix.aix	IBM's version of UNIX.
comp.unix.amiga	Minix, SYSV4 and other *nix on an Amiga.
comp.unix.aux	The version of UNIX for Apple Macintosh II computers.
comp.unix.bsd.386bsd.announce	Announcements pertaining to 386BSD. M
comp.unix.bsd.386bsd.misc	386BSD operating system.
comp.unix.bsd.bsdi.announce	Announcements pertaining to BSD/OS. M
comp.unix.bsd.bsdi.misc	BSD/OS operating system.
comp.unix.bsd.freebsd.announce	Announcements pertaining to FreeBSD. M
comp.unix.bsd.freebsd.misc	FreeBSD operating system.
comp.unix.bsd.misc	BSD operating systems.
comp.unix.bsd.netbsd.announce	Announcements pertaining to NetBSD. M
comp.unix.bsd.netbsd.misc	NetBSD operating system.
comp.unix.dos-under-unix	MS-DOS running under UNIX by whatever means.

comp.unix.internals	Discussions on hacking UNIX internals.
comp.unix.large	UNIX on mainframes and in large networks.
comp.unix.machten	The MachTen operating system and related issues.
comp.unix.misc	Various topics that don't fit other groups.
comp.unix.osf.misc	Various aspects of Open Software Foundation products.
comp.unix.osf.osf1	The Open Software Foundation's OSF/1.
comp.unix.pc-clone.16bit	UNIX on 286 architectures.
comp.unix.pc-clone.32bit	UNIX on 386 and 486 architectures.
comp.unix.programmer	QandA for people programming under Unix.
comp.unix.questions	UNIX neophytes group.
comp.unix.sco.announce	SCO and related product announcements. ᴹ
comp.unix.sco.misc	SCO Unix, Systems, and Environments.
comp.unix.sco.programmer	Programming in and for SCO Environments.
comp.unix.shell	Using and programming the Unix shell.
comp.unix.sys3	System III UNIX discussions.
comp.unix.sys5.misc	Versions of System V which predate Release 3.
comp.unix.sys5.r3	Discussing System V Release 3.
comp.unix.sys5.r4	Discussing System V Release 4.
comp.unix.ultrix	Discussions about DEC's Ultrix.
comp.unix.unixware.announce	Announcements related to UnixWare. ᴹ
comp.unix.unixware.misc	Products of Novell's Unix Systems Group.
comp.unix.user-friendly	Discussion of UNIX user-friendliness.
comp.unix.wizards	For only true Unix wizards. ᴹ
comp.unix.xenix.misc	General discussions regarding XENIX (except SCO).
comp.unix.xenix.sco	XENIX versions from the Santa Cruz Operation.
comp.virus	Computer viruses and security. ᴹ
comp.windows.garnet	The Garnet user interface development environment.
comp.windows.interviews	The InterViews object-oriented windowing system.
comp.windows.misc	Various issues about windowing systems.
comp.windows.news	Sun Microsystems' NeWS window system.
comp.windows.open-look	Discussion about the Open Look GUI.
comp.windows.suit	The SUIT user-interface toolkit.
comp.windows.ui-builders.teleuse	Using/augmenting the TeleUSE UI Builder.
comp.windows.ui-builders.uimx	Using and augmenting the UIM/X UI Builder.
comp.windows.x	Discussion about the X Window System.
comp.windows.x.announce	X Window System announcements. ᴹ
comp.windows.x.apps	Getting and using, not programming, applications for X.
comp.windows.x.i386unix	The XFree86 window system and others.
comp.windows.x.intrinsics	Discussion of the X toolkit.
humanities.answers	Repository for periodic USENET articles. ᴹ
humanities.lit.authors.shakespeare	Poetry, plays, history of Shakespeare.

humanities.misc	General topics in the arts and humanities.
misc.activism.militia	Citizens bearing arms for the common defence. M
misc.activism.progressive	Information for Progressive activists. M
misc.answers	Repository for periodic USENET articles. M
misc.books.technical	Discussion of books about technical topics.
misc.business.consulting	The business of consulting. M
misc.business.facilitators	Discussions for all types of facilitators.
misc.business.records-mgmt	All aspects of professional records management.
misc.consumers	Consumer interests, product reviews, etc.
misc.consumers.house	Discussion about owning and maintaining a house.
misc.creativity	Promoting the use of creativity in all human endeavours.
misc.education	Discussion of the educational system.
misc.education.adult	Adult education and adult literacy practice/research.
misc.education.home-school.christian	Christian home-schooling.
misc.education.home-school.misc	Almost anything about home-schooling.
misc.education.language.english	Teaching English to speakers of other languages.
misc.education.medical	Issues related to medical education.
misc.education.multimedia	Multimedia for education. M
misc.education.science	Issues related to science education.
misc.emerg-services	Forum for paramedics and other first responders.
misc.entrepreneurs	Discussion on operating a business.
misc.entrepreneurs.moderated	Entrepreneur/business topics. M
misc.fitness.aerobic	All forms of aerobic activity.
misc.fitness.misc	All other general fitness topics.
misc.fitness.weights	Bodybuilding, weightlifting, resistance.
misc.forsale.computers.discussion	Discussions only about items for sale.
misc.forsale.computers.mac-specific.cards.misc	Macintosh expansion cards.
misc.forsale.computers.mac-specific.cards.video	Macintosh video cards.
misc.forsale.computers.mac-specific.misc	Other Macintosh equipment.
misc.forsale.computers.mac-specific.portables	Portable Macintosh systems.
misc.forsale.computers.mac-specific.software	Macintosh software.
misc.forsale.computers.mac-specific.systems	Complete Macintosh systems.
misc.forsale.computers.memory	Memory chips and modules for sale and wanted.
misc.forsale.computers.modems	Modems for sale and wanted.
misc.forsale.computers.monitors	Monitors and displays for sale and wanted.
misc.forsale.computers.net-hardware	Networking hardware for sale and wanted.
misc.forsale.computers.other.misc	Miscellaneous other equipment.
misc.forsale.computers.other.software	Software for other systems.

misc.forsale.computers.other.systems	Complete other types of systems.
misc.forsale.computers.pc-specific.audio	PC audio equipment.
misc.forsale.computers.pc-specific.cards.misc	PC expansion cards.
misc.forsale.computers.pc-specific.cards.video	PC video cards.
misc.forsale.computers.pc-specific.misc	Other PC-specific equipment.
misc.forsale.computers.pc-specific.motherboards	PC motherboards.
misc.forsale.computers.pc-specific.portables	Portable PC systems.
misc.forsale.computers.pc-specific.software	PC software.
misc.forsale.computers.pc-specific.systems	Complete PC systems.
misc.forsale.computers.printers	Printers and plotters for sale and wanted.
misc.forsale.computers.storage	Disk, CDROM and tape drives for sale and wanted.
misc.forsale.computers.workstation	Workstation related computer items.
misc.forsale.non-computer	Non-computer items for sale and wanted.
misc.handicap	Items of interest for/about the handicapped. M
misc.headlines	Current interest: drug testing, terrorism, etc.
misc.health.aids	AIDS issues and support.
misc.health.alternative	Alternative, complementary and holistic health care.
misc.health.arthritis	Arthritis and related disorders.
misc.health.diabetes	Discussion of diabetes management in day to day life.
misc.immigration.canada	Canada immigration issues.
misc.immigration.misc	Miscellaneous countries immigration issues.
misc.immigration.usa	USA immigration issues.
misc.industry.pulp-and-paper	Technical topics in the pulp and paper industry.
misc.industry.quality	Quality standards and other issues.
misc.industry.utilities.electric	The electric utility industry.
misc.int-property	Discussion of intellectual property rights.
misc.invest	Investments and the handling of money.
misc.invest.canada	Investing in Canadian financial markets.
misc.invest.funds	Sharing info about bond, stock, real estate funds.
misc.invest.futures	Physical commodity and financial futures markets.
misc.invest.real-estate	Property investments.
misc.invest.stocks	Forum for sharing info about stocks and options.
misc.invest.technical	Analyzing market trends with technical methods.
misc.jobs.contract	Discussions about contract labour.
misc.jobs.misc	Discussion about employment, workplaces, careers.
misc.jobs.offered	Announcements of positions available.

misc.jobs.offered.entry	Job listings only for entry-level positions.
misc.jobs.resumes	Postings of resumes and 'situation wanted' articles.
misc.kids	Children, their behaviour and activities.
misc.kids.computer	The use of computers by children.
misc.kids.consumers	Products related to kids.
misc.kids.health	Children's health.
misc.kids.info	Informational posts related to misc.kids hierarchy. M
misc.kids.pregnancy	Pre-pregnancy planning, pregnancy, childbirth.
misc.kids.vacation	Discussion on all forms of family-oriented vacationing.
misc.legal	Legalities and the ethics of law.
misc.legal.computing	Discussing the legal climate of the computing world.
misc.legal.moderated	All aspects of law. M
misc.misc	Various discussions not fitting in any other group.
misc.news.bosnia	News, articles, reports and information on Bosnia.
misc.news.east-europe.rferl	Radio Free Europe/Radio Liberty Daily Report. M
misc.news.southasia	News from Bangladesh, India, Nepal, etc. M
misc.rural	Devoted to issues concerning rural living.
misc.survivalism	Disaster and long-term survival techniques and theory.
misc.taxes	Tax laws and advice.
misc.test	For testing of network software. Very boring.
misc.test.moderated	Testing of posting to moderated groups. M
misc.transport.air-industry	Airlines, airports, commercial aircraft. M
misc.transport.rail.americas	Railroads and railways in North and South America.
misc.transport.rail.australia-nz	Railways in Australia and New Zealand.
misc.transport.rail.europe	Railroads and railways in all of Europe.
misc.transport.rail.misc	Miscellaneous rail issues and discussions.
misc.transport.trucking	Commercial trucking related issues.
misc.transport.urban-transit	Metropolitan public transportation systems.
misc.wanted	Requests for things that are needed (NOT software).
misc.writing	Discussion of writing in all of its forms.
misc.writing.screenplays	Aspects of writing and selling screenplays.
news.admin.hierarchies	Network news hierarchies.
news.admin.misc	General topics of network news administration.
news.admin.net-abuse.announce	Information regarding network resource abuse. M
news.admin.net-abuse.misc	Network facility abuse, including spamming.
news.admin.technical	Technical aspects of maintaining network news. M
news.announce.conferences	Calls for papers and conference announcements. M
news.announce.important	General announcements of interest to all. M

news.announce.newgroups	Calls for newgroups and announcements of same.
news.announce.newusers	Explanatory postings for new users. M
news.answers	Repository for periodic USENET articles. M
news.groups	Discussions and lists of news groups.
news.groups.questions	Where can I find talk about topic X?
news.groups.reviews	What is going on in group or mailing list named X? M
news.lists	News-related statistics and lists. M
news.lists.ps-maps	Maps relating to USENET traffic flows. M
news.misc	Discussions of USENET itself.
news.newusers.questions	Q and A for users new to the Usenet.
news.software.anu-news	VMS B-news software from Australian National Univ.
news.software.b	Discussion about B-news-compatible software.
news.software.nn	Discussion about the 'nn' news reader package.
news.software.nntp	The Network News Transfer Protocol.
news.software.readers	Discussion of software used to read network news.
rec.animals.wildlife	Wildlife related discussions/information.
rec.answers	Repository for periodic USENET articles. M
rec.antiques	Discussing antiques and vintage items.
rec.antiques.marketplace	Buying/selling/trading antiques.
rec.antiques.radio+phono	Audio devices and materials of yesteryear.
rec.aquaria	Keeping fish and aquaria as a hobby.
rec.arts.animation	Discussion of various kinds of animation.
rec.arts.anime	Japanese animation fen discussion.
rec.arts.anime.info	Announcements about Japanese animation. M
rec.arts.anime.marketplace	Things for sale in the Japanese animation world.
rec.arts.anime.stories	All about Japanese comic fanzines. M
rec.arts.ascii	ASCII art, info on archives, art, and artists. M
rec.arts.bodyart	Tattoos and body decoration discussions.
rec.arts.bonsai	Dwarfish trees and shrubbery.
rec.arts.books	Books of all genres, and the publishing industry.
rec.arts.books.childrens	All aspects of children's literature.
rec.arts.books.hist-fiction	Historical fictions (novels) in general.
rec.arts.books.marketplace	Buying and selling of books.
rec.arts.books.reviews	Book reviews. M
rec.arts.books.tolkien	The works of J.R.R. Tolkien.
rec.arts.comics.alternative	Alternative (non-mainstream) comic books.
rec.arts.comics.creative	Encouraging good superhero-style writing.
rec.arts.comics.dc.lsh	The Legion of Super-Heroes and related characters.
rec.arts.comics.dc.universe	DC Comics' shared universe and characters.
rec.arts.comics.dc.vertigo	Comics from the Vertigo imprint.
rec.arts.comics.elfquest	The Elfquest universe and characters.
rec.arts.comics.info	Reviews, convention information and other comics news. M

rec.arts.comics.marketplace	The exchange of comics and comic related items.
rec.arts.comics.marvel.universe	Marvel Comics' shared universe and characters.
rec.arts.comics.marvel.xbooks	The Mutant Universe of Marvel Comics.
rec.arts.comics.misc	Comic books, graphic novels, sequential art.
rec.arts.comics.other-media	Comic book spinoffs in other media.
rec.arts.comics.strips	Discussion of short-form comics.
rec.arts.dance	Any aspects of dance not covered in another news group.
rec.arts.disney.animation	Animated features, cartoons, short subjects.
rec.arts.disney.announce	FAQs, lists, info, announcements. M
rec.arts.disney.merchandise	Toys, videos, music, books, art, collectibles.
rec.arts.disney.misc	General topics pertinent to the Disney Company.
rec.arts.disney.parks	Parks, resorts, dining, attractions, vacations.
rec.arts.drwho	Discussion about Dr Who.
rec.arts.erotica	Erotic fiction and verse. M
rec.arts.fine	Fine arts and artists.
rec.arts.int-fiction	Discussions about interactive fiction.
rec.arts.manga	All aspects of the Japanese storytelling art form.
rec.arts.marching.band.college	College marching bands.
rec.arts.marching.band.high-school	High school marching bands.
rec.arts.marching.colorguard	Competitive colour guard activity.
rec.arts.marching.drumcorps	Drum and bugle corps.
rec.arts.marching.misc	Marching-related performance activities.
rec.arts.misc	Discussions about the arts not in other groups.
rec.arts.movies.announce	Newsworthy events in the movie business. M
rec.arts.movies.current-films	The latest movie releases.
rec.arts.movies.lists+surveys	Top-N lists and general surveys.
rec.arts.movies.local.indian	Indian movies and the Indian film industry.
rec.arts.movies.misc	General aspects of movies not covered by other groups.
rec.arts.movies.movie-going	Going-to-movies experiences.
rec.arts.movies.past-films	Past movies.
rec.arts.movies.people	People in the movie business.
rec.arts.movies.production	Filmmaking, amateur and professional.
rec.arts.movies.reviews	Reviews of movies. M
rec.arts.movies.tech	Technical aspects of movies.
rec.arts.mystery	Mystery and crime books, plays and films.
rec.arts.poems	For the posting of poems.
rec.arts.prose	Short works of prose fiction and follow-up discussion.
rec.arts.puppetry	For discussion of puppets in any form or venue.
rec.arts.sf.announce	Major announcements of the SF world. M
rec.arts.sf.fandom	Discussions of SF fan activities.
rec.arts.sf.marketplace	Personal for sale notices of SF materials.
rec.arts.sf.misc	Science fiction lovers' news group.
rec.arts.sf.movies	Discussing SF motion pictures.

rec.arts.sf.reviews	Reviews of science fiction/fantasy/horror works.
rec.arts.sf.science	Real and speculative aspects of SF science.
rec.arts.sf.starwars.collecting	Topics relating to Star Wars collecting.
rec.arts.sf.starwars.games	Star Wars games: RPG, computer, card, etc.
rec.arts.sf.starwars.info	General information pertaining to Star Wars. ^M
rec.arts.sf.starwars.misc	Miscellaneous topics pertaining to Star Wars.
rec.arts.sf.tv	Discussing general television SF.
rec.arts.sf.tv.babylon5	Babylon 5 creators meet Babylon 5 fans.
rec.arts.sf.tv.quantum-leap	Quantum Leap TV, comics, cons, etc.
rec.arts.sf.written	Discussion of written science fiction and fantasy.
rec.arts.sf.written.robert-jordan	Books by author Robert Jordan.
rec.arts.startrek.current	New Star Trek shows, movies and books.
rec.arts.startrek.fandom	Star Trek conventions and memorabilia.
rec.arts.startrek.info	Information about the universe of Star Trek. ^M
rec.arts.startrek.misc	General discussions of Star Trek.
rec.arts.startrek.reviews	Reviews of Star Trek books, episodes, films, andc.
rec.arts.startrek.tech	Star Trek's depiction of future technologies.
rec.arts.theatre.misc	Miscellaneous topics and issues in theatre.
rec.arts.theatre.musicals	Musical theatre around the world.
rec.arts.theatre.plays	Dramaturgy and discussion of plays.
rec.arts.theatre.stagecraft	Issues in stagecraft and production.
rec.arts.tv	The boob tube, its history, and past and current shows.
rec.arts.tv.interactive	Developments in interactive television.
rec.arts.tv.mst3k.announce	Mystery Science Theatre 3000 announcements. ^M
rec.arts.tv.mst3k.misc	For fans of Mystery Science Theatre 3000.
rec.arts.tv.soaps.abc	Soap operas produced by or for the ABC network.
rec.arts.tv.soaps.cbs	Soap operas produced by or for the CBS network.
rec.arts.tv.soaps.misc	Postings of interest to all soap opera viewers.
rec.arts.tv.uk.comedy	Regarding UK-based comedy shows.
rec.arts.tv.uk.coronation-st	Regarding the UK based show Coronation Street.
rec.arts.tv.uk.eastenders	Regarding the UK based show Eastenders.
rec.arts.tv.uk.misc	Miscellaneous topics about UK-based television.
rec.arts.wobegon	'A Prairie Home Companion' radio show discussion.
rec.audio.car	Discussions of automobile audio systems.
rec.audio.high-end	High-end audio systems. ^M
rec.audio.marketplace	Buying and selling of home audio equipment.
rec.audio.misc	Post about audio here if you can't post anywhere else.
rec.audio.opinion	Everybody's two bits on audio in your home.
rec.audio.pro	Professional audio recording and studio engineering.

rec.audio.tech	Theoretical, factual, and DIY topics in home audio.
rec.audio.tubes	Electronic audio circuits which use vacuum tubes.
rec.autos.4x4	The on and off-road four-wheel drive vehicle.
rec.autos.antique	Discussing all aspects of automobiles over 25 years old.
rec.autos.driving	Driving automobiles.
rec.autos.makers.chrysler	Dodge, Plymouth, Jeep, Eagle, etc. info/talk.
rec.autos.makers.ford.mustang	Ford Mustangs in all their flavours.
rec.autos.makers.saturn	All about Saturn cars, fans and company.
rec.autos.makers.vw.aircooled	Bug, Bus, Ghia, Squareback, Thing, etc.
rec.autos.makers.vw.watercooled	Golf, Jetta, Corrado, Vanagon, new models, etc.
rec.autos.marketplace	Buy/Sell/Trade automobiles, parts, tools, accessories.
rec.autos.misc	Miscellaneous discussion about automobiles.
rec.autos.rod-n-custom	High performance automobiles.
rec.autos.simulators	Discussion of automotive simulators.
rec.autos.sport.f1	Formula 1 motor racing.
rec.autos.sport.indy	Indy Car motor racing.
rec.autos.sport.info	Auto racing news, results, announcements. [M]
rec.autos.sport.misc	Organized, legal auto competitions.
rec.autos.sport.nascar	NASCAR and other professional stock car racing.
rec.autos.sport.tech	Technical aspects and technology of auto racing.
rec.autos.tech	Technical aspects of automobiles, et al.
rec.autos.vw	Issues pertaining to Volkswagen products.
rec.aviation.announce	Events of interest to the aviation community. [M]
rec.aviation.answers	Frequently asked questions about aviation. [M]
rec.aviation.hang-gliding	Hang-gliding, paragliding, foot-launched flight.
rec.aviation.homebuilt	Selecting, designing, building, and restoring aircraft.
rec.aviation.ifr	Flying under Instrument Flight Rules.
rec.aviation.marketplace	Aviation classifieds.
rec.aviation.military	Military aircraft of the past, present and future.
rec.aviation.misc	Miscellaneous topics in aviation.
rec.aviation.owning	Information on owning airplanes.
rec.aviation.piloting	General discussion for aviators.
rec.aviation.products	Reviews and discussion of products useful to pilots.
rec.aviation.questions	Aviation questions and answers. [M]
rec.aviation.rotorcraft	Helicopters and other rotary wing aircraft.
rec.aviation.simulators	Flight simulation on all levels.
rec.aviation.soaring	All aspects of sailplanes and hang-gliders.
rec.aviation.stories	Anecdotes of flight experiences. [M]
rec.aviation.student	Learning to fly.
rec.aviation.ultralight	Light aircraft in general, all topics.

rec.backcountry	Activities in the Great Outdoors.
rec.bicycles.marketplace	Buying, selling and reviewing items for cycling.
rec.bicycles.misc	General discussion of bicycling.
rec.bicycles.off-road	All aspects of off-road bicycling.
rec.bicycles.racing	Bicycle racing techniques, rules and results.
rec.bicycles.rides	Discussions of tours and training or commuting routes.
rec.bicycles.soc	Societal issues of bicycling.
rec.bicycles.tech	Cycling product design, construction, maintenance, etc.
rec.birds	Hobbyists interested in bird watching.
rec.boats	Hobbyists interested in boating.
rec.boats.building	Boat building, design, restoration, and repair.
rec.boats.cruising	Cruising in boats.
rec.boats.marketplace	Boating products for sale and wanted. M
rec.boats.paddle	Talk about any boats with oars, paddles, etc.
rec.boats.racing	Boat racing.
rec.climbing	Climbing techniques, competition announcements, etc.
rec.collecting	Discussion among collectors of many things.
rec.collecting.cards.discuss	Discussion of sports and non-sports cards.
rec.collecting.cards.non-sports	Non-sports cards.
rec.collecting.coins	Coin, currency, medal, etc. collecting forum.
rec.collecting.dolls	Doll and bear collecting and crafting.
rec.collecting.phonecards	Info and Marketplace group for phonecards.
rec.collecting.sport.baseball	Baseball memorabilia (cards, photos, etc).
rec.collecting.sport.basketball	Basketball memorabilia (cards, photos, etc).
rec.collecting.sport.football	Football memorabilia (cards, photos, etc).
rec.collecting.sport.hockey	Hockey memorabilia (cards, photos, etc).
rec.collecting.sport.misc	Sports memorabilia not in any other group.
rec.collecting.stamps	Discussion of all things related to philately.
rec.crafts.beads	Making, collecting, and using beads.
rec.crafts.brewing	The art of making beers and meads.
rec.crafts.glass	All aspects of glassworking and glass.
rec.crafts.jewelry	All aspects of jewellery making and lapidary work.
rec.crafts.marketplace	Small-scale ads for craft products of all kinds.
rec.crafts.metalworking	All aspects of working with metal.
rec.crafts.misc	Handiwork arts not covered elsewhere.
rec.crafts.polymer-clay	Techniques and resources relating to polymer clay.
rec.crafts.pottery	The ancient art of making clay pots.
rec.crafts.textiles.misc	Fibre and textile crafts not covered elsewhere.
rec.crafts.textiles.needlework	Any form of decorative stitching done by hand.
rec.crafts.textiles.quilting	All about quilts and other quilted items.
rec.crafts.textiles.sewing	Sewing: clothes, furnishings, costumes, etc.
rec.crafts.textiles.yarn	Yarn making and use: spin, dye, knit, weave etc.

rec.crafts.winemaking	The tasteful art of making wine.
rec.drugs.cannabis	The drug cannabis (marijuana).
rec.drugs.misc	Stimulants, sedatives, smart drugs, etc.
rec.drugs.psychedelic	LSD, Ecstasy, magic mushrooms and the like.
rec.equestrian	Discussion of things equestrian.
rec.folk-dancing	Folk dances, dancers, and dancing.
rec.food.chocolate	Chocolate.
rec.food.cooking	Food, cooking, cookbooks, and recipes.
rec.food.drink	Wines and spirits.
rec.food.drink.beer	All things beer.
rec.food.drink.coffee	The making and drinking of coffee.
rec.food.drink.tea	Tea as beverage and culture.
rec.food.historic	The history of food making arts.
rec.food.preserving	Preserving foodstuffs, herbs, and medicinals.
rec.food.recipes	Recipes for interesting food and drink. M
rec.food.restaurants	Discussion of dining out.
rec.food.sourdough	Making and baking with sourdough.
rec.food.veg	Vegetarians.
rec.food.veg.cooking	Vegetarian recipes, cooking, nutrition. M
rec.gambling.blackjack	Analysis of and strategy for blackjack, aka 21.
rec.gambling.craps	Analysis of and strategy for the dice game craps.
rec.gambling.lottery	Strategy and news of lotteries and sweepstakes.
rec.gambling.misc	All other gambling topics including travel.
rec.gambling.other-games	Gambling games not covered elsewhere.
rec.gambling.poker	Analysis and strategy of live poker games.
rec.gambling.racing	Wagering on animal races.
rec.gambling.sports	Wagering on human sporting events.
rec.games.abstract	Perfect information, pure strategy games.
rec.games.backgammon	Discussion of the game of backgammon.
rec.games.board	Discussion and hints on board games.
rec.games.board.ce	The Cosmic Encounter board game.
rec.games.board.marketplace	Trading and selling of board games.
rec.games.bolo	The networked strategy war game Bolo.
rec.games.bridge	Hobbyists interested in bridge.
rec.games.chess.analysis	Analysis of openings/middlegames/endgames.
rec.games.chess.computer	Reports on game servers, databases, software.
rec.games.chess.misc	Forum for news/discussion related to chess.
rec.games.chess.play-by-email	Reports/discussions regarding email chess.
rec.games.chess.politics	News of nat'l/international chess organisations.
rec.games.chinese-chess	Discussion of the game of Chinese chess, Xiangqi.
rec.games.computer.doom.announce	Info/FAQs/reviews about DOOM. M
rec.games.computer.doom.editing	Editing and hacking DOOM-related files.
rec.games.computer.doom.help	DOOM Help Service (new players welcome).
rec.games.computer.doom.misc	Talking about DOOM and ID Software.
rec.games.computer.doom.playing	Playing DOOM and user-created levels.
rec.games.computer.puzzle	Puzzle-solving computer games.

rec.games.computer.xpilot	About the X11 game XPilot.
rec.games.corewar	The Core War computer challenge.
rec.games.design	Discussion of game design related issues.
rec.games.diplomacy	The conquest game Diplomacy.
rec.games.empire	Discussion and hints about Empire.
rec.games.frp.advocacy	Flames and rebuttals about various role-playing systems.
rec.games.frp.announce	Announcements of happenings in the role-playing world. ᴹ
rec.games.frp.archives	Archivable fantasy stories and other projects. ᴹ
rec.games.frp.cyber	Discussions of cyberpunk related roleplaying games.
rec.games.frp.dnd	Fantasy role-playing with TSR's Dungeons and Dragons.
rec.games.frp.gurps	The GURPS role playing game.
rec.games.frp.live-action	Live-action roleplaying games.
rec.games.frp.marketplace	Role-playing game materials wanted and for sale.
rec.games.frp.misc	General discussions of role-playing games.
rec.games.frp.storyteller	World of Darkness and StoryTeller games.
rec.games.go	Discussion about Go.
rec.games.int-fiction	All aspects of interactive fiction games.
rec.games.mecha	Giant robot games.
rec.games.miniatures.historical	Historical and modern tabletop wargaming.
rec.games.miniatures.misc	Miniatures and various tabletop wargames.
rec.games.miniatures.warhammer	Wargaming in the Warhammer Universe.
rec.games.misc	Games and computer games.
rec.games.mud.admin	Administrative issues of multiuser dungeons.
rec.games.mud.announce	Informational articles about multiuser dungeons. ᴹ
rec.games.mud.diku	All about DikuMuds.
rec.games.mud.lp	Discussions of the LPMUD computer role playing game.
rec.games.mud.misc	Various aspects of multiuser computer games.
rec.games.mud.tiny	Discussion about Tiny Muds, like MUSuperhighway, MUSE and MOO.
rec.games.netrek	Discussion of the X window system game Netrek (XtrekII).
rec.games.pbm	Discussion about Play by Mail games.
rec.games.pinball	Discussing pinball-related issues.
rec.games.playing-cards	Recreational (non-gambling) card playing.
rec.games.programmer	Discussion of adventure game programming.
rec.games.roguelike.angband	The computer game Angband.
rec.games.roguelike.announce	Major info about rogue-styled games. ᴹ
rec.games.roguelike.misc	Rogue-style dungeon games without other groups.
rec.games.roguelike.moria	The computer game Moria.
rec.games.roguelike.nethack	The computer game Nethack.

rec.games.roguelike.rogue	The computer game Rogue.
rec.games.trading-cards.announce	Important news about trading card games. ᴹ
rec.games.trading-cards.jyhad	Jyhad trading card game discussions.
rec.games.trading-cards.magic.misc	General 'Magic: the Gathering' postings.
rec.games.trading-cards.magic.rules	'Magic: the Gathering' rules QandA.
rec.games.trading-cards.magic.strategy	'Magic: the Gathering' strategy.
rec.games.trading-cards.marketplace	Sales, auctions, trades of game cards.
rec.games.trading-cards.misc	Other trading card game discussions.
rec.games.trivia	Discussion about trivia.
rec.games.video.3do	Discussion of 3DO video game systems.
rec.games.video.advocacy	Debate on merits of various video game systems.
rec.games.video.arcade	Discussions about coin-operated video games.
rec.games.video.arcade.collecting	Collecting, converting, repairing etc.
rec.games.video.atari	Discussion of Atari's video game systems.
rec.games.video.cd-i	CD-i topics with emphasis on games.
rec.games.video.cd32	Gaming talk, info and help for the Amiga CD32.
rec.games.video.classic	Older home video entertainment systems.
rec.games.video.marketplace	Home video game stuff for sale or trade.
rec.games.video.misc	General discussion about home video games.
rec.games.video.nintendo	All Nintendo video game systems and software.
rec.games.video.sega	All Sega video game systems and software.
rec.games.video.sony	Sony games hardware and software.
rec.games.xtank.play	Strategy and tactics for the distributed game Xtank.
rec.games.xtank.programmer	Coding the Xtank game and its robots.
rec.gardens	Gardening, methods and results.
rec.gardens.orchids	Growing, hybridizing, and general care of orchids.
rec.gardens.roses	Gardening information related to roses.
rec.guns	Discussions about firearms. ᴹ
rec.heraldry	Discussion of coats of arms.
rec.humor	Jokes and the like. May be somewhat offensive.
rec.humor.d	Discussions on the content of recent humour articles.
rec.humor.funny	Jokes that are funny (in the moderator's opinion). ᴹ
rec.humor.oracle	Sagacious advice from the USENET Oracle. ᴹ
rec.humor.oracle.d	Comments about the USENET Oracle's comments.
rec.hunting	Discussions about hunting. ᴹ
rec.hunting.dogs	Hunting topics specifically related to using dogs. ᴹ
rec.juggling	Juggling techniques, equipment and events.
rec.kites	Talk about kites and kiting.
rec.mag	Magazine summaries, tables of contents, etc.
rec.mag.dargon	DargonZine fantasy fiction emag issues and discussion.

rec.martial-arts	Discussion of the various martial art forms.
rec.misc	General topics about recreational/participant sports.
rec.models.railroad	Model railroads of all scales.
rec.models.rc	Radio-controlled models for hobbyists.
rec.models.rc.air	Radio-controlled air models.
rec.models.rc.land	Radio-controlled land models.
rec.models.rc.misc	Radio-controlled miscellaneous items.
rec.models.rc.water	Radio-controlled water models.
rec.models.rockets	Model rockets for hobbyists.
rec.models.scale	Construction of models.
rec.motorcycles	Motorcycles and related products and laws.
rec.motorcycles.dirt	Riding motorcycles and ATVs off-road.
rec.motorcycles.harley	All aspects of Harley-Davidson motorcycles.
rec.motorcycles.racing	Discussion of all aspects of racing motorcycles.
rec.music.a-cappella	Vocal music without instrumental accompaniment.
rec.music.afro-latin	Music with Afro-Latin, African and Latin influences.
rec.music.ambient	Ambient music and artists.
rec.music.artists.beach-boys	The Beach Boys' music and the effect they've had.
rec.music.artists.bruce-hornsby	The music of Bruce Hornsby.
rec.music.artists.queensryche	The Thinking Mind's Metal Band.
rec.music.artists.springsteen	Forum for fans of Bruce Springsteen's music.
rec.music.beatles	Postings about the Fab Four and their music.
rec.music.bluenote	Discussion of jazz, blues, and related types of music.
rec.music.bluenote.blues	The Blues in all forms and all aspects.
rec.music.cd	CDs – availability and other discussions.
rec.music.celtic	Traditional and modern music with a Celtic flavour.
rec.music.christian	Christian music, both contemporary and traditional.
rec.music.classical	Discussion about classical music.
rec.music.classical.guitar	Classical music performed on guitar.
rec.music.classical.performing	Performing classical (including early) music.
rec.music.classical.recordings	Classical music on CD, vinyl, cassette, etc.
rec.music.collecting.cd	Compact discs of collector value.
rec.music.collecting.misc	Music collecting other than vinyl or CD.
rec.music.collecting.vinyl	Collecting vinyl records.
rec.music.compose	Creating musical and lyrical works.
rec.music.country.old-time	Southern fiddle/banjo music and beyond.
rec.music.country.western	CandW music, performers, performances, etc.
rec.music.dementia	Discussion of comedy and novelty music.
rec.music.dylan	Discussion of Bob's works and music.
rec.music.early	Discussion of pre-classical European music.

rec.music.filipino	All types and forms of Filipino music.
rec.music.folk	Folks discussing folk music of various sorts.
rec.music.funky	Funk, soul, rhythm and blues and related.
rec.music.gaffa	Discussion of Kate Bush and other alternative music. ^M
rec.music.gdead	A group for (Grateful) Dead-heads.
rec.music.hip-hop	Hip-Hop music and culture in general.
rec.music.indian.classical	Hindustani and Carnatic Indian classical music.
rec.music.indian.misc	Discussing Indian music in general.
rec.music.industrial	Discussion of all industrial-related music styles.
rec.music.info	News and announcements on musical topics. ^M
rec.music.makers	For performers and their discussions.
rec.music.makers.bagpipe	Music and playing of all types of bagpipes.
rec.music.makers.bands	For musicians who play in groups with others.
rec.music.makers.bass	Upright bass and bass guitar techniques and equipment.
rec.music.makers.bowed-strings	Violin family (current and old) performance.
rec.music.makers.builders	Design, building, repair of musical instruments.
rec.music.makers.dulcimer	Dulcimers and related instruments.
rec.music.makers.french-horn	About horn players and playing.
rec.music.makers.guitar	Electric and acoustic guitar techniques and equipment.
rec.music.makers.guitar.acoustic	Discussion of acoustic guitar playing.
rec.music.makers.guitar.tablature	Guitar tablature/chords.
rec.music.makers.marketplace	Buying and selling used music-making equipment.
rec.music.makers.percussion	Drum and other percussion techniques and equipment.
rec.music.makers.piano	Piano music, performing, composing, learning, styles.
rec.music.makers.songwriting	All about songwriting.
rec.music.makers.synth	Synthesizers and computer music.
rec.music.makers.trumpet	The exchange of trumpet related information.
rec.music.marketplace	Records, tapes, and CDs: wanted, for sale, etc.
rec.music.marketplace.cd	Buying and selling collectible compact discs.
rec.music.marketplace.misc	Buying and selling non-vinyl/CD music.
rec.music.marketplace.vinyl	Buying and selling collectable vinyl records.
rec.music.misc	Music lovers' group.
rec.music.movies	Music for movies and television.
rec.music.newage	'New Age' music discussions.
rec.music.opera	All aspects of opera.
rec.music.phish	Discussing the musical group Phish.
rec.music.progressive	Symphonic rock, art rock, fusion, Canterbury, RIO, etc.
rec.music.promotional	Information and promo materials from record companies. ^M
rec.music.ragtime	Ragtime and related music styles.

rec.music.reggae	Roots, Rockers, Dancehall Reggae.
rec.music.rem	The musical group REM.
rec.music.reviews	Reviews of music of all genres and mediums. M
rec.music.tori-amos	Discussion of the female singer/songwriter Tori Amos.
rec.music.video	Discussion of music videos and music video software.
rec.nude	Hobbyists interested in naturist/nudist activities.
rec.org.mensa	Talking with members of the high IQ society Mensa.
rec.org.sca	Society for Creative Anachronism.
rec.outdoors.fishing	All aspects of sport and commercial fishing.
rec.outdoors.fishing.fly	Fly fishing in general.
rec.outdoors.fishing.saltwater	Saltwater fishing, methods, gear, QandA.
rec.outdoors.national-parks	Activities and politics in national parks.
rec.outdoors.rv-travel	Discussions related to recreational vehicles.
rec.parks.theme	Entertainment theme parks.
rec.pets	Pets, pet care, and household animals in general.
rec.pets.birds	The culture and care of indoor birds.
rec.pets.cats	Discussion about domestic cats.
rec.pets.dogs.activities	Dog events: showing, obedience, agility, etc.
rec.pets.dogs.behavior	Behaviours and problems: housetraining, chewing, etc.
rec.pets.dogs.breeds	Breed specific – breed traits, finding breeders, etc.
rec.pets.dogs.health	Info about health problems and how to care for dogs.
rec.pets.dogs.info	General information and FAQs posted here. M
rec.pets.dogs.misc	All other topics, chat, humour, etc.
rec.pets.dogs.rescue	Information about breed rescue, placing and adopting.
rec.pets.herp	Reptiles, amphibians and other exotic vivarium pets.
rec.photo.advanced	Advanced topics (equipment and technique).
rec.photo.darkroom	Developing, printing and other darkroom issues.
rec.photo.help	Beginners' questions about photography (and answers).
rec.photo.marketplace	Trading of personal photographic equipment.
rec.photo.misc	General issues related to photography.
rec.photo.moderated	The art and science of photography. M
rec.ponds	Pond issues: plants, fish, design, maintenance.
rec.puzzles	Puzzles, problems, and quizzes.
rec.puzzles.crosswords	Making and playing gridded word puzzles.
rec.pyrotechnics	Fireworks, rocketry, safety, and other topics.
rec.radio.amateur.antenna	Antennas: theory, techniques and construction.
rec.radio.amateur.digital.misc	Packet radio and other digital radio modes.
rec.radio.amateur.equipment	All about production amateur radio hardware.

rec.radio.amateur.homebrew	Amateur radio construction and experimentation.
rec.radio.amateur.misc	Amateur radio practices, contests, events, rules, etc.
rec.radio.amateur.policy	Radio use and regulation policy.
rec.radio.amateur.space	Amateur radio transmissions through space.
rec.radio.broadcasting	Discussion of global domestic broadcast radio. M
rec.radio.cb	Citizen-band radio.
rec.radio.info	Informational postings related to radio. M
rec.radio.noncomm	Topics relating to noncommercial radio.
rec.radio.scanner	'Utility' broadcasting traffic above 30 MHz.
rec.radio.shortwave	Shortwave radio enthusiasts.
rec.radio.swap	Offers to trade and swap radio equipment.
rec.roller-coaster	Roller coasters and other amusement park rides.
rec.running	Running for enjoyment, sport, exercise, etc.
rec.scouting	Scouting youth organisations worldwide.
rec.scuba	Hobbyists interested in SCUBA diving.
rec.skiing.alpine	Downhill skiing technique, equipment, etc.
rec.skiing.announce	FAQ, competition results, automated snow reports. M
rec.skiing.backcountry	Backcountry skiing.
rec.skiing.marketplace	Items for sale/wanted.
rec.skiing.nordic	Cross-country skiing technique, equipment, etc.
rec.skiing.resorts.europe	Skiing in Europe.
rec.skiing.resorts.misc	Skiing in other than Europe and North America.
rec.skiing.resorts.north-america	Skiing in North America.
rec.skiing.snowboard	Snowboarding technique, equipment, etc.
rec.skydiving	Hobbyists interested in skydiving.
rec.sport.archery	All aspects of archery for archers of any skill level.
rec.sport.baseball	Discussion about baseball.
rec.sport.baseball.analysis	Analysis and discussion of baseball. M
rec.sport.baseball.college	Baseball on the collegiate level.
rec.sport.baseball.data	Raw baseball data (Stats, birthdays, scheds).
rec.sport.baseball.fantasy	Rotisserie (fantasy) baseball play.
rec.sport.basketball.college	Hoops on the collegiate level.
rec.sport.basketball.europe	A European basketball forum.
rec.sport.basketball.misc	Discussion about basketball.
rec.sport.basketball.pro	Talk of professional basketball.
rec.sport.basketball.women	Women's basketball at all levels.
rec.sport.billiard	Billiard sports, including pool, snooker, carom games.
rec.sport.boxing	Boxing in all its pugilistic facets and forms.
rec.sport.cricket	Discussion about the sport of cricket.
rec.sport.cricket.info	News, scores and info related to cricket. M
rec.sport.disc	Discussion of flying disc based sports.
rec.sport.fencing	All aspects of swordplay.

rec.sport.football.australian	Discussion of Australian (Rules) Football.
rec.sport.football.canadian	All about Canadian rules football.
rec.sport.football.college	US-style college football.
rec.sport.football.fantasy	Rotisserie (fantasy) football play.
rec.sport.football.misc	Discussion about American-style football.
rec.sport.football.pro	US-style professional football.
rec.sport.golf	Discussion about all aspects of golfing.
rec.sport.hockey	Discussion about ice hockey.
rec.sport.hockey.field	Discussion of the sport of field hockey.
rec.sport.misc	Spectator sports.
rec.sport.olympics	All aspects of the Olympic Games.
rec.sport.orienteering	All matters related to the sport of orienteering.
rec.sport.paintball	Discussing all aspects of the survival game paintball.
rec.sport.pro-wrestling	Discussion about professional wrestling.
rec.sport.pro-wrestling.fantasy	Rotisserie league professional wrestling.
rec.sport.rowing	Crew for competition or fitness.
rec.sport.rugby	Discussion about the game of rugby.
rec.sport.rugby.league	Everything related to playing/supporting Rugby League.
rec.sport.rugby.union	Everything related to playing/supporting Rugby Union.
rec.sport.skating.ice.figure	Figure/artistic skating.
rec.sport.skating.ice.recreational	Recreational ice skating.
rec.sport.skating.inline	Inline skating, aka Rollerblading.
rec.sport.skating.misc	Miscellaneous skating topics.
rec.sport.skating.racing	Racing and speed skating.
rec.sport.skating.roller	Conventional (quad) roller skating.
rec.sport.soccer	Discussion about soccer (Association Football).
rec.sport.squash	Forum for all apects of squash.
rec.sport.swimming	Traininĥg for and competing in swimming events.
rec.sport.table-soccer	Table-soccer of all types: football and Subbuteo.
rec.sport.table-tennis	Things related to table tennis (aka Ping Pong).
rec.sport.tennis	Things related to the sport of tennis.
rec.sport.triathlon	Discussing all aspects of multi-event sports.
rec.sport.unicycling	All sorts of fun on one wheel.
rec.sport.volleyball	Discussion about volleyball.
rec.sport.water-polo	Discussion of water polo.
rec.sport.waterski	Waterskiing and other boat-towed activities.
rec.toys.cars	Toy car collecting.
rec.toys.lego	Discussion of Lego, Duplo (and compatible) toys.
rec.toys.misc	Discussion of toys that lack a specific news group.
rec.travel.air	Airline travel around the world.
rec.travel.asia	Travel in Asia.
rec.travel.cruises	Travel by cruise ship.
rec.travel.europe	Travel in Europe.

rec.travel.latin-america	Travel in Caribbean, Central and South America.
rec.travel.marketplace	Tickets and accomodations wanted and for sale.
rec.travel.misc	Everything and anything about travel.
rec.travel.usa-canada	Travel in the United States and Canada.
rec.video	Video and video components.
rec.video.cable-tv	Technical and regulatory issues of cable television.
rec.video.desktop	Amateur, computer-based video editing and production.
rec.video.production	Making professional quality video productions.
rec.video.professional	Professional video, technical and artistic. M
rec.video.releases	Pre-recorded video releases on laserdisc and videotape.
rec.video.satellite.dbs	DBS systems and technologies.
rec.video.satellite.europe	European satellite broadcasting.
rec.video.satellite.misc	Non-TVRO and non-DBS satellite information.
rec.video.satellite.tvro	'Large Dish' ('BUD') systems and technologies.
rec.windsurfing	Riding the waves as a hobby.
rec.woodworking	Hobbyists interested in woodworking.
sci.aeronautics	The science of aeronautics and related technology.
sci.aeronautics.airliners	Airliner technology. M
sci.aeronautics.simulation	Aerospace simulation technology. M
sci.agriculture	Farming, agriculture and related topics.
sci.agriculture.beekeeping	Beekeeping, bee-culture and hive products.
sci.answers	Repository for periodic USENET articles. M
sci.anthropology	All aspects of studying humankind.
sci.anthropology.paleo	Evolution of man and other primates.
sci.aquaria	Only scientifically-oriented postings about aquaria.
sci.archaeology	Studying antiquities of the world.
sci.archaeology.mesoamerican	The field of mesoamerican archaeology.
sci.astro	Astronomy discussions and information.
sci.astro.amateur	Amateur astronomy equipment, techniques, info, etc.
sci.astro.fits	Issues related to the Flexible Image Transport System.
sci.astro.hubble	Processing Hubble Space Telescope data. M
sci.astro.planetarium	Discussion of planetariums.
sci.astro.research	Forum in astronomy/astrophysics research. M
sci.bio.botany	The scientific study of plants.
sci.bio.conservation	Conservation biology research. M
sci.bio.ecology	Ecological research.
sci.bio.entomology.lepidoptera	Lepidoptera: butterflies and moths.
sci.bio.entomology.misc	General insect study and related issues.
sci.bio.ethology	Animal behaviour and behavioural ecology.

sci.bio.evolution	Discussions of evolutionary biology. ᴹ
sci.bio.fisheries	All aspects of fisheries science and fish biology.
sci.bio.food-science	Topics related to food science and technology.
sci.bio.herp	Biology of amphibians and reptiles.
sci.bio.microbiology	Protists, fungi, algae, other microscopic organisms.
sci.bio.misc	Biology and related sciences.
sci.bio.paleontology	Life of the past (but no creation vs evolution!).
sci.bio.phytopathology	All aspects of plant diseases and pests. ᴹ
sci.bio.systematics	Systematics, taxonomy, and the tree of life.
sci.chem	Chemistry and related sciences.
sci.chem.analytical	Analytical chemistry.
sci.chem.electrochem	The field of electrochemistry.
sci.chem.labware	Chemical laboratory equipment.
sci.chem.organomet	Organometallic chemistry.
sci.classics	Studying classical history, languages, art and more.
sci.cognitive	Perception, memory, judgement and reasoning.
sci.comp-aided	The use of computers as tools in scientific research.
sci.cryonics	Theory and practice of biostasis, suspended animation.
sci.crypt	Different methods of data en/decryption.
sci.crypt.research	Cryptography, cryptanalysis, and related issues. ᴹ
sci.data.formats	Modelling, storage and retrieval of scientific data.
sci.econ	The science of economics.
sci.econ.research	Research in all fields of economics. ᴹ
sci.edu	The science of education.
sci.electronics	Circuits, theory, electrons and discussions.
sci.electronics.cad	Schematic drafting, printed circuit layout, simulation.
sci.electronics.repair	Fixing electronic equipment.
sci.energy	Discussions about energy, science and technology.
sci.energy.hydrogen	All about hydrogen as an alternative fuel.
sci.engr	Technical discussions about engineering tasks.
sci.engr.biomed	Discussing the field of biomedical engineering.
sci.engr.chem	All aspects of chemical engineering.
sci.engr.civil	Topics related to civil engineering.
sci.engr.control	The engineering of control systems.
sci.engr.geomechanics	Geomechanics issues and related topics.
sci.engr.heat-vent-ac	Heating, ventilating, air conditioning and refrigeration.
sci.engr.lighting	Light, vision and colour in architecture, media, etc.
sci.engr.manufacturing	Manufacturing technology.

sci.engr.marine.hydrodynamics	Marine hydrodynamics.
sci.engr.mech	The field of mechanical engineering.
sci.engr.metallurgy	Metallurgical engineering.
sci.engr.safety	All aspects of the safety of engineered systems.
sci.engr.semiconductors	Semiconductor devices, processes, materials, physics.
sci.engr.surveying	Measurement and mapping of the earth's surface.
sci.engr.television.advanced	HDTV/DATV standards, equipment, practices, etc.
sci.engr.television.broadcast	Broadcast facility equipment and practices.
sci.environment	Discussions about the environment and ecology.
sci.fractals	Objects of non-integral dimension and other chaos.
sci.geo.earthquakes	For discussion of earthquakes and related matters.
sci.geo.eos	NASA's Earth Observation System (EOS).
sci.geo.fluids	Discussion of geophysical fluid dynamics.
sci.geo.geology	Discussion of solid earth sciences.
sci.geo.hydrology	Surface and groundwater hydrology.
sci.geo.meteorology	Discussion of meteorology and related topics.
sci.geo.oceanography	Oceanography, oceanology and marine science.
sci.geo.petroleum	All aspects of petroleum and the petroleum industry.
sci.geo.satellite-nav	Satellite navigation systems, especially GPS.
sci.image.processing	Scientific image processing and analysis.
sci.lang	Natural languages, communication, etc.
sci.lang.japan	The Japanese language, both spoken and written.
sci.lang.translation	Problems and concerns of translators/interpreters.
sci.life-extension	Slowing, stopping or reversing the ageing process.
sci.logic	Logic – math, philosophy and computational aspects.
sci.materials	All aspects of materials engineering.
sci.materials.ceramics	Ceramic science.
sci.math	Mathematical discussions and pursuits.
sci.math.research	Discussion of current mathematical research. M
sci.math.symbolic	Symbolic algebra discussion.
sci.mech.fluids	All aspects of fluid mechanics.
sci.med	Medicine and its related products and regulations.
sci.med.aids	AIDS: treatment, pathology/biology of HIV, prevention. M
sci.med.cardiology	All aspects of cardiovascular diseases.
sci.med.dentistry	Dentally related topics; all about teeth.
sci.med.diseases.cancer	Diagnosis, treatment, and prevention of cancer.

sci.med.diseases.hepatitis	Hepatitis diseases.
sci.med.diseases.lyme	Lyme Disease: patient support, research and information.
sci.med.immunology	Medical/scientific aspects of immune illness.
sci.med.informatics	Computer applications in medical care.
sci.med.nursing	Nursing questions and discussion.
sci.med.nutrition	Physiological impacts of diet.
sci.med.occupational	Repetitive Strain Injuries (RSI) and job injury issues.
sci.med.orthopedics	Orthopedic Surgery, related issues and management. M
sci.med.pathology	Pathology and laboratory medicine.
sci.med.pharmacy	The teaching and practice of pharmacy.
sci.med.physics	Issues of physics in medical testing/care.
sci.med.psychobiology	Dialog and news in psychiatry and psychobiology.
sci.med.radiology	All aspects of radiology.
sci.med.telemedicine	Hospital/physician networks. No diagnosis questions.
sci.med.transcription	Information for and about medical transcriptionists.
sci.med.vision	Human vision, visual correction, and visual science.
sci.military.moderated	Military technology. M
sci.military.naval	Navies of the world, past, present and future.
sci.misc	Short-lived discussions on subjects in the sciences.
sci.nanotech	Self-reproducing molecular-scale machines. M
sci.nonlinear	Chaotic systems and other nonlinear scientific study.
sci.op-research	Research, teaching and application of operations research.
sci.optics	Discussion relating to the science of optics.
sci.philosophy.tech	Technical philosophy: math, science, logic, etc.
sci.physics	Physical laws, properties, etc.
sci.physics.accelerators	Particle accelerators and the physics of beams.
sci.physics.computational.fluid-dynamics	Computational fluid dynamics.
sci.physics.cond-matter	Condensed matter physics, theory and experiment.
sci.physics.electromag	Electromagnetic theory and applications.
sci.physics.fusion	Info on fusion, esp. 'cold' fusion.
sci.physics.particle	Particle physics discussions.
sci.physics.plasma	Plasma Science and Technology community exchange. M
sci.physics.research	Current physics research. M
sci.polymers	All aspects of polymer science.
sci.psychology.announce	Psychology-related announcements. M

sci.psychology.consciousness	On the nature of consciousness. M
sci.psychology.journals.psyche	E-journal on consciousness. M
sci.psychology.journals.psycoloquy	E-journal on psychology. M
sci.psychology.misc	General discussion of psychology.
sci.psychology.personality	All personality systems and measurement.
sci.psychology.psychotherapy	Practice of psychotherapy.
sci.psychology.research	Research issues in psychology. M
sci.psychology.theory	Theories of psychology and behaviour.
sci.research	Research methods, funding, ethics, and whatever.
sci.research.careers	Issues relevant to careers in scientific research.
sci.research.postdoc	Anything about postdoctoral studies, including offers.
sci.skeptic	Sceptics discussing pseudo-science.
sci.space.news	Announcements of space-related news items. M
sci.space.policy	Discussions about space policy.
sci.space.science	Space and planetary science and related technical work. M
sci.space.shuttle	The space shuttle and the STS programme.
sci.space.tech	Technical and general issues related to space flight. M
sci.stat.consult	Statistical consulting.
sci.stat.edu	Statistics education.
sci.stat.math	Statistics from a strictly mathematical viewpoint.
sci.systems	The theory and application of systems science.
sci.techniques.mag-resonance	Magnetic resonance imaging and spectroscopy.
sci.techniques.mass-spec	All areas of mass spectrometry. M
sci.techniques.microscopy	The field of microscopy.
sci.techniques.spectroscopy	Spectrum analysis.
sci.techniques.testing.misc	General testing techniques in science.
sci.techniques.testing.nondestructive	Nondestructive tests in science.
sci.techniques.xtallography	The field of crystallography.
sci.virtual-worlds	Virtual Reality – technology and culture. M
sci.virtual-worlds.apps	Current and future uses of virtual-worlds technology. M
soc.answers	Repository for periodic USENET articles. M
soc.bi	Discussions of bisexuality.
soc.college	College, college activities, campus life, etc.
soc.college.admissions	The university admissions process.
soc.college.financial-aid	Financial aid issues, college and beyond.
soc.college.grad	General issues related to graduate schools.
soc.college.gradinfo	Information about graduate schools.
soc.college.org.aiesec	The Int'l Assoc. of Business and Commerce Students.
soc.college.teaching-asst	Issues affecting collegiate teaching assistants.
soc.couples	Discussions for couples (cf. soc.singles).
soc.couples.intercultural	Inter-cultural and inter-racial relationships.
soc.couples.wedding	Wedding planning.

soc.culture.afghanistan	Discussion of the Afghan society.
soc.culture.african	Discussions about Africa and things African.
soc.culture.african.american	Discussions about Afro-American issues.
soc.culture.albanian	Albania and Albanians around the world.
soc.culture.algeria	From A to Z about Algeria.
soc.culture.arabic	Technological and cultural issues, *not* politics.
soc.culture.argentina	All about life in Argentina.
soc.culture.asean	Countries of the Assoc. of SE Asian Nations.
soc.culture.asian.american	Issues and discussion about Asian-Americans.
soc.culture.assyrian	Assyrian culture, history, language, current diaspora.
soc.culture.australian	Australian culture and society.
soc.culture.austria	Austria and its people.
soc.culture.baltics	People of the Baltic states.
soc.culture.bangladesh	Issues and discussion about Bangladesh.
soc.culture.belgium	Belgian society, culture(s) and people.
soc.culture.bengali	Sociocultural identity of worldwide Bengali population.
soc.culture.berber	The Berber language, history, and culture.
soc.culture.bolivia	Bolivian people and culture.
soc.culture.bosna-herzgvna	The independent state of Bosnia and Herzegovina.
soc.culture.brazil	Talking about the people and country of Brazil.
soc.culture.british	Issues about Britain and those of British descent.
soc.culture.bulgaria	Discussing Bulgarian society.
soc.culture.burma	Politics, culture, news, discussion about Burma.
soc.culture.cambodia	Cambodia and its people.
soc.culture.canada	Discussions of Canada and its people.
soc.culture.caribbean	Life in the Caribbean.
soc.culture.celtic	Irish, Scottish, Breton, Cornish, Manx and Welsh.
soc.culture.chile	All about Chile and its people.
soc.culture.china	About China and Chinese culture.
soc.culture.colombia	Colombian talk, social, politics, science.
soc.culture.croatia	The lives of people of Croatia.
soc.culture.cuba	Cuban culture, society and politics.
soc.culture.czecho-slovak	Bohemian, Slovak, Moravian and Silesian life.
soc.culture.dominican-rep	The life and people of the Dominican Republic.
soc.culture.ecuador	The culture and people of Ecuador.
soc.culture.egyptian	Egypt, and its society, culture, heritage, etc.
soc.culture.estonia	Estonian culture, language, news, politics. M
soc.culture.europe	Discussing all aspects of all-European society.
soc.culture.filipino	Group about the Filipino culture.
soc.culture.french	French culture, history, and related discussions.
soc.culture.german	Discussions about German culture and history.
soc.culture.greek	Group about Greeks.
soc.culture.haiti	Haiti specific development and cultural issues.

soc.culture.hongkong	Discussions pertaining to Hong Kong.
soc.culture.hongkong.entertainment	Entertainment in Hong Kong.
soc.culture.indian	Group for discussion about India and things Indian.
soc.culture.indian.delhi	Information related to Delhi, capital of India.
soc.culture.indian.info	Info group for soc.culture.indian, etc. M
soc.culture.indian.kerala	Culture of the people of Keralite origin.
soc.culture.indian.marathi	Discussion related to Marathi Culture.
soc.culture.indian.telugu	The culture of the Telugu people of India.
soc.culture.indonesia	All about the Indonesian nation.
soc.culture.iranian	Discussions about Iran and things Iranian/Persian.
soc.culture.iraq	Iraq, its society, culture and heritage.
soc.culture.irish	Ireland and Irish culture.
soc.culture.israel	Israel and Israelis.
soc.culture.italian	The Italian people and their culture.
soc.culture.japan	Everything Japanese, except the Japanese language.
soc.culture.jewish	Jewish culture and religion (cf. talk.politics.mideast).
soc.culture.jewish.holocaust	The Shoah. M
soc.culture.jordan	All topics concerning The Hashemite Kingdom of Jordan.
soc.culture.korean	Discussions about Korea and things Korean.
soc.culture.kurdish	People from Kurdistan and Kurds around the world.
soc.culture.kuwait	Kuwaiti culture, society, and history.
soc.culture.laos	Cultural and social aspects of Laos.
soc.culture.latin-america	Topics about Latin-America.
soc.culture.lebanon	Discussion about things Lebanese.
soc.culture.maghreb	North African society and culture.
soc.culture.magyar	The Hungarian people and their culture.
soc.culture.malagasy	Madagascar and the Malagasy culture.
soc.culture.malaysia	All about Malaysian society.
soc.culture.mexican	Discussion of Mexico's society.
soc.culture.mexican.american	Mexican-American/Chicano culture and issues.
soc.culture.misc	Group for discussion about other cultures.
soc.culture.mongolian	Everything related to Mongols and Mongolia.
soc.culture.native	Aboriginal people around the world.
soc.culture.nepal	Discussion of people and things in and from Nepal.
soc.culture.netherlands	People from the Netherlands and Belgium.
soc.culture.new-zealand	Discussion of topics related to New Zealand.
soc.culture.nigeria	Nigerian affairs, society, cultures, and peoples.
soc.culture.nordic	Discussion about culture up north.
soc.culture.pakistan	Topics of discussion about Pakistan.
soc.culture.palestine	Palestinian people, culture and politics.

soc.culture.peru	All about the people of Peru.
soc.culture.polish	Polish culture, Polish past, and Polish politics.
soc.culture.portuguese	Discussion of the people of Portugal.
soc.culture.puerto-rico	Puerto Rican culture, society and politics.
soc.culture.punjab	Punjab and Punjabi culture.
soc.culture.quebec	Quebec society and culture.
soc.culture.romanian	Discussion of Romanian and Moldavian people.
soc.culture.russian	All things Russian in the broadest sense.
soc.culture.scientists	Cultural issues about scientists and scientific projects.
soc.culture.scottish	Anything regarding Scotland or things Scots.
soc.culture.sierra-leone	The culture of Sierra Leone.
soc.culture.singapore	The past, present and future of Singapore.
soc.culture.slovenia	Slovenia and Slovenian people.
soc.culture.somalia	Somalian affairs, society, and culture.
soc.culture.south-africa	South African society, culture, and politics.
soc.culture.soviet	Topics relating to Russian or Soviet culture.
soc.culture.spain	Spain and the Spanish.
soc.culture.sri-lanka	Things and people from Sri Lanka.
soc.culture.swiss	Swiss culture.
soc.culture.syria	Syrian cultural matters and affairs.
soc.culture.taiwan	Discussion about things Taiwanese.
soc.culture.tamil	Tamil language, history and culture.
soc.culture.thai	Thai people and their culture.
soc.culture.turkish	Discussion about things Turkish.
soc.culture.ukrainian	The lives and times of the Ukrainian people.
soc.culture.uruguay	Discussions of Uruguay for those at home and abroad.
soc.culture.usa	The culture of the United States of America.
soc.culture.venezuela	Discussion of topics related to Venezuela.
soc.culture.vietnamese	Issues and discussions of Vietnamese culture.
soc.culture.welsh	The people, language and history of Wales.
soc.culture.yugoslavia	Discussions of Yugoslavia and its people.
soc.culture.zimbabwe	Culture and other issues pertaining to Zimbabwe.
soc.feminism	Discussion of feminism and feminist issues. M
soc.genealogy.australia+nz	Australia, New Zealand, and their territories.
soc.genealogy.benelux	Genealogy in Belgium, the Netherlands and Luxembourg.
soc.genealogy.computing	Genealogical computing and net resources.
soc.genealogy.french	Francophone genealogy.
soc.genealogy.german	Family history including a German background.
soc.genealogy.hispanic	Genealogy relating to Hispanics.
soc.genealogy.jewish	Jewish genealogy group. M
soc.genealogy.marketplace	Genealogy services and products.
soc.genealogy.medieval	Genealogy in the period from roughly AD500 to AD1600.

soc.genealogy.methods	Genealogical methods and resources. M
soc.genealogy.misc	General genealogical discussions.
soc.genealogy.nordic	Genealogy in the Scandinavian countries.
soc.genealogy.surnames	Surname queries and tafels. M
soc.genealogy.uk+ireland	Genealogy of Britain, Ireland and offshore isles.
soc.history	Discussions of things historical.
soc.history.living	Living history and reenactment, issues and info.
soc.history.moderated	All aspects of history. M
soc.history.science	History of science and related areas.
soc.history.war.misc	History and events of wars in general.
soc.history.war.us-civil-war	Aspects of the US Civil War. M
soc.history.war.vietnam	The Vietnam War. M
soc.history.war.world-war-ii	History and events of World War Two. M
soc.history.what-if	Alternate history.
soc.libraries.talk	Discussing all aspects of libraries.
soc.men	Issues related to men, their problems and relationships.
soc.misc	Socially-oriented topics not in other groups.
soc.motss	Issues pertaining to homosexuality.
soc.net-people	Announcements, requests, etc. about people on the net.
soc.org.nonprofit	Nonprofit organisations.
soc.org.service-clubs.misc	General info on all service topics.
soc.penpals	In search of net.friendships.
soc.politics	Political problems, systems, solutions. M
soc.politics.arms-d	Arms discussion digest. M
soc.religion.bahai	Discussion of the Baha'i Faith. M
soc.religion.christian	Christianity and related topics. M
soc.religion.christian.bible-study	Examining the Holy Bible. M
soc.religion.christian.youth-work	Christians working with young people. M
soc.religion.eastern	Discussions of Eastern religions. M
soc.religion.gnosis	Gnosis, marifat, jnana and direct sacred experience. M
soc.religion.hindu	Discussion about the Hindu dharma, philosophy, culture. M
soc.religion.islam	Discussions of the Islamic faith. M
soc.religion.quaker	The Religious Society of Friends.
soc.religion.shamanism	Discussion of the full range of shamanic experience. M
soc.religion.sikhism	Sikh Religion and Sikhs all over the world. M
soc.religion.unitarian-univ	Unitarian-Universalism and non-creedal religions.
soc.rights.human	Human rights and activism (e.g., Amnesty International).
soc.singles	News group for single people, their activities, etc.
soc.support.fat-acceptance	Self-acceptance for fat people. No diet talk.
soc.support.transgendered	Transgendered and intersexed persons.

soc.support.youth.gay-lesbian-bi	Gay youths helping each other. [M]
soc.veterans	Social issues relating to military veterans.
soc.women	Issues related to women, their problems and relationships.
soc.women.lesbian-and-bi	Lives of lesbian and bisexual women. [M]
talk.abortion	All sorts of discussions and arguments on abortion.
talk.answers	Repository for periodic USENET articles. [M]
talk.bizarre	The unusual, bizarre, curious, and often interesting.
talk.environment	Discussion the state of the environment and what to do.
talk.euthanasia	All aspects of euthanasia.
talk.origins	Evolution versus creationism (sometimes hot!).
talk.philosophy.humanism	Humanism in the modern world.
talk.philosophy.misc	Philosophical musings on all topics.
talk.politics.animals	The use and/or abuse of animals.
talk.politics.china	Discussion of political issues related to China.
talk.politics.crypto	The relation between cryptography and government.
talk.politics.drugs	The politics of drug issues.
talk.politics.european-union	The EU and political integration in Europe.
talk.politics.guns	The politics of firearm ownership and (mis)use.
talk.politics.libertarian	Libertarian politics and political philosophy.
talk.politics.medicine	The politics and ethics involved with health care.
talk.politics.mideast	Discussion and debate over Middle Eastern events.
talk.politics.misc	Political discussions and ravings of all kinds.
talk.politics.soviet	Discussion of Soviet politics, domestic and foreign.
talk.politics.theory	Theory of politics and political systems.
talk.politics.tibet	The politics of Tibet and the Tibetan people.
talk.rape	Discussions on stopping rape; not to be crossposted.
talk.religion.buddhism	All aspects of Buddhism as religion and philosophy.
talk.religion.misc	Religious, ethical, and moral implications.
talk.religion.newage	Esoteric and minority religions and philosophies.
talk.rumors	For the posting of rumours.

Index

E-MAIL
A PRACTICAL GUIDE

SIMON COLLIN

Credit
Card Hotline
Tel: (01865)
314627

If you're an experienced Network Administrator who has decided that E-Mail sounds a good idea, wants to install it but doesn't know where to start, and you're looking for a guide book packed with tips and practical ideas on the whole area of E-Mail then here's your book!

In 250 fact filled pages, let this book show you how to make the most productive use of E-Mail in your business.

Have you just been landed with the job of installing an E-Mail system and need help; look no further, all the information you need is right here.

Managers who have to keep up with their MIS department will also find this book useful as an ideal backgrounder to the whole area of Electronic Mail.

Electronic Mail is one of the fastest-growing areas of computing - don't get left behind - once you've got this book as a guide, you'll wonder how you ever did without it!

0 7506 2112 5, 250 pages, Paperback, April 1995, £24.49
(price includes postage & packing)

E-MAIL
A PRACTICAL GUIDE

SIMON COLLIN

HOW TO ORDER

☎ **Credit Card Hotline:** Tel. (0)1865 314627

✉ **Or send orders to:** Sharon Pitcher, Butterworth-Heinemann, Linacre House, Jordan Hill, Oxford, OX2 8DP quoting ref: Adbanks96

By cheque or credit card (overseas customers please pay by credit card or a cheque drawn in sterling on a UK bank).

Cheques should be made payable to Heinemann Publishers Oxford

Credit Card orders: please state the make of card, number, expiry date and name and address where the card is registered.

THE INTERNET
WITH WINDOWS

COMPUTER WEEKLY
PROFESSIONAL SERIES

GLYN MOODY

The Internet with Windows can be read and used by both Windows 95 and Windows 3.1 users, and the vast bulk of it is applicable to other operating systems as well. In particular, it will be invaluable for those accessing the Internet via CompuServe or the Microsoft Network.

This book:

- Gives simple-to-understand explanations of all the basic Internet concepts, with many practical examples
- Provides a comprehensive guide to accessing 99% of the Internet's resources with just electronic mail
- Gives step-by-step instructions on how to set up the Internet programs contained in Windows 95 and Windows Plus!, and how to obtain and set up equivalent software for Windows 3.1 (which can also be used with Windows 95)
- Explains how to obtain and configure most of the hundred or so Windows Internet shareware programs that are currently available, with detailed tips for using them. These include software for all the main tools - e-mail, Usenet, FTP, telnet, Archie, Gopher, WAIS and the World-Wide Web (WWW) - as well as more unusual ones such as Ping, TraceRoute, Finger, Host Lookup, X.500, Whois, Ph, Chat, IRC, Internet programs that use Virtual Reality, and others that enable you to carry on international conversations for the price of a local call.
- Gives simple instructions on how to set up the leading WWW programs Netscape and Mosaic - both free - and includes step-by-step details of how to write your own Web home page using just a text editor
- Tells you how to find things and people on the Internet, with explicit information about search tools and practical examples

This book assumes no previous expertise apart from some basic familiarity with Windows programs. Successive chapters build to form a complete introduction to all aspects of using the Internet, including elements generally omitted from other books.

Glyn Moody has been writing about computers and communications for fifteen years. His highly-popular Getting Wired page about the Internet appears every Thursday in Computer Weekly, and he also writes for The Guardian, The Daily Telegraph and specialist titles.

1995   0 7506 2099 4   650 pages   236 x 156mm   £22.49 (price includes postage and packing)

More than 1000 Internet addresses in Europe, the USA and Asia
Over 500 Windows 95 screen shots
Full glossary

THE INTERNET
WITH WINDOWS

GLYN MOODY